IN PERSON
30 POETS

FILMED BY PAMELA ROBERTSON-PEARCE

EDITED BY NEIL ASTLEY

BLOODAXE BOOKS

ISBN: 978 1 85224 800 0

First published 2008 by
Bloodaxe Books Ltd,
Highgreen,
Tarset,
Northumberland NE48 1RP.

www.bloodaxebooks.com
For further information about Bloodaxe titles
please visit our website or write to
the above address for a catalogue.

Bloodaxe Books Ltd acknowledges
the financial assistance of
Arts Council England, North East.

Cover design by Neil Astley & Pamela Robertson-Pearce

Book printed in Great Britain by
Bell & Bain Limited, Glasgow, Scotland

DVDs manufactured by
docdata media ltd, Telford, Shropshire

IN PERSON: 30 POETS

COMHAIRLE CHONTAE ÁTHA CLIATH THEAS
SOUTH DUBLIN COUNTY LIBRARIES

CASTLETYMON BRANCH LIBRARY
TO RENEW ANY ITEM TEL: 452 4888

Items should be returned on or before the last date below. Fines, as displayed in the Library, will be charged on overdue items.

PAMELA ROBERTSON-PEARCE is an artist and filmmaker. Her films include *IMAGO: Meret Oppenheim* (1996), on the artist who made the fur-lined teacup, and *Gifted Beauty* (2000), about Surrealist women artists including Leonora Carrington and Remedios Varo. *IMAGO: Meret Oppenheim* won several awards, including the Swiss Film Board's Prize for Outstanding Quality and the Gold Apple Award at the National Educational Film and Video Festival in America. She has shown her work in solo exhibitions in New York and Provincetown (Cape Cod), and in various group shows in the US and Europe. Born in Stockholm, she grew up in Sweden, Spain and England, and then for over 20 years lived mostly in America – also working in Switzerland, Norway and Albania – before moving to Northumberland. She co-edited the anthology *Soul Food: nourishing poems for starved minds* (Bloodaxe Books, 2007) with Neil Astley.

NEIL ASTLEY is editor of Bloodaxe Books, which he founded in 1978, and was given a D.Litt by Newcastle University in 1995 for his pioneering work. He has edited nearly a thousand poetry books and published several anthologies, including *Poetry with an Edge* (1988/1995), *Staying Alive: real poems for unreal times* (2002/2003 USA), *Pleased to See Me: 69 Very Sexy Poems* (2002), *Do Not Go Gentle: poems for funerals* (2003), *Being Alive: the sequel to 'Staying Alive'* (2004), *Passionfood: 100 Love Poems* (2005), *Soul Food: nourishing poems for starved minds* [with Pamela Robertson-Pearce] (2007) and *Earth Shattering: ecopoems* (2007), as well as two poetry collections, *Darwin Survivor* (1988) and *Biting My Tongue* (1995), and two eco-novels, *The End of My Tether* (2002/2003) (shortlisted for the Whitbread First Novel Award), and *The Sheep Who Changed the World* (2005).

CONTENTS

DVD 2

BONUS TRACK
Film by Ivor Bowen

Ken Smith (1938-2003)

NEIL ASTLEY
In Person: Introduction

THE DVD-BOOK

In Person presents contemporary poetry to readers in a totally new way, with short films of 30 living poets reading their work on two DVDs. It is, we believe, the world's first poetry DVD-book: an anthology/DVD combination with all the poems from the films included in the book. No other publisher has attempted anything like this in Britain. No one else has originated and produced short films of major contemporary poets and made these available on DVDs with an anthology including all the texts. *In Person* is, in effect, your own personal interactive poetry festival packaged into a book. There's also a separate "bonus track" at the end: a short film of Ken Smith, made a year before his untimely death. Ken was the first poet to be published by Bloodaxe Books and we wanted to honour his work and memory by including him after the *In Person* films.

Each poet reads for about ten minutes – up to half a dozen poems chosen from across the range of their work – but you can choose which poets to watch and when. We wouldn't expect you to view all the films on either of the two DVDs in one sitting. That would be like sitting through a three-hour poetry marathon. With the DVDs, you can watch a few poets at a time and digest what you've heard before reading the poems on the page; you can experience some readings again if you want to do that before moving on to the next poet. Every poet we've filmed is highly individual and completely different from the next poet; every reading is worth watching, and the wide range of writers reflects both the breadth of the Bloodaxe poetry list and the refreshing diversity of contemporary poetry.

The only other poetry anthology I'm aware of which comes with a DVD of readings is *An Invitation to Poetry* (2004), the third of the *Favorite Poems* anthologies edited by Robert Pinsky and Maggie Dietz, the fruit of the scheme set up by Pinsky when he was America's Poet Laureate. This includes a DVD featuring videos of people from all walks of life reading and talking about their favourite poems, but only a couple of dozen poems from this substantial anthology are given this treatment. Just one of their readers is a poet, an earlier US Poet Laureate, Stanley Kunitz, who reads 'God's Grandeur' by Gerard Manley Hopkins. By coincidence, Kunitz was instrumental in the genesis of our project, which came into being through a whole series of coincidences.

In Person is a collaboration with film-maker Pamela Robertson-Pearce. Her style of filming combines directness and simplicity, sensitivity and warmth – the perfect combination for these intimate readings. It's as if the poet were sitting with you, reading just to you, sometimes adding a comment on the background to a poem.

11

This landmark project also celebrates 30 years of poetry from a pioneering press. Founded in 1978, Bloodaxe has published nearly a thousand titles by three hundred writers. Until now you wouldn't be able to see or hear readings by many of Bloodaxe's international range of poets. *In Person* makes that possible for the first time, presenting readings by 30 essential voices from Britain, Ireland, America, Spain, Hungary, Palestine, Pakistan, China, New Zealand and the Caribbean.

GENESIS

Inspirational figures of another age provided the spark for this 21st-century poetry project. In December 2005, in the course of a week's stay in New York, Pamela and I met a number of remarkable people, including three in particular: the novelist Marianne Hauser, an old family friend; Louise Bourgeois, one of the most inventive, defiantly unconventional artists of modern times, who was 94 that Christmas; and Stanley Kunitz, who'd turned 100 a few months earlier.

Marianne's 95th birthday was also the day of Louise Bourgeois' salon, held on most Sunday afternoons in the house where she has lived since 1962, and where she is still making her art. Her salons enable her to keep in touch with younger artists, writers, musicians, dancers and poets. Pamela had been one of the artists invited to the salon several times over many years, and here our coincidences start coming into play. In 2001 she was awarded a two-year artist's fellowship at the Fine Arts Work Center in Provincetown, Cape Cod, co-founded by Stanley Kunitz, benefiting from a bursary which turned out to be endowed by Louise Bourgeois. Kunitz's summer home for over 50 years was in Provincetown, which was where Pamela first met him and heard him read. I had just published Mary Oliver – who lives in Provincetown – when I first met Pamela, and it was the Cape Cod connection which sparked off our first conversation.

This Sunday follows the usual pattern. Everyone must arrive by 3 PM and be seated when Louise Bourgeois is led into the room. She may look frail, but her mind is alert and her temper as mercurial as ever. She listens carefully as artists take turns to show and talk about their work, alternating with writers and other guests who read poems to the assembled company as chocolates and wine are passed around. Some artists are questioned closely, even sharply, about the work they present. In some ways it's like an old-fashioned drawing-room, highly civilised but also intensely exciting and full of surprises. You don't know what the next person is going to offer: French café songs on an accordion; a laptop guide to an artist's museum of decay in remote woodland; paintings or photographs of sculptures spread out on the table. And poems – all kinds of people from different countries reading poems to each other.

I offer a brief introduction to the work of England's Selima Hill, reading several short poems from her *Portrait of My Lover as a Horse*, but soon sense that my listeners can't quite tune into Hill's wild imagery and outlandish similes. They seem a little baffled by the poems, not quite knowing how to take them. However, my turn isn't over. Louise had been reading a biography of Edna St Vincent Millay, I'm told, and she wants me to read some Millay poems. I can take the floor again after the next artist. An odd-looking collection with a battered green cover is handed to me. It doesn't include any of the Millay poems I know, but sensing interest in an earlier bohemian inhabitant of the Village, I'm pleased to find one poem describing Washington Square. This goes down well, as do others I find to read.

Now I can relax, I think, but soon another visitor is doing a poetry stint, this time reading from a book by Billy Collins. His performance is less than assured, as he freely admits when asked to read one of the poems again. He just likes the work, and wanted to share it. '*Do you know this poet?*' I'm suddenly asked. 'Yes,' I say, 'and I like his work very much.' '*Give him the book,*' our host commands, '*I want him to read this poem.*' The poem is 'Litany', which starts with a couplet quoted from an unconvincing love poem by one of Collins's students: 'You are the bread and the knife / the crystal goblet and the wine.' Collins's ironic send-up of the poetic fallacy needs the right intonation and sardonic delivery for the poem to work; in the first man's reading, the humour struggled to register, and the poem foundered. Fortunate enough to have heard 'Litany' read by Billy Collins a couple of times in England, I know how the poem *should* sound, and so give a droll, almost hammy rendition which I hope even Collins himself would have enjoyed. This time the poem works its magic. Before it had puzzled them, but now it is hilarious. '*Vairy goote, vairy goote,*' says Louise, and I give way to the next guest.

At six o'clock the audience is finished. Suddenly we're no longer part of this rollercoaster meeting of art and poetry, but walking down West 20th Street to catch the subway, back in the so-called real world. After the extraordinary nature of three hours spent not just with Louise Bourgeois but with that afternoon's particular mix of lively people, our minds are buzzing on overdrive as we try to absorb and make sense of the intense experience, the feelings it generated and the questions and contradictions raised. It had included the strangest poetry reading I'd ever been part of, but this had also fired me up. I'd enjoyed reading poetry aloud to such an intimate gathering, and all those present had clearly enjoyed hearing poetry read to them, whether by me or by other guests. And *how* it was read had been just as important; if someone's delivery was flat or failed to carry the music, you might just as well read the poem on the page.

13

What was even stranger to ponder was that this particular set of private readings, along with possibly hundreds of others, including many by eminent visiting poets, had been captured on film, and that these videos of Louise Bourgeois salons formed part of the artist's archive. In Britain we have the Poetry Archive's catalogue of studio recordings available on CD. These need to be ordered on-line because few bookshops are able or willing to stock poetry CDs or cassettes. America's Lannan Foundation has produced excellent videos of poetry readings as well as a set of Bloodaxe's Peter Reading reading his life's work on 22 DVDs, but these are for educational distribution only. In Britain, many readings at festivals and poetry venues are filmed or recorded, but almost always for archive only. Very few recordings, whether audio or video, are readily accessible to the wider public.

As with the Louise Bourgeois archive, what should never be lost is still preserved, yet few people get to see or hear these recordings, often because of over-restrictive copyright control of its dissemination; or because it is too complicated and costly to be copied, packaged and distributed. So we read poetry but rarely get to hear it, and yet poetry is both an oral and an *aural* art. There's poetry on radio but that's usually limited to old favourites read by actors on *Poetry Please,* or British poets reading from new collections on the few other programmes which cover poetry.

Our next day in New York couldn't have been more different. We'd been in touch with Stanley Kunitz's assistant and co-author Genine Lentine over a 100th birthday tribute review of their book *The Wild Braid* I'd written for *Poetry London,*[1] and had been invited for tea at his apartment. By late 2005 Stanley was spending most of his days reading or resting while others looked after his correspondence and general welfare. As well as reading any book, newspaper or magazine he happened to find by his armchair, he loved listening to poems. Genine would read him poems by the writers he admired most, along with new poems from the many books and magazines he was sent by younger poets. She was reading whole books to him in instalments; most recently, *Moby-Dick.* And Stanley himself could still recite poetry with gusto, as we discovered in the course of a wonderful hour spent in his company.

We had brought copies of two anthologies in which I'd included his work, and he was soon persuaded to read us some of the poems. Tracing the words with a shaky, gnarled finger, he read each line of 'Touch Me' in a quavering voice, but with a power and feeling which seemed to connect with the source of

> Words plucked out of the air
> some forty years ago
> when I was wild with love
> and torn almost in two...

And putting the book down, he intoned the last few lines from memory:

> Darling, do you remember
> the man you married? Touch me,
> remind me who I am.

We were so captivated that I found myself almost holding my breath, not wanting to miss the tiniest nuance. Then Stanley wanted me to read some of the poems I especially liked from the two anthologies, and I chose Robert Frost's 'Stopping by Woods on a Snowy Evening', Gjertrud Schnackenberg's 'Snow Melting' and Brendan Kennelly's 'Begin'. This time I was reading poems to just three people – including one of the poets I most admired in the world – and as I read each line, I was acutely aware of the extraordinary nature of the occasion, and the need to give of my best if the reading were to pass muster. I remember concentrating hard on giving just the right weight to the sounds of the poems, the rhymes, chimes, assonances and other musical effects which only reading aloud can fully sound. I wanted to give something back to Stanley, and to share this with the others just as we'd shared his reading.

Afterwards, we talked about how amazing it would have been to have filmed Stanley giving that magical reading to three people; and also how filming such an intimate encounter would have required particular sensitivity and tact.

FILMING WRITERS

Before we left New York, Pamela would see Marianne Hauser again, possibly for the last time. Marianne also had been a formidable reader, but at 95 she was in failing health, and Pamela wished she had been able to film her friend years earlier. The idea of filming Bloodaxe's writers grew from these conversations. When both Marianne Hauser and Stanley Kunitz died the following summer, the latter just two months short of his 101st birthday, we felt the urgency of capturing the older poets on film for posterity. As well as filming the older writers, we wanted to catch some of the poets who visit Britain from overseas each year to give readings. However, we didn't want to point a camera at them at a public event, nor did we want to film people in the artificial environment of a recording studio; what we wanted was something more like the intimate reading Stanley Kunitz had given us.

We were still thinking then of an archive of filmed readings by some of the many poets published by Bloodaxe, with video samples posted on the website, but by the time we started the actual filming, this idea had grown to include the DVD-book – or more precisely, a growing film archive from which video footage for DVD-books could be sourced. Such an archive would also be an invaluable resource for any future advances in media technology.

Where possible we filmed the poets in their own homes. With visiting writers caught on the hoof, we had to find a quiet place somewhere else. Because the writer wasn't invaded by a whole film crew, the dynamic was much more relaxed. I had met all but four of the poets at least once, and in most cases we had known each other for many years; some had become lifelong friends. Agreeing upon the right choice of poems was not difficult. All they had to do was make themselves comfortable, and read. We filmed them reading the poems one at a time. If someone was nervous, the first takes could be warm-up readings, and those poems were read again at the end of the session. Some writers were totally at ease with being filmed, like Philip Levine, who told us: 'I'm not sitting in front of a camera. I'm sitting in front of two people.'

We did what we could to minimise background noise, where possible using rooms away from busy streets. If there was a sudden, totally unexpected loud noise, like a revving motorbike or someone shouting, we had to stop and reshoot the interrupted poem. When we filmed Philip Levine in Brooklyn, we had to contend with a police helicopter which kept returning to frustrate our endeavours, but in the end were able to get good takes of all five of his poems. Filming other poets on the Suffolk coast and Dublin Bay, we sometimes felt stalked by seagulls.

The outside world will always make its presence heard, however quiet the location. In London, for example, hardly a minute passes without the sound of an ambulance or police siren; even in quieter parts like Hampstead, you can hear planes climbing high above the city every couple of minutes. If you live there, you tend to block out such noises, they are just part of the urban soundscape. These are the sounds we live with every day, and it's only when making recordings that you become acutely conscious of them. Even weather can be noisy. In the film of Micheal O'Siadhail, the mid-afternoon light fades in his attic study as the sky darkens over Dublin; then driving rain lashes the skylight as he reads the last poem, 'Only End'. The storm made filming impossible after that, but we were happy to keep that final poem with its atmospheric accompaniment.

I remember being captivated many years ago by a radio programme which included a recording of Robert Frost reading poems in his rural home, punctuated by occasional farmyard noises, from chickens to a distant saw. These made Frost's presence feel even more real: this was the great man himself saying his poems in the place where he wrote them. This natural background acoustic didn't detract from the reading: in many ways it actually enhanced it, placing Frost not just in the farmhouse but in time, at that point in his life. Once I'd recalled that programme, I became much less anxious about our recordings. Now I don't even mind occasional background noises in some of the films; they add a little colour to the sound palette. We don't live in a world without these kinds of background sounds – indeed, this *is* the soundtrack of the modern world – so why pretend otherwise?

Likewise, Pamela's whole approach to filmmaking is informal and straightforward, involving no artifice, visual trickery or use of extraneous material. Not unlike an alternative documentary film-maker, she puts the viewer inside the room with the person being filmed. Her camera becomes your eyes and ears as the poet reads to both of us, but there's no pretending that the film frame is the total world. Sometimes the poet may speak to us between poems, offstage as it were, or one of us may say something in response to what's just been said or read, and if that engagement connects with comments she wants to keep as part of the film, then what we say is included as well.

Once we had filmed a number of poets in this way, it became clear that our still evolving format was enabling the writer to give a reading which was quite unlike anything either of us – or the poet – had seen or experienced. Viewing our footage poet by poet, I remembered my own experience of reading at Louise Bourgeois' salon, and how the poetry had to be read aloud for both sound and syntax for the audience to "get" it; they had to hear, feel and follow the music and the narrative simultaneously. Over the years I've heard many poets murdering their poems at readings, not just the whiners, droners and monotoners, but mad mutterers and speed-readers, and worst of all, those poets infected with that irritating 60s habit of reading every line exactly the same way, as one long drone, but with a sharp drop at the end, like a priest incanting a prayer.

But the poets we've filmed are all exceptionally good readers. And now, watching all these films as I've been putting this anthology together, I've become more fully aware of its educational and cultural significance: that these films show, more clearly than any project I've known, that hearing poetry read aloud – and read well – must be essential to anyone's appreciation or understanding of this oral art, and especially when the readers are the poets themselves.

FROM ARCHIVE TO DVD

The idea of producing DVD-books from our film archive was sparked off by two things coming together. The first of these was Galway Kinnell's latest collection, *Strong Is Your Hold*, offered to Bloodaxe by his American publisher Houghton Mifflin as a book with an audio CD. He reads all the poems in the collection on the accompanying CD, which is pouched inside the back cover. If we could publish books with CDs, then why not DVDs?

The second factor was that Bloodaxe Books celebrates its 30th birthday in 2008. For our 10th birthday in 1988 I had produced *Poetry with an Edge*, an anthology of 56 of the poets published by

Bloodaxe in its first ten years. The updated and expanded edition of *Poetry with an Edge* published for the 15th birthday in 1993 included 90 of Bloodaxe's poets, and even then, that was just a selection. To mark the 21st birthday in 1999 I edited *New Blood*, an anthology of new Bloodaxe writers who had published their first collections during the previous ten years, 38 poets in all, the Bloodaxe poets from the so-called 'New Generation' of the 1990s.

Bloodaxe has now published nearly a thousand titles by over 300 writers. This means it is no longer possible to publish a "representative" anthology like *Poetry with an Edge*. Something very different was needed for the 30th birthday, and I didn't see the need for yet another "birthday book" in any case. What was more important was to do something which would build upon the work done by Bloodaxe since *Poetry with an Edge* to broaden the readership of poetry.

Introducing more readers to the diverse spectrum of contemporary poetry has always been central to Bloodaxe's publishing strategy. In recent years, as well as publishing a wide range of collections by new and established poets from Britain, America and many other countries, Bloodaxe has produced international anthologies like *Staying Alive* and *Being Alive* which have introduced many thousands of new readers to contemporary poetry from around the world.

Bloodaxe has always taken an innovative, many-stranded approach to poetry publishing. Using the latest technology in filming, film editing and DVD production for *In Person* is the latest example of this. The DVD-book enables thousands of people to see and hear these particular poets reading their work, but more importantly – in the wider educational context – it shows why poetry must be read aloud.

Choosing which 30 poets to include in our 30th birthday DVD-book was always going to be an impossible task, especially given the number of poets Bloodaxe publishes and the range and quality of the list. The first priority had to be to include as many of the older poets as possible in this first DVD-book: a third of them are over 70. Secondly, over the course of the 18 months available to us, we would film poets who were visiting Britain to give readings, as well as poets we might be able to link up with on our own trips to America. And thirdly, we wanted to include as many as possible of the poets whose books have formed an integral part of the Bloodaxe publishing programme over the past 30 years. To cover all three groups adequately we would have needed to include 60 poets, not 30. However, we are continuing to film the poets, and will have more than enough films in a couple of years for a second DVD-book of equal quality. As it stands, the diverse combination of writers we've been able to show in this DVD-book offers readers a snapshot of contemporary poetry in 2006-08.

Four out of the 30 short films present the poets' work bilingually. Menna Elfyn's reading alternates between her Welsh poems and their English translations. Joan Margarit reads in Catalan in tandem with his translator Anna Crowe reading her English translations. Palestinian poet Taha Muhammad Ali reads in Arabic and then re-inhabits each poem as it is read in English by his translator Peter Cole. Yang Lian introduces his work in English, and reads the poems in Chinese. The anthology presents all their poems in both languages in a parallel-text format, enabling you to follow either language as the poems are read on the film.

All the other readings are in English only, and in many varieties of English: not just poems read in Scottish, Welsh and Irish English by Jackie Kay, W.N. Herbert, Gwyneth Lewis, Brendan Kennelly and Micheal O'Siadhail, but also George Szirtes' Hungarian-inflected English, Benjamin Zephaniah's melding of Jamaican and Birmingham, and the Caribbean lilt of John Agard and James Berry. The musical range of American voices is just as diverse, ranging from urban Detroit (Philip Levine) to the Ozark Mountains (C.D. Wright).

THE ORAL ART

As I have said, every one of these writers is a powerful reader of poetry, and seeing and listening to their readings, anyone should gain a much greater appreciation not just of their poetry but of how the best modern poetry is conceived, written, spoken and *sounded*.

Apart from one recording taken from a live public performance, all the films present informal, one-to-one readings. You hear how the poems sound; you see how the poets read and present their work. T.S. Eliot once described poetry as 'one person talking to another', while W.H. Auden believed it was essential to hear poetry read aloud, for 'no poem, which when mastered, is not better heard than read is good poetry'. *In Person* presents the oral art of poetry in that spirit.

The 'singer everyone has heard' of Robert Frost's poem 'The Oven Bird' is both bird and poet. Frost believed that the poet's own song must carry the rhythms of human speech, as Richard Wilbur explains:

> In a famous early letter to a friend, Frost distinguished between his own practice and that of Swinburnian poets for whom 'the music of words was a matter of harmonised vowels and consonants'. For Frost, the earthier objective was 'to make sound out of what I may call the sound of sense' – which meant that the sounds and rhythms of his poems were to echo or evoke the natural intonations of animated speech. [...] In his turning away from abstract musicality, and his basing of poetry in everyday speech, Frost was one of the great invigorators of modern verse.[2]

Yet some of the strongest and most invigorating readings I've heard in my life were by the great Northumbrian poet Basil Bunting, a modernist with Swinburnian sympathies which would seem to set him at odds with Frost. Meaning and musicality came together in Bunting's readings. He believed that poetry had to be read aloud because 'the meaning of poetry...is in the sound':

Poetry, like music, is to be heard. It deals in sound – long sounds and short sounds, heavy beats and light beats, the tone relations of vowels, the relations of consonants to one another which arc likc instrumental colour in music. Poetry lies dead on the page, until some voice brings it to life, just as music, on the stave, is no more than instructions to the player. A skilled musician can imagine the sound, more or less, and a skilled reader can try to hear, mentally, what his eyes see in print: but nothing will satisfy either of them till his ears hear it as real sound in the air. Poetry must be read aloud.

Reading in silence is the source of half the misconceptions that have caused the public to distrust poetry. Without the sound, the reader looks at the lines as he looks at prose, seeking a meaning. Prose exists to convey meaning, and no meaning such as prose conveys can be expressed as well in poetry. That is not poetry's business.[3]

One of Bloodaxe's first titles was an LP record, produced in 1980, of Bunting reading his epic poem *Briggflatts* (which features the Viking king Eric Bloodaxe); in 2000 Bloodaxe published his *Complete Poems* with a cassette; in 2009 there will be a separate edition of *Briggflatts* with an audio CD at the back of the book.

Some of the other great readers I've heard seemed to almost embody their poetry as they read, notably Sorley Maclean, who rocked back and forth with the lilt of each line, and Ted Hughes, whose readings seemed infused with the original force which had fired the poems. When Robert Garioch and Norman MacCaig read their poems, they brought out the warmth and wit of their work. With other writers it was their diction, tone, narrative style or humour – as well as the music of their voice – which illuminated the poetry as they read: I'm thinking here in particular of readings by Anne Carson, Michael Donaghy, Paul Durcan, Seamus Heaney, Geoffrey Hill, Michael Longley, Derek Mahon, Paul Muldoon, Sharon Olds, Alice Oswald and Matthew Sweeney, as well as many by Bloodaxe's poets – not just the 30 *In Person* writers, but other brilliant readers, from Kamau Brathwaite to Carolyn Forché. In the case of the late and much lamented Michael Donaghy, giving readings almost entirely from memory added another dimension to the poet's work; and the same is true of Brendan Kennelly, Sinéad Morrissey, Ruth Padel and Benjamin Zephaniah.

In Ireland, the oral tradition is still so much part of the culture that many poets know their work by heart, and have such an intimate knowledge and sense of the poems they've memorised that they don't read the poems, they *say* them, and freed from the need to read their words from the page they are able to present the narrative much more freely, almost like storytellers. Brendan Kennelly, for example, knows hundreds of poems by heart, not only his own work but numerous poems by writers from Shakespeare and Milton to Yeats, Eliot, MacNeice and Kavanagh. He has given many readings without books and lectures without notes quoting great chunks of verse from memory. For our film, he chose five poems to say, and then recited them, one after another, in a single take.

Basil Bunting was critical of readings by actors with 'the defects of their profession' who were 'apt to make poetry sound theatrical', but conceded that 'actors and poets alike, if they but speak the lines, will give you more of a poem than you can get by reading it in silence'. In recent years Josephine Hart has staged readings in London theatres and at the British Library by eminent actors who know how to read poetry well. She has also produced *Catching Life by the Throat: How to Read Poetry and Why*, an anthology of eight poets with live readings by her actor-readers on an accompanying CD, a copy of which was sent to every secondary school in Britain. She wrote of this initiative to have poetry heard in the classroom:

> The sense of sound, and what Robert Frost described as 'the sound of sense', is lost unless we hear it. The loss is incalculable. Increasingly our inner ear is failing and an entire sound archive from which great poetry was not only created, but appreciated and understood, is fading away. For centuries this inner ear was trained through the speaking of poetry out loud, the oral tradition not a discipline but a voluptuous joy as we absorbed into memory the resonance of sound.
>
> The echo chambers of our minds are becoming silent. Children can leave school, or indeed university, without hearing some of the greatest lines ever written, by some of the greatest poets in this or any other language, lines mostly written to be 'sounded out'.[4]

What Josephine Hart says about the need to hear the work of our greatest poets is equally true of the best poets of our own time, and I am indebted to her for drawing my attention to what Seamus Heaney has written about the 'crucial moment of illumination' he experienced as an undergraduate on hearing T.S. Eliot's poetry spoken aloud. In his essay 'Learning from Eliot', Heaney describes the effect first of reading Eliot's essays, including his

> definition of the faculty that he called 'the auditory imagination'. This was 'the feeling for syllable and rhythm, penetrating far below the conscious levels of thought and feeling, invigorating every word; sinking to the most primitive and forgotten, returning to an origin and bringing something back...[fusing] the most ancient and civilised mentalities.' [...]
>
> At this stage of readiness to listen, I was also lucky enough to hear Eliot's poetry read aloud by the actor Robert Speaight. I had made an introductory foray into *Four Quartets* but was finding it difficult to retain any impression unified and whole in my mind. The bigness of the structure, the opacity of the thought, the complexity of the organisation of these poems held you at bay; yet while they daunted you, they promised a kind of wisdom – and it was at this tentative stage that I heard the whole thing read aloud. That experience taught me, in the words, of the poem, 'to sit still'. To sit, in fact, all through an afternoon in Belfast, in an upstairs flat, with a couple of graduate students in biochemistry, people with a less professional anxiety about understanding the poetry than I had, since in their unprofessional but rewarding way they still assumed that mystification was par for the course in modern poetry.
>
> What I *heard* made sense. [...] This procedure is available through a silent reading, of course, since (to quote again from Eliot's own definition of 'auditory imagination') it operates below the level of sense; but it operates much more potently when the poem is spoken aloud.[5]

A DVD-anthology of poetry has all kinds of benefits, not only educational and cultural, but democratic. It makes it possible for people to experience readings by poets they might never had an opportunity to see, as well as to give a platform to poets from overseas whose books receive little exposure here.

Around half a million poetry books are sold in Britain each year, so the numbers of people who attend poetry readings must be tiny compared with the number who buy or read poetry books. But not everyone lives in a town or city with a good reading series or a literature festival. In England there are wonderful poetry festivals in Aldeburgh and Ledbury, as well as Poetry International in London every two years. Scotland has StAnza in St Andrews, while Ireland has Cúirt in Galway, Cuisle in Limerick, Poetry Now in Dún Laoghaire and the Dublin Writers Festival. I've experienced many excellent readings over the years at these festivals in particular, as well as at Newcastle's Morden Tower, where I heard my first poetry reading in 1975.

Every time I've been lucky enough to be at an exceptional reading I've felt sad afterwards that so many others had missed out on it. When I've tried to describe such events, my attempts have met with blank looks. With this project of filming poets, I feel that now, at last, I'm finally able to share that experience with thousands of others. So offering these films of 30 remarkable readings by some of the best poets in the world – for the price of a book – feels almost like a revolutionary act.

NOTES

1. 'In the presence of a master and seer, listening to distilled wisdom of a lifetime's service to poetry: Neil Astley celebrates Stanley Kunitz's 100th year', *Poetry London*, 52 (Autumn 2005), 31-32.

2. 'Richard Wilbur on Robert Frost', in *Poetry Speaks*, ed. Elise Paschen & Rebekah Presson Mosby (Sourcebooks, USA, 2001).

3. Basil Bunting: 'The Poet's Point of View' (1966), in *Strong Words: modern poets on modern poetry*, ed. W.N. Herbert & Matthew Hollis (Bloodaxe Books, 2000), 80-82.

4. Josephine Hart: 'Sound, sense and sensibility', *The Guardian* (11 November 2006).

5. Seamus Heaney: 'Learning from Eliot', *Finders Keepers: Selected Prose 1971-2001* (Faber & Faber, 2002), 34-36.

PAMELA ROBERTSON-PEARCE
The Film-maker's View

While I worked on this project as a film-maker, I felt privileged to be able to experience so many personal readings by poets, mostly in their own homes and environments.

I have always read poetry, and go to poetry readings as well as to poetry festivals, but have rarely had the opportunity to be read to aloud in such an intimate setting, and to enjoy that very special relationship between writer and listener.

As the Chinese proverb has it, 'the great musician also needs a great listener'.

I love having poetry, stories or novels read to me in the evenings. It is one of my favourite moments of the day, and feels like a bond and reverberation with the past and my childhood, when the written word was only accessible to me through bedtime stories read aloud, in one of two languages, Swedish or English. Later I read a great deal to my own child. I think this really helped foster our shared love of books and reading.

Neil already knew the work of the poets we filmed, and had known most of the writers for many years. For me it felt like a great honour to be read to by them, and in many cases it was the first time I had heard these particular poets reading their work. Not only was I filming them but I was responding to every line I was hearing, and this made the readings feel even more intimate for the poets – and so also for the viewer of these films. The poets were not just reading to a camera but to a camera person sitting directly in front of them who was visibly responsive. I had to remain absolutely silent as I concentrated on the filming, but several of the poets said their reading became more intensely personal as they registered my facial mime behind the camera: if a line in a poem especially moved, shocked, surprised or delighted me, my expression showed this immediately.

I hope that you as a reader and viewer of this DVD-book will enjoy sharing this delicious experience and cornucopia of poets served up to you in your own home.

ACKNOWLEDGEMENTS

In Person is dedicated to all the writers, translators and artists whose work has been published by Bloodaxe Books, and to everyone who has worked for Bloodaxe over the past 30 years. We also dedicate it to the memory of two great lovers of poetry who helped with the filming arrangements for three of the poets, Anthony Minghella and Dr Robert Woof.

Many other people and organisations helped the project in a variety of ways. As well as the poets who gave generously of their time and hospitality, we would like to thank the following in particular: The Academy Hotel, Aldeburgh Poetry Trust (Naomi Jaffa, Michael Laskey, Dean Parkin, Judy Braggins), Apples & Snakes (Geraldine Collinge), Myra Barr, Paul Beasley, Judi Benson, Peter and Terry Born, Bobbie Bristol, Ivor Bowen, Karen Cattini, Noah Fisher, Peter Lucas, Paul Martin, William and Cynthia Morrison-Bell, Barbara Russell and Brad Foster, Brid O'Siadhail, Simon Powell, Elizabeth Sandie, Soho Theatre, Debbie Taylor, Ty Newydd (Sally Baker), and the Wordsworth Trust (Richard Stanton).

Special thanks are also due to Arts Council England (and to Rachael Ogden, Kate Griffin and Holly Hooper in particular) for assistance given to Bloodaxe's international translation and DVD project through Grants for the arts funded by the National Lottery.

NOTE ON THE TEXTS

Collections cited after each poem title in the anthology are the books (some not published by Bloodaxe) in which these poems were first published. If these collections are now out of print, the preceding note on the author will give the current source of the work. The Bibliography on pages 263-72 lists every title published by Bloodaxe from 1978 to 2008.

Note from Adrian Mitchell: 'None of my poems is to be used in connection with any examination whatsoever. I'm happy if people who like them choose to learn them, recite them or sing them in schools. But please don't make anyone study them or write essays about them. Why? Because examinations were a social experiment which has failed dismally.'

DVD 1

FLEUR ADCOCK
Filmed in London, 29 June 2007

FLEUR ADCOCK writes about men and women, childhood, identity, roots and rootlessness, memory and loss, animals and dreams, as well as our interactions with nature and place. Her poised, ironic poems are remarkable for their wry wit, conversational tone and psychological insight, unmasking the deceptions of love or unravelling family lives.

Born in New Zealand in 1934, she spent the war years in England, returning with her family to New Zealand in 1947. There she later married the poet Alistair Campbell, and they had two sons. She emigrated to Britain with her younger son Andrew in 1963, working as a librarian in London until 1979. In 1977-78, she took a year off to be writer-in-residence at Charlotte Mason College of Education, Ambleside, when she wrote the Lake District poems of *Below Loughrigg*, the second title to be published by Bloodaxe Books (this included 'Weathering'). She was Northern Arts Literary Fellow in 1979-81, living in Newcastle, becoming a freelance writer after her return to London. She received an OBE in 1996, and the Queen's Gold Medal for Poetry in 2006.

All her collections were published by Oxford University Press until they shut down their poetry list in 1999. I first met Fleur in 1977 when I produced a pamphlet for her reading at Morden Tower in Newcastle. Subsequently Bloodaxe was able to publish her pamphlets *Below Loughrigg* (1979), *Hotspur* (1986) and *Meeting the Comet* (1988), as well as her translations of medieval Latin lyrics, *The Virgin & the Nightingale* (1983). All the poems included in this DVD-book are from her *Poems 1960-2000* (2000).

Much of her work relates to family history, and a thread of family connections runs through the poems here. When we filmed her in June 2007 she was anxiously awaiting a phone call announcing the birth in New Zealand of a new granddaughter, Rosa. The first poem she reads, 'For a Five-Year-Old' was written for her son Andrew, Rosa's father (and dedicatee of another touching early poem, 'For Andrew'). 'For Heidi with Blue Hair' relates to her goddaughter. 'Counting' is about the birth of her first son Gregory, written for a commission when he was in his 30s. 'Where They Lived' recalls a visit to a street in Manchester where her grandparents lived until 1914, when they left for New Zealand with Fleur's father, then aged 10. A sepia photograph of him (then aged 24) can be seen on the sideboard behind her in the film. The two children in 'The Video' are Laura and Ceri, daughters of her niece Sarah, second daughter of her sister, the novelist Marilyn Duckworth.

For a Five-Year-Old
TIGERS 1967

A snail is climbing up the window-sill
into your room, after a night of rain.
You call me in to see, and I explain
that it would be unkind to leave it there:
it might crawl to the floor; we must take care
that no one squashes it. You understand,
and carry it outside, with careful hand,
to eat a daffodil.

I see, then, that a kind of faith prevails:
your gentleness is moulded still by words
from me, who have trapped mice and shot wild birds,
from me, who drowned your kittens, who betrayed
your closest relatives, and who purveyed
the harshest kind of truth to many another.
But that is how things are: I am your mother,
and we are kind to snails.

The Pangolin
TIGERS 1967

There have been all those tigers, of course,
and a leopard, and a six-legged giraffe,
and a young deer that ran up to my window
before it was killed, and once a blue horse,
and somewhere an impression of massive dogs.
Why do I dream of such large, hot-blooded beasts
covered with sweating fur and full of passions
when there could be dry lizards and cool frogs,
or slow, modest creatures, as a rest
from all those panting, people-sized animals?
Hedgehogs or perhaps tortoises would do,
but I think the pangolin would suit me best:
a vegetable animal, who goes
disguised as an artichoke or asparagus-tip
in a green coat of close-fitting leaves,
with his flat shovel-tail and his pencil-nose:
the scaly anteater. Yes, he would fit
more aptly into a dream than into his cage
in the Small Mammal House; so I invite him
to be dreamt about, if he would care for it.

28

An Illustration to Dante
THE SCENIC ROUTE 1974

Here are Paolo and Francesca
whirled around in the circle of Hell
clipped serenely together
her dead face raised against his.
I can feel the pressure of his arms
like yours about me, locking.

They float in a sea of whitish blobs –
fire, is it? It could have been
hail, said Ruskin, but Rossetti
'didn't know how to do hail'.
Well, he could do tenderness.
My spine trickles with little white flames.

Weathering
BELOW LOUGHRIGG 1979

Literally thin-skinned, I suppose, my face
catches the wind off the snow-line and flushes
with a flush that will never wholly settle. Well:
that was a metropolitan vanity,
wanting to look young for ever, to pass.

I was never a Pre-Raphaelite beauty,
nor anything but pretty enough to satisfy
men who need to be seen with passable women.
But now that I am in love with a place
which doesn't care how I look, or if I'm happy,

happy is how I look, and that's all.
My hair will turn grey in any case,
my nails chip and flake, my waist thicken,
and the years work all their usual changes.
If my face is to be weather-beaten as well

that's little enough lost, a fair bargain
for a year among lakes and fells, when simply
to look out of my window at the high pass
makes me indifferent to mirrors and to what
my soul may wear over its new complexion.

For Heidi with Blue Hair

THE INCIDENT BOOK 1986

When you dyed your hair blue
(or, at least, ultramarine
for the clipped sides, with a crest
of jet-black spikes on top)
you were sent home from school

because, as the headmistress put it,
although dyed hair was not
specifically forbidden, yours
was, apart from anything else,
not done in the school colours.

Tears in the kitchen, telephone calls
to school from your freedom-loving father:
'She's not a punk in her behaviour;
it's just a style.' (You wiped your eyes,
also not in a school colour.)

'She discussed it with me first –
we checked the rules.' 'And anyway, Dad,
it cost twenty-five dollars.
Tell them it won't wash out –
not even if I wanted to try.'

It would have been unfair to mention
your mother's death, but that
shimmered behind the arguments.
The school had nothing else against you;
the teachers twittered and gave in.

Next day your black friend had hers done
in grey, white and flaxen yellow –
the school colours precisely:
an act of solidarity, a witty
tease. The battle was already won.

Where They Lived

LOOKING BACK 1997

That's where they lived in the 1890s.
They don't know that we know,
or that we're standing here, in possession
of some really quite intimate information
about the causes of their deaths,
photographing each other in a brisk wind
outside their terrace house, both smiling
(not callously, we could assure them),
our hair streaming across our faces
and the green plastic Marks and Spencer's bag
in which I wrapped my camera against showers
ballooning out like a wind-sock
from my wrist, showing the direction
of something that's blowing down our century.

Counting

TIME-ZONES 1991

You count the fingers first: it's traditional.
(You assume the doctor counted them too,
when he lifted up the slimy surprise
with its long dark pointed head and its father's nose
at 2.13 a.m. – 'Look at the clock!'
said Sister: 'Remember the time: 2.13.')

Next day the head's turned pink and round;
the nose is a blob. You fumble under the gown
your mother embroidered with a sprig of daisies,
as she embroidered your own Viyella gowns
when you were a baby. You fish out
curly triangular feet. You count the toes.

'There's just one little thing,' says Sister:
'His ears – they don't quite match. One
has an extra whorl in it. No one will notice.'
You notice like mad. You keep on noticing.
Then you hear a rumour: a woman in the next ward
has had a stillbirth. Or was it something worse?

You lie there, bleeding gratefully.
You've won the Nobel Prize, and the VC,
and the State Lottery, and gone to heaven.
Feed-time comes. They bring your bundle –
the right one: it's him all right.
You count his eyelashes: the ideal number.

You take him home. He learns to walk.
From time to time you eye him,
nonchalantly, from each side.
He has an admirable nose.
No one ever notices his ears. No one
ever stands on both sides of him at once.

He grows up. He has beautiful children.

The Video

LOOKING BACK 1997

When Laura was born, Ceri watched.
They all gathered around Mum's bed –
Dad and the midwife and Mum's sister
and Ceri. 'Move over a bit,' Dad said –
he was trying to focus the camcorder
on Mum's legs and the baby's head.

After she had a little sister,
and Mum had gone back to being thin,
and was twice as busy, Ceri played
the video again and again.
She watched Laura come out, and then,
in reverse, she made her go back in.

Things

THE INNER HARBOUR 1979

There are worse things than having behaved foolishly in public.
There are worse things than these miniature betrayals,
committed or endured or suspected; there are worse things
than not being able to sleep for thinking about them.
It is 5 a.m. All the worse things come stalking in
and stand icily about the bed looking worse and worse and worse.

JOHN AGARD

Filmed in London, 10 October 2007

JOHN AGARD has been subverting British poetry for over 30 years with his mischievous, satirical fables which overturn all our expectations. He is a prolific poet and children's writer, and a charismatic performer who gives numerous readings every year in Britain and around the world. He takes part in the annual Poetry Live tour, reading 'Half-Caste' and other work to thousands of students who study his poetry on GCSE English courses.

Born in Guyana in 1949, he worked as journalist before moving to England in 1977, where he became a touring lecturer for the Commonwealth Institute, visiting nearly 2000 schools to promote Caribbean culture and poetry. In 1998 he was writer-in-residence for the BBC with the Windrush Project, and in 2007 was poet-in-residence with the National Maritime Museum in Greenwich, whose archives include documentation of the slave trade. He lives with the poet Grace Nichols and family in Sussex.

I first met him at an extraordinary five-poet reading at Newcastle's Live Theatre in Newcastle in June 1992, the last in a programme of events organised by Northern Arts for visiting poet Kamau Brathwaite. The other three readers were James Berry, Fred D'Aguiar and Grace Nichols. At that time he had published two collections with Serpent's Tail, *Mangoes and Bullets* (1985) and *Lovelines for a Goat-Born Lady* (1990). I was so knocked out by the reading that I told him I wished Bloodaxe had published his work; and said the same to James Berry. Both writers sent me their next collections.

His Bloodaxe titles are *From the Devil's Pulpit* (1997), *Weblines* (2000) and *We Brits* (2006), with two further books due in 2009, *Clever Backbone*, a sequence of new poems relating to Darwin and evolution, and *Alternative Anthem*, a DVD-book selection from previous books with films of live performances.

The first four poems in our film are from *We Brits*, which gives an outsider's inside view of British life in poems which both challenge and cherish our peculiar culture and hallowed institutions. Some explore hidden connections in British history, while others are wildly inventive forays into comic territory: Shakespeare addresses the tabloids; Jesus, Buddha and Mohammed arrive in Britain at Gatwick, Heathrow and Dover; and all the foreign words flee the English dictionary. The last poem, 'Bridge Builder', is the final climactic poem in *From the Devil's Pulpit*, poems offering a Devil's eye view of the world, sweeping from Genesis across time.

The film shows excerpts from a live performance, part of a poetry evening presented by Apples & Snakes at Soho Theatre.

Talking to Plants
WE BRITS 2006

Always talk to your plants.
Sit back and watch them flourish.
Good advice. Of course we presume
that all plants speak English.

Speak slowly, watch them bloom.
If necessary shout each syllable.
Their little ears are ready vessels
for a shower of the Queen's vowels.

Never mind if it's a China rose
or an African violet.
Better yet, recite a bit of English Lit.
See abundance spring at your fingertip.

So I spoke like an Oxford don
to my wilting rhododendron.
It wilted more. As for my drooping shrub,
my words only seem to draw more slugs.

O plants, what is it that makes you grow?
I watch my immigrant neighbour's patio
with a sense of distant envy.
Tell me, plants, must I address you in Punjabi?

Reporting from the Frontline of the Great Dictionary Disaster
WE BRITS 2006

Why has the English dictionary grown so thin?
Why is it weeping between its covers?
Because today is the day
all words of foreign origin
return to their native borders.
Linguists are rioting in the streets.
Crossword lovers are on hunger strike.
But words are voting with their feet
and familiar objects across the British Isles
have staged a mass evacuation.

Anoraks
have been seen flying off backs
remaking their Innuit tracks.

Bananas
hands forming a queue
are now bound for a Bantu rendezvous.

Hammocks
leave bodies in mid-swing
and billow back to a Carib beginning.

Pyjamas
without regard to size or age
take off on a Hindu pilgrimage.

Sofas
huddle themselves into caravans,
their destination – the Arabian sands.

Even Baguettes
(as we speak) grab the chance
to jump the channel for the south of France.

This is a tragedy
turning into a comedy
for reports are reaching us by satellite
that in the wee hours of the night
the ghosts of ancient Greeks and Romans
have been preparing an epic knees-up
to mark the homecoming of their word-hoard.
Stay tuned for live and direct coverage
on this day a dictionary mourns its language.

The Ascent of John Edmonstone

WE BRITS 2006

*(The freed black slave who taught Darwin
taxidermy at Edinburgh – 1826.)*

My name rings no bell
in the ears of science
but footnotes know me well –

footnotes where history
shows its true colours
and passing reference is flesh

for I am John Edmonstone,
whose name is little known
to evolution's white ladder.

But Darwin will remember me,
just say the black man who taught him
Egypt's ancient art of taxidermy.

To think that we should meet
in Edinburgh of all places
few doors apart on Lothian Street.

No mention then of savage races.
In those days we were two bird-stuffers
mounting mortality in feathers.

We were each other's missing link
colleagues upright on the chain of being
a pair of wingless apes condemned to think.

Alternative Anthem
WE BRITS 2006

Put the kettle on
Put the kettle on
It is the British answer
to Armageddon.

Never mind taxes rise
Never mind trains are late
One thing you can be sure of
and that's the kettle, mate.

It's not whether you lose
It's not whether you win
It's whether or not
you've plugged the kettle in.

May the kettle ever hiss
May the kettle ever steam
It is the engine
that drives our nation's dream.

Long live the kettle
that rules over us
May it be limescale free
and may it never rust.

Sing it on the beaches
Sing it from the housetops
The sun may set on empire
but the kettle never stops.

Bridge Builder

FROM THE DEVIL'S PULPIT 1997

Bridge-builder I am
between the holy and the damned
between the bitter and the sweet
between the chaff and the wheat

Bridge-builder I am
between the goat and the lamb
between the sermon and the sin
between the princess and Rumpelstiltskin

Bridge-builder I am
between the yoni and the lingam
between the darkness and the light
between the left hand and the right

Bridge-builder I am
between the storm and the calm
between the nightmare and the sleeper
between the cradle and the Reaper

Bridge-builder I am
between the hex and the hexagram
between the chalice and the cauldron
between the gospel and the Gorgon

Bridge-builder I am
between the serpent and the wand
between the hunter and the hare
between the curse and the prayer

Bridge-builder I am
between the hanger and the hanged
between the water and the wine
between the pearls and the swine

Bridge-builder I am
between the beast and the human
for who can stop the dance
of eternal balance?

ELIZABETH ALEXANDER
Filmed in Grasmere, Cumbria, 24 October 2006

ELIZABETH ALEXANDER is a leading American poet whose work has been inspired by a wide range of influence, from history, literature, art and music, dreams and stories to the 'rich infinity' of the African American experience. Hers is a vital and vivid poetic voice on race, gender, politics and motherhood. Many of her poems bring history alive and singing into the present in highly musical, sharply contemporary narratives which use many different forms and voices to cover subjects ranging from slave rebellions, the Civil Rights movement, Muhammed Ali and Toni Morrison to the lives of jazz musicians and the 'Venus Hottentot', a 19th-century African woman exhibited at carnivals (also the subject of a poem by Jackie Kay).

She has published four collections of poetry in the US, *Venus Hottentot* (1990), *Body of Life* (1996), *Antebellum Dream Book* (2001) and *American Sublime* (2005), as well as a book of essays on African American artistic life through literature, painting, film and popular media, *The Black Interior* (Graywolf Press, 2004). Her first British publication, *American Blue: Selected Poems* 2006), draws on all these. The anthology *Bloodaxe Poetry Introductions: 1* (2006) includes a selection of her poems with extracts from an interview and an essay on African American poetry.

She was born in 1962 in Harlem, New York, grew up in Washington, DC, and studied at the universities of Yale, Boston and Pennsylvania. She lives in New Haven, Connecticut, and is Professor of African-American Studies at Yale University. She has received many awards, including, mostly recently, an inaugural Alphonse Fletcher, Sr Award for work 'that contributes to improving race relations in American society', and a fellowship at the Radcliffe Institute in 2007-08. Her latest titles are *Power & Possibility: Essays, Reviews and Interviews* (University of Michigan Press, 2007) and a collaboration with poet Marilyn Nelson and artist Floyd Cooper, *Miss Crandall's School for Young Ladies & Little Misses of Color* (Wordsong, 2007).

In the film she reads poems from three of the collections covered by *American Blue*. 'Translator' is from a long sequence, *Amistad*, about a rebellion in 1839 aboard a Spanish schooner taking slaves from Africa to Cuba; the ship was seized by the US Navy and taken to New Haven, Connecticut, but after a series of trials and appeals, the captives were eventually freed and returned to Sierra Leone.

We met for the first time in 2006 before her first UK reading at Dove Cottage, Grasmere, and filmed her in the library of the Jerwood Centre.

Smile

AMERICAN SUBLIME 2005

When I see a black man smiling
like that, nodding and smiling
with both hands visible, mouthing

'Yes, Officer', across the street,
I think of my father, who taught us
the words 'cooperate', 'officer',

to memorise badge numbers,
who has seen black men shot at
from behind in the warm months north.

And I think of the fine line –
hairline, eyelash, fingernail paring –
the whisper that separates

obsequious from *safe*. Armstrong,
Johnson, Robinson, Mays.
A woman with a yellow head

of cotton candy hair stumbles out
of a bar at after-lunchtime
clutching a black man's arm as if

for her life. And the brother
smiles, and his eyes are flint
as he watches all sides of the street.

Ars Poetica #92: Marcus Garvey on Elocution

AMERICAN SUBLIME 2005

Elocution means to speak out.
That is to say, if you have a tale to tell,
tell it and tell it well.

This I was taught.

To speak properly you must have sound and good teeth.
You must have clear nostrils.
Your lungs must be sound.
Never try to make a speech on a hungry stomach.

Don't chew your words but talk them out plainly.
Always see that your clothing is properly arranged before you get on a platform.
You should not make any mistake in pronouncing your words
because that invites amusement for certain people.

To realise I was trained for this,
expected to speak out, to speak well.
To realise, my family believed
I would have words for others.

An untidy leader is always a failure.
A leader's hair should always be well kept.
His teeth must also be in perfect order.
Your shoes and other garments must also be clean.
If you look ragged, people will not trust you.

My father's shoe-shine box:
black Kiwi, cordovan Kiwi,
the cloths, the lambswool brush.

My grandmother's dressing table:
potions for disciplining
anything scraggle or stray.

For goodness sake, always speak out,
said Marcus Garvey,
said my parents,
said my grandparents,
and meant it.

Ars Poetica #100: I Believe
AMERICAN SUBLIME 2005

Poetry, I tell my students,
is idiosyncratic. Poetry

is where we are ourselves
(though Sterling Brown said

'Every "I" is a dramatic "I"'),
digging in the clam flats

for the shell that snaps,
emptying the proverbial pocketbook.

Poetry is what you find
in the dirt in the corner,

overhear on the bus, God
in the details, the only way

to get from here to there.
Poetry (and now my voice is rising)

is not all love, love, love,
and I'm sorry the dog died.

Poetry (here I hear myself loudest)
is the human voice,

and are we not of interest to each other?

Translator

(JAMES COVEY: *from 'Amistad'*)
AMERICAN SUBLIME 2005

I was stolen from Mendeland as a child
then rescued by the British ship *Buzzard*
and brought to Freetown, Sierra Leone.

I love ships and the sea, joined this crew
of my own accord, set sail as a teen,
now re-supplying in New York Harbor.

When the white professor first came to me
babbling sounds, I thought he needed help
until *weta*, my mother's six, hooked my ear

and I knew what he was saying, and I knew
what he wanted in an instant, for we had heard
wild tales of black pirates off New London,

the captives, the low black schooner like
so many ships, an infinity of ships fatted
with Africans, men, women, children

as I was. Now it is my turn to rescue.
I have not spoken Mende in some years,
yet every night I dream it, or silence.

To New Haven, to the jail. To my people.
Who am I now? This them, not them. We burst
with joy to speak and settle to the tale:

We killed the cook, who said he would cook us.
They rubbed gunpowder and vinegar in our wounds.
We were taken away in broad daylight.

And in a loud voice loud as a thousand waves
I sing my father's song. It shakes the jail.
I sing from my entire black body.

Race

ANTEBELLUM DREAM BOOK 2001

Sometimes I think about Great-Uncle Paul who left Tuskegee,
Alabama to become a forester in Oregon and in so doing
became fundamentally white for the rest of his life, except
when he traveled without his white wife to visit his siblings –
now in New York, now in Harlem, USA – just as pale-skinned,
as straight-haired, as blue-eyed as Paul, and black. Paul never told anyone
he was white, he just didn't say that he was black, and who could imagine,
an Oregon forester in 1930 as anything other than white?
The siblings in Harlem each morning ensured
no one confused them for anything other than what they were, black.
They were black! Brown-skinned spouses reduced confusion.
Many others have told, and not told, this tale.
When Paul came East alone he was as they were, their brother.

The poet invents heroic moments where the pale black ancestor stands up
on behalf of the race. The poet imagines Great-Uncle Paul
in cool, sagey groves counting rings in redwood trunks,
imagines pencil markings in a ledger book, classifications,
imagines a sidelong look from an ivory spouse who is learning
her husband's caesuras. She can see silent spaces
but not what they signify, graphite markings in a forester's code.

Many others have told, and not told, this tale.
The one time Great-Uncle Paul brought his wife to New York
he asked his siblings not to bring their spouses,
and that is where the story ends: ivory siblings who would not
see their brother without their telltale spouses.
What a strange thing is "race", and family, stranger still.
Here a poem tells a story, a story about race.

House Party Sonnet: '66
THE VENUS HOTTENTOT 1990

Small, still. Fit through the banister slit.
Where did our love go? Where did our love go?
Scattered high heels and the carpet rolled back.
Where did our love go? Where did our love go?
My brother and I, tipping down from upstairs
Under the cover of 'Where Did Our Love Go?'
Cat-eyed Supremes wearing siren-green gowns.
Pink curls of laughter and hips when they shake
Shake a tambourine *where did our love go?*
Where did our love go? Where did our love go?
Stale chips next morning, shoes under the couch,
Smoke-smelling draperies, water-paled Scotch.
Matches, stray earrings to find and to keep –
Hum of invisible dancers asleep.

Little Slave Narrative #1: Master
AMERICAN SUBLIME 2005

He would order the women to pull up their clothes
'in Alabama style', as he called it. He would whip them

for not complying. He taught bloodhounds
to chase down negro boys, hence the expression

'hell-hounds on my trail'. He was fond of peach brandy,
put ads in the paper: *Search high, search low*

for my runaway Isaac, my runaway Joe,
his right cheek scarred, occasioned by buckshot,

runaway Ben Fox, very black, chunky made,
two hundred dollars live, and if dead,

bring his dead body, so I may look at it.

JAMES BERRY
Filmed in London, 27 June 2007

JAMES BERRY was born in 1924 in Jamaica where he grew up in a tiny seaside village. He learnt to read before he was four years old, mostly from the Bible, which he often read aloud to his mother's friends. When he was 17, he went to work in America, but hated the way black people were treated there, and returned to Jamaica after four years. In 1948, he made his way to Britain, and took a job working for British Telecom. He lives in London.

One of the first black writers in Britain to achieve wider recognition, he rose to prominence in 1981 when he won the National Poetry Competition. His numerous books include two seminal anthologies of Caribbean poetry, *Bluefoot Traveller* (1976) and *News for Babylon* (Chatto, 1984), and six collections of poetry, including *Fractured Circles* (1979) and *Lucy's Letters and Loving* (1982) from New Beacon Books, *Chain of Days* (Oxford University Press, 1985), and *Hot Earth Cold Earth* (1995) and *Windrush Songs* (2007) from Bloodaxe. He has published several books of poetry and short stories for children, and won many literary prizes. He was awarded the OBE in 1990.

The first two poems he reads on the film are from *Hot Earth Cold Earth*, which celebrates the divided world of a lifelong outsider, a poet of two tongues, 'Hot Earth' Creole and 'Cold Earth' English. These are followed by four poems from *Windrush Songs* giving voice to the people who came on the first ships from the Caribbean, whose journeys held strange echoes of earlier sea voyages which had brought ancestors from Africa to the slave plantations. Berry came to Britain on the next ship after the *Windrush* and shared many of the experiences that prompted this migration in search of change and a better life. His book explores the different reasons his fellow travellers had for leaving the Caribbean when they rushed to get on the boat. The poems also look back on slavery and individual experiences of hardship and trying to make a living: *'Mi one milkin cow just die! / Gone, gone – and leave me / Like hurricane disaster!'*

I first heard him read at Newcastle's Live Theatre in Newcastle in June 1992, the last in a programme of events organised by Northern Arts for visiting poet Kamau Brathwaite, an extraordinary reading which also featured John Agard, Fred D'Aguiar and Grace Nichols. He submitted the manuscript of his next book to Bloodaxe, and *Hot Earth Cold Earth* followed in 1995, including a large selection of new poems as well as the best work from his previous collection *Chain of Days*, which OUP had allowed to go out of print.

Defendant in a Jamaican Court

HOT EARTH COLD EARTH 1995

Yes I did chop him, sar.
I chop him.
I woz full-full
of the vexation of spirit, sar.

I woz beyon all ow I know me, sar –
over the odda side cut off
from all mi goodness
and I couldn steady mi han firm, sar.

I chop him shoulder.
I let mi distric man blood stream down.

Him did storm up mi bad-bad waters
that I couldn settle –
that flood me, sar –
that mek one quick-quick terrible shut-eye
when all mi badness did rule.

Words of a Jamaican Laas Moment Them

HOT EARTH COLD EARTH 1995

When I dead
mek rain fall.
Mek the air wash.
Mek the lan wash good-good.
Mek dry course them run, and run.

As laas breath gone
mek rain burst –
hilltop them work
waterfall, and all
the gully them gargle fresh.

Mek breadfruit limb them drip,
mango limb them drip. Cow, hog, fowl
stan still, in the burst of clouds.
Poinciana bloom them soak off, clean-clean.
Grass go unda water.

46

Instant I gone
mek all the Island wash – wash away
the mess of my shortcomings –
all the brok-up things I did start.
Mi doings did fall short too much.
Mi ways did hurt mi wife too oftn.

To Travel This Ship
WINDRUSH SONGS 2007

To travel this ship, man
I gladly strip mi name
of a one-cow, two-goat an a boar pig
an sell the land piece mi father lef
to be on this ship and to be a debtor.

Man, jus fa diffrun days
I woulda sell, borrow or thief
jus fa diffrun sunrise an sundown
in annodda place wid odda ways.

To travel this ship, man
I woulda hurt, I woulda cheat or lie,
I strip mi yard, mi friend and cousin-them
To get this yah ship ride.

Man – I woulda sell mi modda
Jus hopin to buy her back.
Down in dat hole I was
I see this lickle luck, man,
I see this lickle light.

Man, Jamaica is a place
Where generations them start out
Havin notn, earnin notn,
And – dead – leavin notn.

I did wake up every mornin
and find notn change.
Children them shame to go to school barefoot.
Only a penny to buy lunch.

Man, I follow this lickle light for change.
I a-follow it, man!

Englan Voice

WINDRUSH SONGS 2007

I prepare – an prepare well – fe Englan.
Me decide, and done leave behine
all the voice of ol slave-estate bushman.

None of that distric bad-talk in Englan,
that bush talk of ol slave-estate man.

Hear me speak in Englan, an see
you dohn think I a Englan native.

Me nah go say
'Bwoy, how you du?'
me a-go say 'How are you old man?'

Me nah go say
'Wha yu nyam las night?'
me a-go say 'What did you have for supper?'

Patois talk is bushman talk –
people who talk patois them dam lazy.

Because mi bush voice so settle in me
an might let me down in-a Englan
me a-practise.

Me a-practise talk like teacher
till mi Englan voice come out-a me
like water from hillside rock.

Even if you fellows here
dohn hear mi Englan voice
I have it – an hear it in mi head!

In the Land and Sea Culture-crossed

WINDRUSH SONGS 2007

In the land and sea culture-crossed
we call to the hearts of difference.
Restless, we widen our boundaries.
Expansion may be for self-loving, yet
our world is smaller and closer
and, in gesturing, we touch different other.

A voice in me says:
Completeness comes from
a balance of allness.
All faces and conditions you not
only inherit but with them must find
agreement and oneness.

A voice in me says: Who is not
a beginner, seeking balance?
Who does not want to be heights and depths of music
harmonious with all difference?

A voice in me says:
We will change wildness to love,
into rejuvenation.
There is madness in self-love
we will change it to sanity.
We will release change in each other.

As the ground catches the rotten fruit
for its centre to grow again, and
as only our *negative* selves are hurt by cleansing
for the expansion of self essence,
oh, let us more and more know.

Let us strive for
a coming together of allness in the self,
as, at peace with our centre
inhabiting all faces
inhabiting the core of all centres
being at home with allness
we strive to become habitation of allness.

New Space

WINDRUSH SONGS 2007

I lived where the day's light was
a clean and open transparency
so clear I should see into level distances
and, from hilltops,
know every fluttering wing,
every leaf down to the sprawling sea.

I should know every sky glow
and be dreaming in
the white sheeting of moonlight –
moonlight's wide sheeting.

I should be well washed
by clean green spaces and the gargle
of clear and stony streams, invisible
on sheer bird-throated land.

I should sway and echo with
the ancient sea's voice
and its depths, pregnant with life
more varied than the air holds –

longing to stand on the feet of a passing day
        and be carried
                where all new time is stored.

DAVID CONSTANTINE
Filmed in Oxford, 28 October 2007

DAVID CONSTANTINE is an English poet known also for his transla-
tions of poets such as Enzensberger, Goethe, Hölderlin, Kleist and
Jaccottet. His poetry stands outside the current literary climate, and
like the work of the European and English poets who have nour-
ished him, it is informed by a profoundly humane vision of the
world. Its mood is often one of unease, elegiac or comically edged,
barbed with pain or tinged with pleasure. His poems hold a wor-
ried and restless balance between celebration and anxiety, restraint
and longing. His early influences included Graves, Lawrence and
Edward Thomas, poets he admired 'for their passion and attention
to the real and the mythic world'; other poets important for him
and his work would include Keats, Wordsworth, Clare and Hardy.

Born in 1944 in Salford, Lancashire, he read Modern Languages
at Oxford, and lectured in German at Durham (1969-81) and Oxford
(1981-2000). He is a Fellow of the Queen's College, Oxford; a free-
lance writer and translator, based in Oxford and Scilly; and co-
editor with Helen Constantine of *Modern Poetry in Translation*.

I first met him in the 70s when working on *Stand*, which pub-
lished his poem sequence, 'In Memoriam 8571 Private J.W. Gleave'.
He had published very few poems at that time. In 1979 I asked if
he would send me some poems for my anthology *Ten North-East
Poets* (1980). All these were so strong that I asked to see more, and
was astonished to discover that he had a full manuscript of poems,
very few of which anyone had wanted to publish, such was the
difference between his work and what editors preferred then. His
first collection, *A Brightness to Cast Shadows* (1980), was launched
at Durham University with my anthology and very well received.

Bloodaxe has since published seven more poetry collections by him,
as well as his *Collected Poems* (2004), which includes all the poems
he reads in the film. In 1998 he was joint winner of the European
Translation Prize for his translation of Friedrich Hölderlin's *Selected
Poems* (1990; new edition, 1996), and he won the Poetry Society's
Corneliu M. Popescu Prize for European Poetry Translation in
2003 for his translation of Hans Magnus Enzensberger's *Lighter
Than Air* (2002). His other Bloodaxe titles are *Hölderlin's Sophocles*,
his English translations of Hölderlin's German versions of Soph-
ocles' *Oedipus* and *Antigone* (2001); two editions in the Bloodaxe
Contemporary French Poets series, *Spaced, Displaced* by Henri
Michaux (with Helen Constantine, 1992) and *Under Clouded Skies /
Beauregard* by Philippe Jaccottet (with Mark Treharne, 1994); his
novel *Davies* (1985); and *A Living Language* (2004), his Newcastle /
Bloodaxe poetry lectures.

Watching for Dolphins

WATCHING FOR DOLPHINS 1983

In the summer months on every crossing to Piraeus
One noticed that certain passengers soon rose
From seats in the packed saloon and with serious
Looks and no acknowledgement of a common purpose
Passed forward through the small door into the bows
To watch for dolphins. One saw them lose

Every other wish. Even the lovers
Turned their desires on the sea, and a fat man
Hung with equipment to photograph the occasion
Stared like a saint, through sad bi-focals; others,
Hopeless themselves, looked to the children for they
Would see dolphins if anyone would. Day after day

Or on their last opportunity all gazed
Undecided whether a flat calm were favourable
Or a sea the sun and the wind between them raised
To a likeness of dolphins. Were gulls a sign, that fell
Screeching from the sky or over an unremarkable place
Sat in a silent school? Every face

After its character implored the sea.
All, unaccustomed, wanted epiphany,
Praying the sky would clang and the abused Aegean
Reverberate with cymbal, gong and drum.
We could not imagine more prayer, and had they then
On the waves, on the climax of our longing come

Smiling, snub-nosed, domed like satyrs, oh
We should have laughed and lifted the children up
Stranger to stranger, pointing how with a leap
They left their element, three or four times, centred
On grace, and heavily and warm re-entered,
Looping the keel. We should have felt them go

Further and further into the deep parts. But soon
We were among the great tankers, under their chains
In black water. We had not seen the dolphins
But woke, blinking. Eyes cast down
With no admission of disappointment the company
Dispersed and prepared to land in the city.

52

Something for the Ghosts
SOMETHING FOR THE GHOSTS 2002

Here's something for the ghosts who are
No one now and can't come up against
The edge of anyone else: that heavy skirt,
Your bare cold feet come out from under it,
Their print, black wet, on the slabs of slate

For days. Poor ghosts, where they are mine and thine
Flit like snowflakes, drift like mist, not like
My grasp of your black hair, the rain in it,
The smell of the rain that I breathed in after
For days. Poor gibbering ghosts, when they have done

Their best with bits of sound to shape someone
They knew or thought they knew or wished they had
It never amounts to anything more than this
Ghost of a mouth with questions in such as
Who were you and who did you think I was?

Legger
SOMETHING FOR THE GHOSTS 2002

Casting him off from the sympathetic horses
They shoved him gently into the low hole
Telling him the drift, such as it was, would help him
And that the level of the water would not rise or fall.

He went in snug as a shuttle with a lantern in the bows
About as bright as the light on a glow-worm's tail
And lay on his back the way they had said he must
And began to leg his longboat through the hill

Mile after mile, only as fast as Shanks's
And the sun came and went and the same old stars
Shifted their quarters slowly as it is fixed they will
And he continued his course out of sight of theirs

Treading the slimy ceiling in his hobnail boots
Like a living dead as though to slide the lid
He trod and trod and the heavy water
Squeezed past him with a shudder on either side.

I have had a picnic on that sunny hill
And read 'The Lady of Shalott' to a romantic girl
Hoping it would undress her and lay her down
Smiling under my shadow and my smile

And all the while those thousands of fathoms down
Under the severed ends of sinister lodes
His legs even in his dreams, even dead asleep,
Were trudging along the roof of his one and only road

Long since without even a fag end of light
Even the kindness of dumb animals long since gone from mind
Under the weight of millions of years of rock
And twenty hundred of christian humankind.

He will be a wonder when he comes out of the hill
On our side berthing in the orange water
In the old wharfs among the sunken skeletons
Of the ancient narrowboats, strange as Arthur

In his overalls and the soles of his boots and the soles
Of his feet worn through and no light in his eyes
Under the interest of our savants and our developers
Grinning with horror, rictus of the bad old days.

Common and Particular

SOMETHING FOR THE GHOSTS 2002

I like these men and women who have to do with death,
Formal, gentle people whose job it is,
They mind their looks, they use words carefully.

I liked that woman in the sunny room
One after the other receiving such as me
Every working day. She asks the things she must

And thanks me for the answers. Then I don't mind
Entering your particulars in little boxes,
I like the feeling she has seen it all before,

There is a form, there is a way. But also
That no one come to speak up for a shade
Is like the last, I see she knows that too.

I'm glad there is a form to put your details in,
Your dates, the cause. Glad as I am of men
Who'll make a trestle of their strong embrace

And in a slot between two other slots
Do what they have to every working day:
Carry another weight for someone else.

It is common. You are particular.

New Year Behind the Asylum
SOMETHING FOR THE GHOSTS 2002

There was the noise like when the men in droves
Are hurrying to the match only this noise was
Everybody hurrying to see the New Year in
In town under the clock but we, that once,

He said would I come our usual Saturday walk
And see it in out there in the open fields
Behind the asylum. Even on sunny days
How it troubled me more and more the nearer we got

And he went quiet and as if he was ashamed
For what he must always do, which was
Go and grip the bars of the iron gates and stand
Staring into the garden until they saw him.

They were like the animals, so glad and shy
Like overgrown children dressed in things
Handed down too big or small and they came in a crowd
And said hello with funny chunnering noises

And through the bars, looking so serious,
He put his empty hand out. But that night
We crept past quickly and only stopped
In the middle of the empty fields and there

While the clock in the square where the normal people stood
And all the clocks in England were striking twelve
We heard the rejoicings for the New Year
From works and churches and the big ships in the docks

So faint I wished we were hearing nothing at all
We were so far away in our black fields
I felt we might not ever get back again
Where the people were and it was warm, and then

Came up their sort of rejoicing out of the asylum,
Singing or sobbing I don't know what it was
Like nothing on earth, their sort of welcoming in
Another New Year and it was only then

When the bells and the cheerful hooters couldn't be heard
But only the inmates, only the poor mad people
Singing or sobbing their hearts out for the New Year
That he gripped me fast and kissed my hair

And held me in against him and clung on tight to me
Under a terrible number of bare stars
So far from town and the lights and house and home
And shut my ears against the big children crying

But listened himself, listened and listened
That one time. And I've thought since and now
He's dead I'm sure that what he meant was this:
That I should know how much love would be needed.

IMTIAZ DHARKER
Filmed in London, 11 March 2008

IMTIAZ DHARKER's cultural experience spans three countries. Born in 1954 in Lahore, Pakistan, she grew up a Muslim Calvinist in a Lahori household in Glasgow, later eloping with a Hindu Indian to live in Bombay. She now lives between Mumbai (where she makes documentary films), London and Wales. It is from this life of transitions that she draws her main themes: childhood, exile, journeying, home, displacement, religious strife and terror. 'I knew I didn't belong in one place,' she has said, 'but I began to feel strongly that this wasn't a bad thing...My real country and culture is movement, transition, crossing over.'

She is also an accomplished artist, and her drawings form an integral part of her books. Her first collection *Purdah* was published by Oxford University Press in India in 1989, and her second, *Postcards from god*, by Penguin India in 1994. After Michael Hulse judged the All India Poetry Competition with her in 1995, he sent me his copies of these two books, suggesting that Bloodaxe should consider publishing them in Britain. Some months later Jo Shapcott returned from India with the same recommendation. I arranged to meet Imtiaz on her next trip to London, in 1996, and we agreed that Bloodaxe would publish an edition combining the poems of *Purdah* and *Postcards from god* in 1997, including not just the drawings from the Indian edition of *Postcards from god* but also those relating to *Purdah* which OUP had not included. Bloodaxe has since published two subsequent collections with their drawings, *I speak for the devil* (2001) and *The terrorist at my table* (2006), with Penguin India publishing their own editions a year later.

In *Purdah*, she is a traveller between cultures, while in *Postcards from god*, she imagines an anguished god surveying a world stricken by fundamentalism. In *I speak for the devil*, the woman's body is a territory, a thing that is possessed, owned by herself or by another. Her sequence from that book, *They'll say, 'She must be from another country'* (she reads its title-poem in the film) traces a journey, starting with a striptease where the claims of nationality, religion and gender are cast off, to allow an exploration of new territories, the spaces *between* countries, cultures and religions.

The terrorist at my table asks crucial questions about how we live now – working, travelling, eating, listening to the news, preparing for attack. What do any of us know about the person who shares this street, this house, this table, this body? When life is in the hands of a fellow-traveller, a neighbour, a lover, son or daughter, how does the world shift and reform itself around our doubt, our belief?

Blessing

PURDAH 1989

The skin cracks like a pod.
There never is enough water.

Imagine the drip of it,
the small splash, echo
in a tin mug,
the voice of a kindly god.

Sometimes, the sudden rush
of fortune. The municipal pipe bursts,
silver crashes to the ground
and the flow has found
a roar of tongues. From the huts,
a congregation: every man woman
child for streets around
butts in, with pots,
brass, copper, aluminium,
plastic buckets,
frantic hands,

and naked children
screaming in the liquid sun,
their highlights polished to perfection,
flashing light,
as the blessing sings
over their small bones.

Honour killing
I SPEAK FOR THE DEVIL 2001

At last I'm taking off this coat,
    this black coat of a country
    that I swore for years was mine,
    that I wore more out of habit
    than design.
    Born wearing it,
    I believed I had no choice.

I'm taking off this veil,
    this black veil of a faith
    that made me faithless
    to myself,
    that tied my mouth,
    gave my god a devil's face,
    and muffled my own voice.

I'm taking off these silks,
    these lacy things
    that feed dictator dreams,
    the mangalsutra and the rings
    rattling in a tin cup of needs
    that beggared me.

I'm taking off this skin,
    and then the face, the flesh,
    the womb.

Let's see
    what I am in here
    when I squeeze past
    the easy cage of bone.

Let's see
    what I am out here,
    making, crafting,
    plotting
    at my new geography.

The terrorist at my table

THE TERRORIST AT MY TABLE 2006

I slice sentences to turn them into
onions. On this chopping board, they
seem more organised,
as if with a little effort
I could begin
to understand their shape.

At my back, the news is the same
as usual. A train
blown up, hostages taken.
Outside, in Pollokshields, the rain.

I go upstairs, come down.
I go to the kitchen.
When things are in their place,
they look less difficult.
I cut and chop. I don't need to see,
through onion tears,
my own hand power the knife.

Here is the food. I put it on the table.
The tablecloth is fine cutwork,
sent from home. Beneath it, Gaza
is a spreading watermark.

Here are the facts, fine
as onion rings.
The same ones can come chopped
or sliced.

Shoes, kitchens, onions can be left
behind, but at a price.
Knowledge is something you can choose
to give away,
but giving and taking leave a stain.

Who gave the gift of Palestine?

Cut this. Chop this,
this delicate thing
haloed in onion skin.

Your generosity turns my hands
to knives,
the tablecloth to fire.

Outside, on the face of Jerusalem,
I feel the rain.

How to cut a pomegranate

THE TERRORIST AT MY TABLE 2006

'Never,' said my father,
'Never cut a pomegranate
through the heart. It will weep blood.
Treat it delicately, with respect.

Just slit the upper skin across four quarters.
This is a magic fruit,
so when you split it open, be prepared
for the jewels of the world to tumble out,
more precious than garnets,
more lustrous than rubies,
lit as if from inside.
Each jewel contains a living seed.
Separate one crystal.
Hold it up to catch the light.
Inside is a whole universe.
No common jewel can give you this.'

Afterwards, I tried to make necklaces
of pomegranate seeds.
The juice spurted out, bright crimson,
and stained my fingers, then my mouth.

I didn't mind. The juice tasted of gardens
I had never seen, voluptuous
with myrtle, lemon, jasmine,
and alive with parrots' wings.

The pomegranate reminded me
that somewhere I had another home.

They'll say, 'She must be from another country'

I SPEAK FOR THE DEVIL 2001

When I can't comprehend
why they're burning books
or slashing paintings,
when they can't bear to look
at god's own nakedness,
when they ban the film
and gut the seats to stop the play
and I ask why
they just smile and say,
'She must be
from another country.'

When I speak on the phone
and the vowel sounds are off
when the consonants are hard
and they should be soft,
they'll catch on at once
they'll pin it down
they'll explain it right away
to their own satisfaction,
they'll cluck their tongues
and say,
'She must be
from another country.'

When my mouth goes up
instead of down,
when I wear a tablecloth
to go to town,
when they suspect I'm black
or hear I'm gay
they won't be surprised,
they'll purse their lips
and say,
'She must be
from another country.'

When I eat up the olives
and spit out the pits
when I yawn at the opera
in the tragic bits
when I pee in the vineyard
as if it were Bombay,

62

flaunting my bare ass
covering my face
laughing through my hands
they'll turn away,
shake their heads quite sadly,
'She doesn't know any better,'
they'll say,
'She must be
from another country.'

Maybe there is a country
where all of us live,
all of us freaks
who aren't able to give
our loyalty to fat old fools,
the crooks and thugs
who wear the uniform
that gives them the right
to wave a flag,
puff out their chests,
put their feet on our necks,
and break their own rules.

But from where we are
it doesn't look like a country,
it's more like the cracks
that grow between borders
behind their backs.
That's where I live.
And I'll be happy to say,
'I never learned your customs.
I don't remember your language
or know your ways.
I must be
from another country.'

MAURA DOOLEY
Filmed in London, 8 October 2007

MAURA DOOLEY's poetry is remarkable for embracing both lyricism and political consciousness, for its fusion of head and heart. These qualities have won her wide acclaim. Helen Dunmore (in *Poetry Review*) admired her 'sharp and forceful' intelligence. Adam Thorpe praised her ability 'to enact and find images for complex feelings... Her poems have both great delicacy and an undeniable toughness ...she manages to combine detailed domesticity with lyrical beauty, most perfectly in the metaphor of memory' (*Literary Review*).

Born in Truro in 1957, she grew up in Bristol. She was co-director with her husband David Hunter of the Arvon Foundation's Lumb Bank centre in Yorkshire for five years until 1987, and then Literature Officer of London's South Bank Centre. She is now a freelance writer and lectures at Goldsmiths' College in London.

I first met her at Lumb Bank when she had published some fine poems in magazines, and encouraged her to send a collection to Bloodaxe when she felt ready. Her first pamphlet collection, *Ivy Leaves & Arrows* (1986) from Bloodaxe was followed by her first full-length collection, *Explaining Magnetism*, in 1991. Her second collection, *Kissing a Bone* (1996), was shortlisted for the T.S. Eliot Prize. The poems she reads on the film are all included in *Sound Barrier: Poems 1982-2002* (2002), except for a recent poem, 'The Elevator', from her latest collection, *Life Under Water* (2008). Her other books include two Bloodaxe anthologies, *Making for Planet Alice: New Women Poets* (1997) and *The Honey Gatherers: A Book of Love Poems* (2002), and *How Novelists Work* (2000) from Seren.

Interviewed by Lidia Vianu in 2003, she described her reading and influences: 'Growing up I read Philip Larkin, William Blake, W.B. Yeats, and Seamus Heaney most of all. Then the Metaphysicals, Miroslav Holub, Wallace Stevens, the New York School and Rimbaud. At school we read T.S. Eliot and D.H. Lawrence. All men, you'll notice. It's different now. We just did not have so many women in print then. But I'd say that music and song lyrics were at least as strong an influence at that time: Bob Dylan, Van Morrison, Elvis Costello, Joni Mitchell...then the end of a strong moment in the British folk scene, reggae and the beginnings of punk. I read Sylvia Plath when I was very young but didn't understand her till later. Then I read Paul Muldoon, Medbh McGuckian, early Derek Walcott, Michael Longley, Fleur Adcock, Gillian Clarke, Anne Sexton and at this time discovering some great work through translation: Marina Tsvetaeva, Czesław Miłosz, Nina Cassian. In the late 80s I was stunned by C.K. Williams and Sharon Olds: lots of the Americans.'

What Every Woman Should Carry

KISSING A BONE 1996

My mother gave me the prayer to Saint Theresa.
I added a used tube ticket, kleenex,
several Polo mints (furry), a tampon, pesetas,
a florin. Not wishing to be presumptuous,
not trusting you either, a pack of 3.
I have a pen. There is space for my guardian
angel, she has to fold her wings. Passport.
A key. Anguish, at what I said/didn't say
when once you needed/didn't need me. Anadin.
A credit card. His face the last time,
my impatience, my useless youth.
That empty sack, my heart. A box of matches.

History

KISSING A BONE 1996

It's only a week but already you are slipping
down the cold black chute of history. Postcards.
Phonecalls. It's like never having seen the Wall,
except in pieces on the dusty shelves of friends.

Once I queued for hours to see the moon in a box
inside a museum, so wild it should have been kept
in a zoo at least but there it was, unremarkable,
a pile of dirt some god had shaken down.

I wait for your letters now: a fleet of strange cargo
with news of changing borders, a heart's small
journeys. They're like the relics of a saint.
Opening the dry white papers is kissing a bone.

Dancing at Oakmead Road

KISSING A BONE 1996

Sometimes I think of its bright cramped spaces,
the child who grew there and the one we lost,
how when we swept up for its newest lover
the empty rooms were still so full of us.

The honeyed boards I knew would yet hold close
our dusts, some silver from my father's head,
the resin of the wood would somehow catch
in patina the pattern of his tread.

That time in the back room, laughing and drunk,
Geraldo and his orchestra, a tune
that had you up and waltzing and me quiet,
my throat so achey at the sight of you,

glimpsing for a second how it might have been
before his mouth went down on yours, before
the War, before the children broke into
the dance, before the yoke of work. Before.

Freight

KISSING A BONE 1996

I am the ship in which you sail,
little dancing bones,
your passage between the dream
and the waking dream,
your sieve, your pea-green boat.
I'll pay whatever toll your ferry needs.
And you, whose history's already charted
in a rope of cells, be tender to
those other unnamed vessels
who will surprise you one day,
tug-tugging, irresistible,
and float you out beyond your depth,
where you'll look down, puzzled, amazed.

The Weighing of the Heart

SOUND BARRIER 2002

What does the heart weigh?
More than the pull of your small
hand on mine? More than your head's
light heaviness on my shoulder?

Under the tender pressure of sleep
my old wool jacket becomes
your memory of consolation, comfort,
that ancient sweetness of love and tweed.

Remembering this, watching you,
I lose my place entirely, not knowing
whose the head, whose the sleeve,
whose the big hand and whose the small.

The Ancients measured a good heart
against the slightest puff of down,
in the gleam and glitter of delicate scales.
Like Thoth, we watch and wait.

What does the heart weigh?
Less than your head's tiny burden,
for lighter than a feather is love
and this the Egyptians knew.

The Elevator
LIFE UNDER WATER 2008

As an oyster opens,
wondrous, and through mud
lets glitter that translucent
promise, so the lift doors
close and I am inside
alone with Leonard Cohen.

Vertigo, fear, desire.
I could unpeel myself here,
not just down to the honest
freckled skin of me but through
the sticky layers of a past.

Surely he'd know me anywhere?

Remember that time in the Colston Hall,
how you sang only to me?

The Albert Hall, when I blagged
a press seat and you never once
took your eyes from my shining face?

Here, now, today, in Toronto,
how did you find me?
How did you know I'd be here?

He looks to where I stand
in the radiant silence,
the earth falling away beneath us,
till the silvery gates slide open
to release him. He steps out.
He steps out and I stand still.

'D'you know where you're going?'
he asks.
'Is this where you wanted to be?'

Up on the Roof

KISSING A BONE 1996

You wonder why it is they write of it, sing of it,
till suddenly you're there, nearest you can get
to flying or jumping and you're alone, at last,
the air bright. Remembering this, I go
with my too-light jacket up to the sixth floor,
out onto the roof and I freeze under the stars
till he comes with my too-heavy jacket, heavier
and heavier, as he tries to muffle my foolishness.
A blanket on a fire (he says) and it's true
I am left black, bruised a little, smouldering.

You can sit with a book up there and reel in
life with someone else's bait. You can let your eyes
skim the river, bridges, banks, a seagull's parabola.
At night, you can watch the sky, those strange galaxies
like so many cracks in the ceiling spilling secrets
from the flat above. You can breathe. You can dream.

But he turns to me, as you'd coax a child
in the back of a stuffy car: *we could play I-Spy?*
I look at the black and blue above and the only
letter I find is 'S'. I cannot name
the dust of starlight, the pinheaded planets,
but I can join the dots to make a farming tool,
the belt of a god: all any of us needs is work,
mystery, a little time alone up on the roof.

HELEN DUNMORE
Filmed in Bristol, 25 June 2007

HELEN DUNMORE is best-known as a novelist, but had published four poetry books with Bloodaxe before her first novel appeared: *Zennor in Darkness* (1993), which was set in a Cornish village during the First World War when D.H. Lawrence and his wife Frieda lived there, and were suspected of being German spies. She has since published nine more novels, including *A Spell of Winter*, which won the first Orange Prize for fiction in 1996, as well as three books of short stories, and numerous novels, short story collections and books for children. Her most recent novel *Counting the Stars* (2008) features the Roman poet Catullus, and his older married lover Clodia Metelli, the Lesbia of his poems.

Helen Dunmore is as spellbinding a storyteller in her poetry as in her novels. Her poetry shows a sensuous use of language and alertness to all the senses characteristic of all her writing. Her haunting poems draw us into darkness, engaging our fears and hopes. Many explore the fleetingness of life, its sweetness and intensity, the short time we have on earth and the pleasures of the earth, with death as the frame which sharpens everything and gives it shape.

Poetry was very important to her from childhood. 'I began by listening to and learning by heart all kinds of rhymes and hymns and ballads, and then went on to make up my own poems, using the forms I'd heard. Writing these down came a little later.' Being part of a large extended family was a strong influence on both her life and her writing: 'In a large family you hear a great many stories. You also come to understand very early that stories hold quite different meanings for different listeners, and can be recast from many viewpoints.'

She was born in 1952 in Beverley, Yorkshire. After studying at York University, and working in Finland for two years, she settled in Bristol. I first read her poems as typescripts submitted to *Stand* in the late 70s, and met her when she was encouraged to join the magazine as a co-editor, a position she wisely decided not to take up. Instead, she stayed in Bristol, married and started raising a family. She continued to write and publish poems in magazines, working towards her first collection, *The Apple Fall*, published by Bloodaxe in 1983; she also wrote two novels ('fortunately neither survives') and some of the stories later published in *Love of Fat Men* (1997). She has published eight books of poetry with Bloodaxe, most recently *Out of the Blue: Poems 1975-2001* (2001) and *Glad of These Times* (2007). All the poems she reads on the film are from those two books.

Wild strawberries

THE RAW GARDEN 1988

What I get I bring home to you:
a dark handful, sweet-edged,
dissolving in one mouthful.

I bother to bring them for you
though they're so quickly over,
pulpless, sliding to juice,

a grainy rub on the tongue
and the taste's gone. If you remember
we were in the woods at wild strawberry time

and I was making a basket of dockleaves
to hold what you'd picked,
but the cold leaves unplaited themselves

and slid apart, and again unplaited themselves
until I gave up and ate wild strawberries
out of your hands for sweetness.

I lipped at your palm –
the little salt edge there,
the tang of money you'd handled.

As we stayed in the wood, hidden,
we heard the sound system below us
calling the winners at Chepstow,
faint as the breeze turned.

The sun came out on us, the shade blotches
went hazel: we heard names
bubble like stock-doves over the woods

as jockeys in stained silks gentled
those sweat-dark, shuddering horses
down to the walk.

When You've Got

RECOVERING A BODY 1994

When you've got the plan of your life
matched to the time it will take
but you just want to press SHIFT / BREAK
and print over and over
this is not what I was after
this is not what I was after,

when you've finally stripped out the house
with its iron-cold fireplace,
its mouldings, its mortgage,
its single-skin walls
but you want to write in the plaster
'This is not what I was after,'

when you've got the rainbow-clad baby
in his state-of-the-art pushchair
but he arches his back at you
and pulps his Activity Centre
and you just want to whisper
'This is not what I was after,'

when the vacuum seethes and whines in the lounge
and the waste-disposal unit blows,
when tenners settle in your account
like snow hitting a stove,
when you get a chat from your spouse
about marriage and personal growth,

when a wino comes to sleep in your porch
on your Citizen's Charter
and you know a hostel's opening soon
but your headache's closer
and you really just want to torch
the bundle of rags and newspaper

and you'll say to the newspaper
'This is not what we were after,
this is not what we were after.'

72

Candle poem

(after Sa'di Yusuf)
BESTIARY 1997

A candle for the ship's breakfast
eaten while moving southward
through mild grey water
with the work all done,
a candle for the house seen from outside,
the voices and shadows
of the moment before coming home,

a candle for the noise of aeroplanes
going elsewhere, passing over,
for delayed departures, embarrassed silences
between people who love one another,
a candle for sandwiches in service stations
at four a.m., and the taste of coffee
from plastic cups, thickened with sugar
to keep us going,

a candle for the crowd around a coffin
and the terrible depth it has to fall
into the grave dug for everyone,
the deaths for decades to come,
our deaths; a candle for going home
and feeling hungry after saying
we would never be able to eat the ham,
the fruit cake, those carefully-buttered buns.

City lilacs

GLAD OF THESE TIMES 2007

In crack-haunted alleys, overhangs,
plots of sour earth that pass for gardens,
in the space between wall and wheelie bin,

where men with mobiles make urgent conversation,
where bare-legged girls shiver in April winds,
where a new mother stands on her doorstep and blinks
at the brightness of morning, so suddenly born –

73

in all these places the city lilacs are pushing
their cones of blossom into the spring
to be taken by the warm wind.

Lilac, like love, makes no distinction.
It will open for anyone.
Even before love knows that it is love
lilac knows it must blossom.

In crack-haunted alleys, in overhangs,
in somebody's front garden
abandoned to crisp packets and cans,

on landscaped motorway roundabouts,
in the depth of parks
where men and women are lost in transactions
of flesh and cash, where mobiles ring

and the deal is done – here the city lilacs
release their sweet, wild perfume
then bow down, heavy with rain.

Glad of these times

GLAD OF THESE TIMES 2007

Driving along the motorway
swerving the packed lanes
I am glad of these times.

Because I did not die in childbirth
because my children will survive me
I am glad of these times.

I am not hungry, I do not curtsey,
I lock my door with my own key
and I am glad of these times,

glad of central heating and cable TV
glad of e-mail and keyhole surgery
glad of power showers and washing machines,

74

glad of polio inoculations
glad of three weeks' paid holiday
glad of smart cards and cashback,

glad of twenty types of yoghurt
glad of cheap flights to Prague
glad that I work.

I do not breathe pure air or walk green lanes,
see darkness, hear silence,
make music, tell stories,

tend the dead in their dying
tend the newborn in their birthing,
tend the fire in its breathing,

but I am glad of my times,
these times, the age
we feel in our bones, our rage

of tyre music, speed
annulling the peasant graves
of all my ancestors,

glad of my hands on the wheel
and the cloud of grit as it rises
where JCBs move motherly
widening the packed motorway.

Dolphins whistling
GLAD OF THESE TIMES 2007

Yes, we believed that the oceans were endless
surging with whales, serpents and mermaids,
demon-haunted and full of sweet voices
to lure us over the edge of the world,

we were conquerors, pirates, explorers, vagabonds
war-makers, sea-rovers, we ploughed
the wave's furrow, made maps
that led others to the sea's harvest

and sometimes we believed we heard dolphins whistling,
through the wine-dark waters we heard dolphins whistling.

We were restless and the oceans were endless,
rich in cod and silver-scaled herring
so thick with pilchard we dipped in our buckets
and threw the waste on the fields to rot,

we were mariners, fishers of Iceland, Newfoundlanders
fortune-makers, sea-rovers, we ploughed
the wave's furrow and earned our harvest
hungrily trawling the broad waters,

and sometimes we believed we heard dolphins whistling,
through blue-green depths we heard dolphins whistling.

The catch was good and the oceans were endless
so we fed them with run-off and chemical rivers
pair-fished them, scoured the sea-bed for pearls
and searched the deep where the sperm-whale plays,

we were ambergris merchants, fish farmers, cod-bank strippers
coral-crushers, reef-poisoners, we ploughed
the sea's furrow and seized our harvest
although we had to go far to find it

for the fish grew small and the whales were strangers,
coral was grey and cod-banks empty,
algae bloomed and the pilchards vanished
while the huer's lookout was sold for a chalet,

and the dolphins called their names to one another
through the dark spaces of the water
as mothers call their children at nightfall
and grow fearful for an answer.

We were conquerors, pirates, explorers, vagabonds
war-makers, sea-rovers, we ploughed
the wave's furrow, drew maps
to leads others to the sea's harvest,

and we believed that the oceans were endless
and we believed we could hear the dolphins whistling.

MENNA ELFYN

Filmed in Llanystumdwy, Wales, 22 June 2007

MENNA ELFYN is a poet and playwright who writes with passion of the Welsh language and Welsh identity. She is the best-known and most translated of all modern Welsh-language poets. The international range of her subjects, inventiveness and generosity of vision place her among Europe's leading poets.

Hers is a poetry of daringly imaginative leaps, exploring both inner and outer landscapes, taking exuberant liberties with language, and presenting her translators with formidable challenges. Her questing eye, affectionately critical of many domestic presumptions, restlessly interrogates horizons that others have ignored or taken as read. But wherever she finds herself – and as a reader she is in demand all over the world – she never loses sight of Wales.

Born in 1951, she grew up in bilingual communities in the Swansea Valley and at Peniel near Carmarthen. Learning the harp she also found music in the written word: 'Writing is something like music especially if you write in Welsh, one of the oldest recorded living languages in Europe. The language of the home was Welsh but English was the dominant language of work and school.'

She graduated in Welsh at University College Swansea, and has lived in Llandyssul for many years. Twice imprisoned for language campaigns, she has worked on many Welsh television projects, including a documentary filmed in Vietnam. She was Wales's National Children's Laureate in 2002, and received a Creative Wales Award in 2008. She is Director of the MA in Creative Writing at Trinity College, Carmarthen and Writing Fellow at Swansea University.

She has published eight collections and three children's novels in Welsh, and also co-edited *The Bloodaxe Book of Modern Welsh Poetry* (2003) with John Rowlands. Her poetry is available in two bilingual selections, *Eucalyptus: Detholiad o Gerddi / Selected Poems 1978-1994* from Gomer, and *Perfect Blemish: New & Selected Poems / Perffaith Nam: Dau Ddetholiad & Cherddi Newydd 1995-2007* from Bloodaxe. The latter includes work from two earlier bilingual collections published by Bloodaxe, *Cell Angel* (1996) and *Blind Man's Kiss / Cusan Dyn Dall* (2001), and newer work from *Perffaith Nam* (2005).

Her translators have included some of Wales's most distinguished modern poets: Elin ap Hywel, Joseph Clancy, Gillian Clarke, Tony Conran, Nigel Jenkins, Robert Minhinnick and R.S. Thomas.

Menna is a regular tutor at Tŷ Newydd, Llanystumdwy, the National Writers' Centre for Wales near Criceith. We filmed her in the library at Tŷ Newydd, a large house which was once David Lloyd George's home. All the poems and translations she reads in the film are from *Perfect Blemish / Perffaith Nam*.

77

Gwely Dwbwl

CELL ANGEL 1996

Ddealles i erioed unbennaeth y gwely dwbwl.
Nid lluosog mo'r aelodau'n cysgu. Ar wasgar

digymar ydynt, a'u ffiniau'n codi sofraniaeth –
disyfl dan ddwfe heb i wladfa dwy genedl

negydu rhandiroedd sy'n ffrwythlon. Clymbleidir
weithiau, a thro arall bydd blas wermod ar dafod

wrth gael coes yn rhydd, neu lithro ar gulfor matras.
Mor unplyg yw trwmgwsg. Er nesed ei nwydau, dyheu

am ymbellhau a wnawn wedyn. Osgoi penelin ar ffo,
cnwch ysgwydd ar letraws. Gorgyffwrdd yw trafferth

perthynas. Gadael dim ond lled cornel. Ac eto, yn dy absen,
a'r hunan bach mewn gwely, rhy fawr yw i un grynhoi

ei holl hunaniaeth. Lled ofni a wnaf ar obennydd –
na ddaw'r tresmaswr byth rhagor i'r plu aflonydd

a thry'r gwely heb dy gymalau yn wainbren
heb gyllell. A'm gadael yn breuddwydio

am y cnawd deheuig a'r anghenus ymlid –
yn anhrefn perffaith o dan y cwrlid.

Cyplau

CUSAN DYN DALL 2001

Murddun yw byw. Ninnau, mynnwn ei drwsio
at ddiddosrwydd. Gyda'n dwylo ei saernïo

at frig adeilad. Nes clymu o dano nenbren
a wylia holl fynd a dod ein byw heb wybren.

Double Bed

CELL ANGEL 1996

I never understood the tyranny of the double bed.
Sleeping limbs are single, on the move

unpartnered, in territory held
staunch beneath the duvet, uncolonised by the nation-state's

pillage of fruitful land. Coalition
sometimes, other times wormwood on the tongue

struggling to free a leg or to slip the straits of the mattress.
How sound is the deepest sleep, though passion unites us, after

we keep our distance. Avoid the flying elbow,
the sharp shoulder-blade. Overlap is the hard part

of belonging. Left with nothing but a corner. Yet, you away,
my small self in bed, it's too big to gather

an identity. On my pillow I'm half afraid
the trespasser won't come back to the restless feathers

and the bed without your body is a wooden
scabbard. I'm left dreaming

of the articulate flesh, desire's needling,
the perfect disarray beneath the covers.

Translated by Gillian Clarke

Couplings

BLIND MAN'S KISS 2001

Life is a house in ruins. And we mean to fix it up
and make it snug. With our hands we knock it into shape

to the very top. Till beneath this we fasten a roofbeam
that will watch the coming and going of our skyless life,

Dau rwymyn cam. Naddwyd hwy yn gyfan
yn gyffion cytûn. Yn drawstiau llyfn a llydan.

Cyfarfod dau. Dyna'r grefft a fagwn wrth amgáu
dros ffrâm ddau gnawd. Gan asio'r llyfnus gyplau

sydd weithiau'n enfysu'n un. Ar ogwydd, uwch yr oerfyd
geubrennau'n chwiffio serch. Yna'n stond am ennyd.

A'r to mor elwig ar dro yn gwichian cariad
wrth ddwrdio'r gwyfyn draw. I aros tro ei gennad.

Cusan Hances

CUSAN DYN DALL 2001

> *Mae cerdd mewn cyfieithiad fel cusan drwy hances.*
> R.S. THOMAS

Anwes yn y gwyll?
Rhyw bobl lywaeth oeddem

yn cwato'r gusan ddoe.
Ond heddiw, ffordd yw i gyfarch

ac ar y sgrin fach, gwelwn
arweinwyr y byd yn trafod,

hulio hedd ac anwes las;
ambell un bwbach. A'r delyneg

o'i throsi nid yw ond cusan
drwy gadach poced, medd ein prifardd.

Minnau, sy'n ymaflyd cerdd ar ddalen
gan ddwyn i gôl gariadon-geiriau.

A mynnaf hyn. A fo gerdd bid hances
ac ar fy ngwefus

sws dan len.

two crooked segments. They are fitted together,
timbers in concord. Smooth beams, and wide.

Two in touch. That's the craft we nurture in folding
doubled flesh on a frame. Conjoining the smooth couplings

that sometimes arch into one. Aslant above a cold world,
hollow wood wafting passion. Then stock still for a time.

And how clear-cut the roof, creaking love at times,
as it chides the worm to keep off and await its turn.

Translated by Joseph P. Clancy

Handkerchief Kiss

BLIND MAN'S KISS 2001

> *A poem in translation is like kissing through a handkerchief.*
> R.S. THOMAS

A caress in the dark.
What a tame lot we were,

with our secretive yesterday's kisses.
Today, it's a common greeting,

and we watch on the small screen
world leaders deal peace

with a cold embrace,
or an adder's kiss. The lyric

translated is like kissing
through a hanky, said the bard.

As for me, I hug those poems between pages
that bring back the word-lovers.

Let the poem carry a handkerchief
and leave on my lip

its veiled kiss.

Translated by Gillian Clarke

Iâ Cymru

PERFFAITH NAM 2005

Eira'r oen a iâ, dau efaill yn wir,
Rhew yn y glesni olaf, dan ei sang –
Ymddatod wnânt eu beichiau, gadael tir.

Anadl o'r anialwch, yn blasau sur,
Cnu o gusanau dros ehangder maith,
Eira'r oen a iâ, dau efaill yn wir.

Fflochau'n arwynebu eu pigau ir,
Beddargraff pob teyrnas, yn toddi'n llif,
Ymddatod wnânt eu beichiau, gadael tir.

Cotwm tylwyth teg, gwawn yn pefrio'n glir,
Cloeon ar led, pob Enlli fach ar ffo,
Eira'r oen a iâ, dau efaill yn wir.

Meirioli gwlad? Ai dyma arian cur?
Pob Cantre'r Gwaelod yn ddinas dan do?
Ymddatod wnânt eu beichiau, gadael tir.

O'r Pegwn pell, glasddwr yw'n hanes hir,
Wrth ymryddhau, bydd llithro ach i'r lli;
Eira'r oen a iâ, dau efaill yn wir,
Ymddatod wnânt eu beichiau, gadael tir.

Welsh Ice

PERFECT BLEMISH 2007

They're becoming the same, Welsh ice and spring frost,
both worn underfoot to a blue wafer.
How alike as they leave us, how soon they'll be lost.

Only bitterest breath comes over the glacier
where kisses are white wreaths upon a white coast.
They're becoming the same, Welsh ice and spring frost.

A kingdom must start or finish in flood.
There's some iceberg with our epitaph written on its crown.
How alike as they leave us, how deep they'll go down.

We're scarcely a cobweb, a rumour of ghosts,
and a country might vanish at the turn of a key.
They're becoming the same, Welsh ice, spring frosts.

History thaws. But when has mercury shown
mercy or memory of what it murders?
They're alike as they leave us, how soon they'll be gone.

It starts at the Pole in a kind of unlocking
and soon we're a legend beneath a blue level.
They're becoming the same, Welsh ice and spring frost;
so alike as they leave us, so soon to be lost.

Translated by Robert Minhinnick

W.N. HERBERT
Filmed in North Shields, 5 December 2007

W.N. HERBERT is a highly versatile poet who writes both in English and Dundonian Scots. Born in 1961 in Dundee, he established his reputation with several small press booklets, including *Dundee Doldrums*, *Sharawaggi* and *Anither Music*, selections from which appeared in his first full-length collection from Bloodaxe, *Forked Tongue* (1994). He has since published four more bulky English/Scots collections with Bloodaxe, *Cabaret McGonagall* (1996), *The Laurelude* (1998), *The Big Bumper Book of Troy* (2002) and *Bad Shaman Blues* (2007). Two of his collections have been shortlisted for the T.S. Eliot Prize. He also co-edited (with Matthew Hollis) *Strong Words: modern poets on modern poetry* (Bloodaxe Books, 2000).

In 1992 he published a study of Hugh MacDiarmid, *To Circumjack MacDiarmid* (Oxford University Press), and later took the great Scots socialist poet's *Hymns to Lenin* as a launchpad for one of his own best-known poems, 'A Three Year Ode'. Inspired by both MacDiarmid and Edwin Morgan, he has extended and refreshed the vernacular tradition of Robert Fergusson and Robert Burns, mastering the forms they excelled in using, notably their ballad stanzas, in poems of delicacy and linguistic purity, as well as re-working the terrible verse of William McGonagall to great comic effect. He has said: 'Scots is a language capable of doing more than English, capable of doing something different from English that criticises and, ultimately, extends English. That is the spirit in which I write Scots poetry.'

More recently his poetic territory has shifted south of the border to his adopted home on Tyneside as well as to England's wettest county, Cumbria, where he was Wordsworth fellow at Dove Cottage, Grasmere for two years, finding inspiration both from rain ('The Black Wet') and from the life and work of local boys William Wordsworth and Stan Laurel.

He writes phantasmagorical satires, in which real and imagined characters wreak havoc with cherished myths. Sometimes reflective, sometimes subversively mischievous, he registers or rails against displacement and resettlement. But he can also be tenderly lyrical, offering fond homage (as in his chocolate mousse parody of Burns) as well as terrier wit. *The Guardian* has described his poetry as 'a weird mix of Desperate Dan, MacDiarmid and Dostoyevsky'.

Bill Herbert is Professor of Poetry and Creative Writing at Newcastle University. He lives in a converted lighthouse overlooking the River Tyne at North Shields. We filmed him in his study at the very top of the house, the walls of which are criss-crossed with salvaged ship timbers.

Corbandie

CABARET McGONAGALL 1996

See thi corbie oan thi wire
i thi bullyragglan wund
wi a braichum up o feathirs roond'iz heid:

syne he pints intil thi blast
lyk a collie oan thi brae
at thi cloods that spleet lyk sheep aboot'iz neb;

syne he stauchers, steps, and flauchters
till he dips his heid an grips:
ut's as near's he gets tae flehan oan thi spot.

But he wullna let ut gae
an be breeshilt by thi breeze
tho ut gees um coordy-licks wi aa uts micht,

till thi meenut that he waants tae,
syne thon burd wull spang thi lift
lyk a fleck o ess that's fleean up thi lum.

An sae ut'll be wi you, ma luve,
an thi bairn in yir wame
i thi hanlawhile that lichters you o hur;

fur therr's naebody sall ken
o thi cause that maks hur cry
'Here comes in corbandie' – an be boarn.

corbandie: in argument, some great difficulty which opposes a plausible hypothesis; *corbie*: a raven; *bullyragglan*: noisy, abusive wrangling; *braichum up*: an untidy wrapping up against the weather; *stauchers*: staggers; *flauchters*: flutters; *breeshilt*: rustled, hurried; *coordy-licks*: blows to incite one to fight; *spang*: leap elastically; *ess*: ash; *lum*: chimney; *wame*: womb; *hanlawhile*: short space of time; *lichters*: delivers.

The Black Wet

THE LAURELUDE 1998

It's raining stair-rods and chairlegs,
it's raining candelabra and microwaves,
it's raining eyesockets.
When the sun shines through the shower
it's raining the hair of Sif,
each strand of which is real gold
(carat unknown).

It's raining jellyfish,
it's raining nuts, bolts and pineal glands,
it's raining a legion of fly noyades,
it's raining marsupials and echnidae,
it's raining anoraks in profusion.
It's siling, it's spittering, it's stotting, it's teeming,
it's pouring, it's snoring, it's plaining, it's Spaining.

People look up, open their mouths momentarily,
and drown.
People look out of windows and say,
'Send it down, David.'
Australians remark, 'Huey's missing the bowl.'
Americans reply, 'Huey, Dewie and Louie
are missing the bowl.'

It is not merely raining,
it's Windering and Thirling, it's Buttering down.
It's raining lakes, it's raining grass-snakes,
it's raining Bala, Baikal, and balalaikas,
it's raining soggy sidewinders and sadder adders.
It's raining flu bugs, Toby jugs and hearth-rugs,
it's raining vanity.

The sky is one vast water-clock
and it's raining seconds, it's raining years:
already you have spent more of your life looking at the rain
that you have sleeping, cooking, shopping and making love.
It's raining fusilli and capeletti,
it's raining mariners and albatrosses,
it's raining iambic pentameters.

Let's take a rain-check:
it's raining houndstooth and pinstripe,
it's raining tweed. This is the tartan of McRain.

This is the best test of the wettest west:
it is not raining locusts – just.
Why rain pests
when you can rain driving tests?

It is raining through the holes in God's string vest.

NOTE: *The black wet* (Scots) – rain as opposed to snow.

To a Mousse

THE LAURELUDE 1998

O queen o sludge, maist royal mousse,
yir minions bear ye ben thi hoose,
O quakin sheikess, lavish, loose,
          dessert o fable:
ye pit thi bumps back oan ma goose
          and shauk ma table.

Ye lang cloacal loch o choc,
grecht flabby door at which Eh knock,
and wi ma spunie seek a lock
          tae mak ye gape,
ye flattened, tockless cuckoo clock
          that drives me ape.

Come let me lift ye tae ma mooth
and pree yir pertness wi ma tooth –
ye slake ma hunger and ma drouth
          wi wan sma bite:
come pang ma toomness tae thi outh
          wi broon delight.

Let ane and aa dig in thir spades
and cerve oot chocolate esplanades,
and raise thir umber serenades
          at ilka sip:
sweet Venus, queen o cocoa glades
          and thi muddied lip!

pang: stuff; *toomness:* emptiness; *outh:* utmost.

Song of the Longboat Boys

THE BIG BUMPER BOOK OF TROY 2002

Well we've been sailing all day through the ice and snow,
we've got this little wooden compass tells us where to go;
now some folks say we like to ravish and rage
but a viking's got a right to earn a living wage
in

> *Northumberland thumber thumberberland*
> *Northumberland thumber thumberberland.*

Well our boss is Erik Bloodaxe he's a bit of a dork:
he wants to settle down in this place called York,
but we're all far too young we wanna filch and fight
and gan oot wi the lasses on a Saturday night
in the

> *Bigg Bigg Bigg Bigg Mar-ket Biggbigg Mar-ket*
> *Bigg Bigg Bigg Bigg Mar-ket Biggbigg Mar-ket.*

Well we hear there's aal these lads who like to dress in gray
and sing their Christmas carols in the kirk aal day:
they get a lot of leather and they call it a book,
then they cover it in gold – we'd like to take a look
in

> *Lindisfarne disfarne Lindisdisfarne*
> *Lindisfarne disfarne Lindisdisfarne.*

Well Olaf's got an axe and Gunnar's got a spear
and you oughta see our boat cause we made it last year;
we're gonna crack your skull and burn your neighbourhood
but then we'll build this cool store and sell you bits of wood
in

> *Northumberland thumber thumberberland*
> *Northumberland thumber thumberberland*
> *Northumberland thumber thumberberland*
> *Northumberland thumber thumberberland...*

(Continue until interrupted by a chorus of Geordies):

'Woh! We're gannin to IKEA! Doodleoodleoodoo...
Woh! We're gan to buy some flat-packs! Doodleoodleoodoo...'

Slow Animals Crossing

THE BIG BUMPER BOOK OF TROY 2002

Lemurs somehow, at that lilt of the road
up and sideways at the trees, stooping through
the farmyard on the way to Derrybeg.
Surely there are slower creatures who could cross:
turtles with their solemn wiping gait
or sloths who swim as though to sink
is no disgrace, such aqualungs of air would be
trapped among their matted spider hair.
I think of water since that night was full of it
and white frogs leapt into my lights
like chewing gum attempting
to free itself from tarmac. And I think of lemurs
whenever I see that sign with its red letters
because of the night, and the story
of the three men walking home, and the man
on the left said 'goodnight' to someone, and
the man on the right, 'goodnight' to someone else
and the man in the middle asked who
were they talking to? And one had seen a man
and one had seen a woman, and both
described the third man's parents, turning off
at the road to the graveyard. And when I thought
of lemurs I'd forgotten they were named
for the Latin word for spirits, and I only saw,
crawling slowly in my mind across the night road
back to my parents' house and my daughter,
the bandit eyes and banded tails and soft grey backs
and the white hands of lemurs, delicately placed
upon the twist and the shrug of the road.

Bad Shaman Blues

BAD SHAMAN BLUES 2007

Well ma ma bought me a bodhran but Eh cannae keep thi beat
and when Eh see a sickie kiddie Eh jist stert tae greet –
Eh've gote thi bad shaman blues (bad shaman blues).
Eh tak ma magic mushrooms and begin tae fleh
but then Eh croodle in thi corner while meh harnies freh,
coz that's thi bad shaman blues (yeah that's thi bad shaman blues).

Well aa guid people wi-ah porridge in yir theghs
get up and gang tae work
while Eh leh here and waatch thi crab-sun rehz
coz Eh am jist a jerk.
And that's thi mewly droolin pewly foolin
bad shaman blues
yeah that's thi grown man yelpin poor Van Helsin
bad shaman blues.

Well some people think Eh'm evil but they huvnae gote a clue
coz at thi furst apparition Eh jist weeja tae thi loo –
Eh've gote thi bad shaman poos (bad shaman poos).
And Eh mak ut tae thi bathroom in ma sleepin bag
whaur thi knotholes in thi flairboards they continue tae nag
'Ye've gote thi bad shaman blues' (bad shaman blues).
Aa guid people wi pehs fur ehz
ut's time tae stoap fur lunch
Eh'll tell ye nae truths and Eh'll tell ye nae lehs
Eh'm whit thi monsters munch.
Coz that's thi pukey rooky plukey stookie
bad shaman blues
yeah that's thi black-ah mass and Quatermassin
bad shaman blues.

Well Eh see thi dots and spirals and Eh waant tae hide
Eh've gote three white feathirs that'll smother meh pride
cause that's whit bad shamans use (bad shamans use).
Doon below thi river whaur thi auld queen sits
see me queuein fir a stewin lyk a hopeless wee shit
coz that's whit bad shamans do (yeah that's whit bad shamans do).

Well aa guid people wi sliders fur spines
drehv aff and pick up yir kids
cause thi wey Eh huvtae pey meh lehbrury fines
meh pants ur fuhl o skids.
But that's thi tottery snortery, toss him oot thi coterie
bad shaman blues,
yeah that's thi Scooby Gang and Whovian, act lyk you're Venusian
bad shaman blues.

Well Eh meet a lot o people wi sticks fur heids
and a lot o them ur nutters and a few ur deid
but that's thi bad shaman blues (bad shaman blues).
And hoo thi hell's a gimp lyk me a-gonnae help a man
wha's soul's an ell o charcoal and ut jist fell in thi sand?
but that's whit bad shamans do (yeah that's whit bad shamans do).

Aa guid people wi yir heids a-fuhl o mince
get oot and beh some tat
while Eh think things that mak thi spiders wince
and act lyk Eh'm a bat.
Coz that's thi moanin groanin helpline phonin
bad shaman blues,
yeah that's thi Mulder and Scully, older than Oor Wullie
bad shaman blues.

A lot o weemen blame me fur behaviour beh thir ex-es
Eh'm itherwise an oabject o disdain fur baith thi sexes –
that's jist thi bad shaman blues (it's jist thi bad shaman blues).
Eh like tae think it helps tae write yir symptoms doon
but Eh feel lyk Eh'm thi public fiss of Eccles thi Goon
sae Eh scrieve these bad shaman blues (scrieve these bad shaman blues).
Aa guid people wi hough fur herts
jist get yirsels tae sleep
Eh've a vigil set wi Virgil whaur thi Devil farts
that Eh'm too feart tae keep.
But that's the violet-shrinkin, cannae stop thinkin
bad shaman blues
ut's jist thi Buffy-lovin, Tufty-clubbin
bad shaman blues.

(diminuendo)

It's thi chittery flittery wittery skittery
bad shaman blues
it's the shamble-lyk-a-shot-stirk, Randall and-ah Hopkirk
bad shaman blues
thi hokum-frichtenin, scrotum-tichtenin
bad shaman blues
thi lab-rat yellow, Abbot and Costello
bad shaman blues

bad shaman blues
bad shaman blues
bad shaman blues

who's bad?

SELIMA HILL

Filmed in London, 2 November 2007

SELIMA HILL's poetry has been called wanton, wildly imaginative, tender, intelligent, dangerous, defiant, subversive and startling. All these qualities are strongly present throughout *Gloria*, a comprehensive selection published by Bloodaxe in 2008 drawn from ten formally diverse and thematically unified collections, each offering wild variations on her abiding themes: women's identities, love and loss, repression and abuse, family conflict and mental illness, men, animals and human civilisation. All the poems she reads in the film are included in *Gloria*.

In *Modern Women Poets* (2005), Deryn Rees-Jones writes that 'Hill's early use of Egyptian imagery deliberately estranged her from the logic and proportion of the classical world, setting it up...as a trope for femininity, as well as using it as a device to give distance from autobiographical experience...Hill returns repeatedly to fragmented narratives, charting extreme experience with a dazzling excess.'

She has said that the characters in her poems are ways of writing about herself: 'The only energy we have is the energy of our own lives. But sometimes autobiography is not true enough. In order to be ruthlessly accurate (which is my aim) it is sometimes necessary to fictionalise: in this way I feel free. (I do not want to hurt anyone: Art is not an excuse for hurting anyone...)'

Born in 1945, she was rescued from a burning house as a baby, and grew up in a family of painters on farms in England and Wales. She has lived in Dorset for many years. After working with children for much of her life, she became a freelance writer. She has collaborated with several artists, worked on multimedia projects with the Royal Ballet, Welsh National Opera and BBC Bristol, and taught creative writing for the Poetry School and in hospitals and prisons.

She published two collections with Chatto, *Saying Hello at the Station* (1984) and *My Darling Camel* (1988), and would have published *The Accumulation of Small Acts of Kindness* (1991) with Bloodaxe, until she realised that it was a book, not a pamphlet. Her switch to Bloodaxe came with her next collection, *A Little Book of Meat* (1993), which was followed by *Trembling Hearts in the Bodies of Dogs: New & Selected Poems* (1994), *Violet* (1997), *Bunny* (2001), *Portrait of My Lover as a Horse* (2002), *Lou-Lou* (2004), *Red Roses* (2006), *Gloria: Selected Poems* (2008) and *The Hat* (2008).

Violet was shortlisted for all three of Britain's main poetry prizes; *Bunny* won the Whitbread Poetry Award and was also shortlisted for the T.S. Eliot Prize. The horse on the front cover of *Portrait of My Lover as a Horse* was photographed in the drawing-room at Highgreen Manor.

Don't Let's Talk About Being in Love
A LITTLE BOOK OF MEAT 1993

Don't let's talk about being in love, OK?
– about *me* being in love, in fact, OK?
about your bloated face, like a magnolia;
about marsupials,
whose little blunted pouches
I'd like to crawl inside, lips first;
about the crashing of a million waterfalls
– as if LOVE were a dome of glass beneath a lake
entered through a maze of dripping tunnels
I hoped and prayed I'd never be found inside.

At night I dream that your bedroom's crammed with ducks.
You smell of mashed-up meal and scrambled egg.
Some of the ducks are broody, and won't stand up.
And I dream of the fingers of your various wives
reaching into your private parts like beaks.
And you're lying across the bed like a man shouldn't be.
And I'm startled awake by the sound of creaking glass
as if the whole affair's about to collapse
and water come pouring in with a rush of fishes
going *slurpetty-slurpetty-slurp* with their low-slung mouths.

Cow
A LITTLE BOOK OF MEAT 1993

I want to be a cow
and not my mother's daughter.
I want to be a cow
and not in love with you.
I want to feel free to feel calm.
I want to be a cow who never knows
the kind of love you 'fall in love with' with;
a queenly cow, with hips as big and sound
as a department store,
a cow the farmer milks on bended knee,
who when she dies will feel dawn
bending over her like lawn to wet her lips.

I want to be a cow,
nothing fancy –
a cargo of grass,
a hammock of soupy milk
whose floating and rocking and dribbling's undisturbed
by the echo of hooves to the city;
of crunching boots;
of suspicious-looking trailers parked on verges;
of unscrupulous restaurant-owners
who stumble, pink-eyed, from stale beds
into a world of lobsters and warm telephones;
of streamlined Japanese freighters
ironing the night,
heavy with sweet desire like bowls of jam.

The Tibetans have 85 words for states of consciousness.
This dozy cow I want to be has none.
She doesn't speak.
She doesn't do housework or worry about her appearance.
She doesn't roam.
Safe in her fleet
of shorn-white-bowl-like friends,
she needs, and loves, and's loved by,
only this –
the farm I want to be a cow on too.

Don't come looking for me.
Don't come walking out into the bright sunlight
looking for me,
black in your gloves and stockings and sleeves
and large hat.
Don't call the tractorman.
Don't call the neighbours.
Don't make a special fruit-cake for when I come home:
I'm not coming home.
I'm going to be a cowman's counted cow.
I'm going to be a cow
and you won't know me.

Desire's a Desire

A LITTLE BOOK OF MEAT 1993

It taunts me
like the muzzle of a gun;
it sinks into my soul like chilled honey
packed into the depths of treacherous wounds;
it wraps me up in cold green sheets
like Indian squaws
who wrap their babies in the soft green sheathes of irises
that smell of starch;
it tattooes my shins;
it itches my thighs
like rampant vaginal flora;
it tickles my cheeks
like silkworms munching mulberry leaves
on silk farms;
it nuzzles my plucked armpits like fat dogs;
it plays me
like a piano being played
by regimented fingers
through pressed sheets;
it walks across my back
like geese at dawn,
or the gentle manners
of my only nurse,
who handles me like glass, or Bethlehem.

My skin is white.
I neither eat nor sleep.
My only desire's a desire
to be free from desire.

Being a Wife

TREMBLING HEARTS IN THE BODIES OF DOGS 1994

So this is what it's like being a wife.
The body I remember feeling as big as America in,
the thighs so far away
his hand had to ride in an aeroplane to get there;
the giggles I heard adults giggling with
I was puzzled about,
and felt much too solemn to try;
buttons unbuttoned by somebody else, not me;
the record-player
neither of us were able to stop what we were doing
to turn off;
the smell of fish
I dreaded I'd never get used to,
the peculiar, leering, antediluvian taste
I preferred not to taste;
the feeling of being on the edge of something
everyone older than us,
had wasted,
and not understood,
as we were about to do;
his pink hand gripping my breast
as if his life depended on it;
the shame of the thought of the mirror
reflecting all this,
seem long ago,
yet somehow authentic and right.
Being a wife is like acting being a wife,
and the me that was her with him in the past is still me.

Why I Left You

VIOLET 1997

When you had quite finished
dragging me across your bed
like a band of swaggering late-night removal men
dragging a piano
the size and shape of the United States of America
across a tent,

I left the room,
and slipped into the garden,
where I gulped down whole mouthfuls of delicious aeroplanes
that taxied down my throat
still wrapped in sky
with rows of naked women in their bellies
telling me to go,
and I went,
and that's why I did it,
and everything told me so –
tracks that I knew the meaning of
like the tracks of a wolf
wolf-hunters know the exact colour of
by the tracks of the tracks alone.
You get a feeling for it.
You stand in the garden at night
with blood getting crisp on your thighs
and feel the stars spiralling right down
out of the sky into your ears,
burrowing down inside your ears
like drip-fed needles
saying *Get out. Now.*
By 'you' I mean me.
One of us had to:
I did.

The World's Entire Wasp Population
VIOLET 1997

This feeling I can't get rid of,
this feeling that someone's been reading
my secret diary
that I kept in our bedroom
because I thought nobody else but us
would want to go in there,
except it's not my diary,
it's my husband,
I'd like you to smear this feeling
all over and into her naked body like jam
and invite the world's entire wasp population,
the sick, the halt, the fuzzy,
to enjoy her.

PRAWNS DE JO
BUNNY 2001

Because she was wrong,
because it was all her fault right from the beginning,
because she was ashamed of even thinking about it,
and should never have been his daughter in the first place;
because she was ugly
and he was magnificent
and she was the scum of the earth,
it must never be mentioned:
the unforgettable smell of the singeing baby,
the unforgettable sight of billowing curtains like brides,
the cot,
the charred muslin,
the endless procession of leggy inquisitive flies,
the orange buzz of the electric fire,
and how she'd sit for hours squeezing oranges,
and how she'd sit and fan the flies away,
and hurry down the streets with aching breasts
to part the veil of flies to please the doctors,
the orange ash, the orange carrot-juice,
are never to be mentioned. In that case
what is she to do with the head
that has to be oiled and covered and never mentioned,
as crisp as the colour of violets sprinkled with salt
that grow in the dark
to within half an inch of her brain,
as the colour of prawns sprinkled with salt and pepper
and served to the rats at a diner named PRAWNS DE JO;
that somebody feels beside herself with guilt about
and wheels her off to the sun-tanned arms of a specialist
and all she wants is for him to unpeel it off
and patch it up with a patch from the lawn of her leg,
but he's kitting her out with a rat-sized wig instead
that she keeps in a box
like pet pubic hair
she's secretly proud of because she is horrified by
but never wears because what's the use of a head
with a tuft of hair like a hat from a cracker on top
that's always about to come skew and slither off;
and what's the use of a scar if it's not to be mentioned,
and the milling of flies
and the sight of the flame-proof fireman
with a baby slung over his shoulder as if she's a pig?
And what's the use of the hand-knitted matinee jacket
the surgeon had to pick out with a pair of tweezers?

98

JANE HIRSHFIELD
Filmed in London, 29 October 2006

Jane Hirshfield is an American poet, critic and anthologist who trained as a Zen Buddhist. Her poems are both sensual meditations and passionate investigations which reveal complex truths in language luminous and precise. Rooted in the living world, they celebrate and elucidate a hard-won affirmation of our human fate.

Born of a rigorous questioning of heart, spirit and mind, they have become indispensible to many American readers in navigating their own lives. Hers is a poetry of clarity and hybrid vigour, drawing deeply on English and American traditions but also those of world poetry. The poetries of modern and classical Greece, of Horace and Catullus, of classical China and Japan and Eastern Europe all resonate in Hirshfield's structures of thought and in her sensibilities.

Born in 1953 in New York, she has lived in northern California since 1974, for the past 20 years in a small white cottage looking out on fruit trees, old roses and Mt Tamalpais. In 2004, after including four of her poems in my anthology *Being Alive*, I sought out the other collections of hers I didn't have, and was about to write to ask if Bloodaxe could publish her in Britain when a letter from her arrived out of the blue, with a copy of one of her books, introducing her work and asking if I would consider publishing her poetry; she had also just been invited to read at StAnza, Scotland's poetry festival in St Andrews, the following year.

Her first UK publication, *Each Happiness Ringed by Lions: Selected Poems*, was launched at StAnza in 2005, drawing on five previous collections: *Alaya* (1982), *Of Gravity & Angels* (1988), *The October Palace* (1994), *The Lives of the Heart* (1997) and *Given Sugar, Given Salt* (2001). Her latest collection, *After*, was published in the US by HarperCollins and by Britain by Bloodaxe in 2006, and was shortlisted for the T.S. Eliot Prize. In 2007 she gave the Newcastle/Bloodaxe Poetry Lectures, published in 2008 as *Hiddenness, Uncertainties, Surprise: Three Generative Energies of Poetry*.

Her collection of essays, *Nine Gates: Entering the Mind of Poetry* was published by HarperCollins in 1997. She has edited and co-translated several books collecting the work of women poets of the past: *The Ink Dark Moon: Love Poems by Ono no Komachi and Izumi Shikibu, Women of the Ancient Court of Japan* (1990); *Women in Praise of the Sacred: 43 Centuries of Spiritual Poetry by Women* (1994); and *Mirabai: Ecstatic Poems* (2004). Her own poetry was translated into Polish by Czesław Miłosz, who also wrote the introduction to her Polish Selected Poems.

The Envoy
GIVEN SUGAR, GIVEN SALT 2001

One day in that room, a small rat.
Two days later, a snake.

Who, seeing me enter,
whipped the long stripe of his
body under the bed,
then curled like a docile house-pet.

I don't know how either came or left.
Later, the flashlight found nothing.

For a year I watched
as something – terror? happiness? grief? –
entered and then left my body.

Not knowing how it came in,
Not knowing how it went out.

It hung where words could not reach it.
It slept where light could not go.
Its scent was neither snake nor rat,
neither sensualist nor ascetic.

There are openings in our lives
of which we know nothing.

Through them
the belled herds travel at will,
long-legged and thirsty, covered with foreign dust.

The Poet
THE LIVES OF THE HEART 1997

She is working now, in a room
not unlike this one,
the one where I write, or you read.
Her table is covered with paper.
The light of the lamp would be

100

tempered by a shade, where the bulb's
single harshness might dissolve,
but it is not, she has taken it off.
Her poems? I will never know them,
though they are the ones I most need.
Even the alphabet she writes in
I cannot decipher. Her chair –
Let us imagine whether it is leather
or canvas, vinyl or wicker. Let her
have a chair, her shadeless lamp,
the table. Let one or two she loves
be in the next room. Let the door
be closed, the sleeping ones healthy.
Let her have time, and silence,
enough paper to make mistakes and go on.

The Weighing

THE OCTOBER PALACE 1994

The heart's reasons
seen clearly,
even the hardest
will carry
its whip-marks and sadness
and must be forgiven.

As the drought-starved
eland forgives
the drought-starved lion
who finally takes her,
enters willingly then
the life she cannot refuse,
and is lion, is fed,
and does not remember the other.

So few grains of happiness
measured against all the dark
and still the scales balance.

The world asks of us
only the strength we have and we give it.
Then it asks more, and we give it.

Burlap Sack

AFTER 2006

A person is full of sorrow
the way a burlap sack is full of stones or sand.
We say, 'Hand me the sack,'
but we get the weight.
Heavier if left out in the rain.
To think that the sand or stones are the self is an error.
To think that grief is the self is an error.
Self carries grief as a pack mule carries the side bags,
being careful between the trees to leave extra room.
The mule is not the load of ropes and nails and axes.
The self is not the miner nor builder nor driver.
What would it be to take the bride
and leave behind the heavy dowry?
To let the thin-ribbed mule browse in tall grasses,
its long ears waggling like the tails of two happy dogs?

Pyracantha and Plum

AFTER 2006

Last autumn's chastened berries still on one tree,
spring blossoms tender, hopeful, on another.
The view from this window
much as it was ten years ago, fifteen.
Yet it seems this morning
a self-portrait both clearer and darker,
as if while I slept some Rembrandt or Brueghel
had walked through the garden, looking hard.

Tree

GIVEN SUGAR, GIVEN SALT 2001

It is foolish
to let a young redwood
grow next to a house.

Even in this
one lifetime,
you will have to choose.

That great calm being,
this clutter of soup pots and books –

Already the first branch-tips brush at the window.
Softly, calmly, immensity taps at your life.

It Was Like This: You Were Happy
AFTER 2006

It was like this:
you were happy, then you were sad,
then happy again, then not.

It went on.
You were innocent or you were guilty.
Actions were taken, or not.

At times you spoke, at other times you were silent.
Mostly, it seems you were silent – what could you say?

Now it is almost over.

Like a lover, your life bends down and kisses your life.

It does this not in forgiveness –
between you, there is nothing to forgive –
but with the simple nod of a baker at the moment
he sees the bread is finished with transformation.

Eating, too, is a thing now only for others.

It doesn't matter what they will make of you
or your days: they will be wrong,
they will miss the wrong woman, miss the wrong man,
all the stories they tell will be tales of their own invention.

Your story was this: you were happy, then you were sad,
you slept, you awakened.
Sometimes you ate roasted chestnuts, sometimes persimmons.

JACKIE KAY
Filmed in Manchester, 23 November 2007

JACKIE KAY was an adopted child of Scottish/Nigerian descent brought up by Scottish parents. With humour and emotional directness, her poetry explores gender, sexuality, identity, racism and cultural difference as well as love and music. Her poems draw on her own life and the lives of others to make a tapestry of voice and communal understanding. The title of her short story collection, *Why Don't You Stop Talking* (Picador, 2002) could almost be a comment on her poems: their urgency of voice and their recognition of the urgency in all voice, particularly the need to be heard, to have voice. It is through talking her characters into being that she creates her own sense of self through her poems, which are conversational in tone but with jazz-inflected rhythms.

Like many books by new writers published by Bloodaxe over the years, her first collection landed on my desk as an unsolicited manuscript, in 1989. I didn't know at the time but several other editors had already turned it down. After we'd worked on the manuscript over several months, *The Adoption Papers* was published in 1991, and has gone on to sell over 18,000 copies. Adapted from a BBC radio play, its title-sequence tells the story of a black girl's adoption. A stage version of *The Adoption Papers* was brilliantly effective at Manchester's Royal Exchange Theatre in 2007.

Jackie has always felt a strong bond with Bloodaxe, both because I responded to her work and wanted to publish her when she was an unknown writer and also because of the consistent support and recognition Bloodaxe has given to women writers. Other publishers had to be disappointed when they wanted to publish her poetry later, including some who had actually rejected *The Adoption Papers*.

She has published five other poetry books with Bloodaxe: *Other Lovers* (1993), *Off Colour* (1998), *Life Mask* (2005) and *Darling: New & Selected Poems* (2007), which have sold thousands of copies each; and *The Lamplighter* (2008), her play and multi-layered epic poem on women and slavery, published with a CD of the much acclaimed BBC radio play. Her other books include *Trumpet* (1998) and a second book of stories, *Wish I Was Here* (2006), both from Picador.

Born in 1961 in Edinburgh, she grew up in Glasgow, studying at the Royal Scottish Academy of Music and Drama and at Stirling University. She has written widely for stage, radio and television, and has won the Signal Poetry Award twice – in 1993 and 1999 – for her books of poetry for children. Her other awards include the *Guardian* Fiction Prize, Somerset Maugham Award, Cholmondeley Award and Decibel Writer of the Year. In 2006 she was made an MBE for services to literature. She lives in Manchester.

from The Adoption Papers
Chapter 3: The Waiting Lists
THE ADOPTION PAPERS 1991

The first agency we went to
didn't want us on their lists,
we didn't live close enough to a church
nor were we church-goers
(though we kept quiet about being communists).
The second told us
we weren't high enough earners.
The third liked us
but they had a five-year waiting list.
I spent six months trying not to look
at swings nor the front of supermarket trolleys,
not to think this kid I've wanted could be five.
The fourth agency was full up.
The fifth said yes but again no babies.
Just as we were going out the door
I said oh you know we don't mind the colour.
Just like that, the waiting was over.

This morning a slim manilla envelope arrives
postmarked Edinburgh: one piece of paper
I have now been able to look up your microfiche
(as this is all the records kept nowadays).
From your mother's letters, the following information:
Your mother was nineteen when she had you.
You weighed eight pounds four ounces.
She liked hockey. She worked in Aberdeen
as a waitress. She was five foot eight inches.

I thought I'd hid everything
that there wasnie wan
giveaway sign left

I put Marx Engels Lenin (no Trotsky)
in the airing cupboard – she'll no be
checking out the towels surely

All the copies of the *Daily Worker*
I shoved under the sofa
the dove of peace I took down from the loo

A poster of Paul Robeson
saying give him his passport
I took down from the kitchen

I left a bust of Burns
my detective stories
and the Complete Works of Shelley

She comes at 11.30 exactly.
I pour her coffee
from my new Hungarian set

And foolishly pray she willnae
ask its origins – honestly
this baby is going to my head.

She crosses her legs on the sofa
I fancy I hear the *Daily Workers*
rustle underneath her

Well she says, you have an interesting home
She sees my eyebrows rise.
It's different she qualifies.

Hell and I've spent all morning
trying to look ordinary
– a lovely home for the baby.

She buttons her coat all smiles
I'm thinking
I'm on the home run

But just as we get to the last post
her eye catches at the same times as mine
a red ribbon with twenty world peace badges

Clear as a hammer and sickle
on the wall.
Oh, she says are you against nuclear weapons?

To Hell with this. Baby or no baby.
Yes I says. Yes yes yes.
I'd like this baby to live in a nuclear free world.

Oh. Her eyes light up.
I'm all for peace myself she says,
and sits down for another cup of coffee.

In Jackie Kay's *The Adoption Papers* sequence, the voices of
the three speakers are distinguished typographically, including:

DAUGHTER: Palatino typeface
ADOPTIVE MOTHER: Gill typeface

In my country
OTHER LOVERS 1993

walking by the waters
down where an honest river
shakes hands with the sea,
a woman passed round me
in a slow watchful circle,
as if I were a superstition;

or the worst dregs of her imagination,
so when she finally spoke
her words spliced into bars
of an old wheel. A segment of air.
Where do you come from?
'Here,' I said, 'Here. These parts.'

Somebody else
OFF COLOUR 1998

If I was not myself, I would be somebody else.
But actually I am somebody else.
I have been somebody else all my life.

It's no laughing matter going about the place
all the time being somebody else:
people mistake you; you mistake yourself.

Late Love
LIFE MASK 2005

How they strut about, people in love,
how tall they grow, pleased with themselves,
their hair, glossy, their skin shining.
They don't remember who they have been.

How filmic they are just for this time.
How important they've become – secret, above
the order of things, the dreary mundane.
Every church bell ringing, a fresh sign.

How dull the lot that are not in love.
Their clothes shabby, their skin lustreless;
how clueless they are, hair a mess; how they trudge
up and down streets in the rain,

remembering one kiss in a dark alley,
a touch in a changing-room, if lucky, a lovely wait
for the phone to ring, maybe, baby.
The past with its rush of velvet, its secret hush

already miles away, dimming now, in the late day.

The Spare Room
LIFE MASK 2005

When my lover found a brand-new lover,
on the longest day of the year by far,
she asked if I would move into the spare room.

That first night I was awake and then asleep,
and then awake, very hot and very cold;
I turned and tossed in the small white room.

Halfway through the night, still black outside,
the air held its chilly breath and I held my head,
wide, wide awake in the pale spare room.

After a long, long while daylight spilled.
I climbed out of the spare room bed.
I stood staring at the bed, at the dented pillows.

Last night I must have turned from her side to mine
from the blank wall to the blind window, spoon to moon,
as if two people had slept in the spare room bed.

Twelve Bar Bessie

OTHER LOVERS 1993

See that day, Lord, did you hear what happened then.
A nine o'clock shadow always chases the sun.
And in the thick heavy air came the Ku Klux Klan
To the tent where the Queen was about to sing her song.

They were going to pull the Blues Tent down.
Going to move the Queen out of the town.
Take her twelve bar beat and squash it into the ground.
She tried to get her Prop Boys together, and they got scared.

She tried to get the Prop Boys together, and they got scared.
She said Boys, Boys, get those men out of here.
But they ran away and left the Empress on her own.
She went up to the men who had masks over their head

With her hand on her hips she cursed and she hollered,
'I'll get the whole damn lot of you out of here now
If I have to. You are as good as dead.
You just pick up the sheets and run. Go on.'

That's what she done. Her voice was cast-iron.
You should have seen them. You should have seen them.
Those masks made of sheets from somebody's bed.
Those masks flying over their heads. Flapping.

They was flapping like some strange bird migrating.
Some bird that smelt danger in the air, a blue song.
And flew. Fast. Out of the small mid western town.
To the sound of black hands clapping.

And the Empress saying, 'And as for you' to the ones who did nothing.

109

Old Tongue

LIFE MASK 2005

When I was eight, I was forced south.
Not long after, when I opened
my mouth, a strange thing happened.
I lost my Scottish accent.
Words fell off my tongue:
eedyit, dreich, wabbit, crabbit
stummer, teuchter, heidbanger,
so you are, so am ur, see you, see ma ma,
shut yer geggie or I'll gie you the malkie!

My own vowels started to stretch like my bones
and I turned my back on Scotland.
Words disappeared in the dead of night,
new words marched in: ghastly, awful,
quite dreadful, *scones* said like *stones.*
Pokey hats into ice cream cones.

Oh where did all my words go –
my old words, my lost words?
Did you ever feel sad when you lost a word,
did you ever try and call it back
like calling in the sea?
If I could have found my words wandering,
I swear I would have taken them in,
swallowed them whole, knocked them back.

Out in the English soil, my old words
buried themselves. It made my mother's blood boil.
I cried one day with the wrong sound in my mouth.
I wanted them back; I wanted my old accent back,
my old tongue. My dour soor Scottish tongue.
Sing-songy. I wanted to *gie it laldie.*

Darling

DARLING 2007

You might forget the exact sound of her voice
or how her face looked when sleeping.
You might forget the sound of her quiet weeping
curled into the shape of a half moon,

when smaller than her self, she seemed already to be leaving
before she left, when the blossom was on the trees
and the sun was out, and all seemed good in the world.
I held her hand and sang a song from when I was a girl –

Heel y'ho boys, let her go boys –
and when I stopped singing she had slipped away,
already a slip of a girl again, skipping off,
her heart light, her face almost smiling.

And what I didn't know or couldn't say then
was that she hadn't really gone.
The dead don't go till you do, loved ones.
The dead are still here holding our hands.

BRENDAN KENNELLY
Filmed in Boston, Massachusetts, 8 September 2007

BRENDAN KENNELLY is one of Ireland's most distinguished poets, as well as a dramatist, critic, renowned teacher and cultural commentator. Born in 1936 in Ballylongford, Co. Kerry, he was Professor of Modern Literature at Trinity College, Dublin from 1973 until his retirement in 2005. He is a much loved public figure in Ireland, and a popular guest on television programmes.

Most of his work is concerned with the people, landscapes, wildlife and history of Ireland, and with language, religion and politics. 'His poems shine with the wisdom of somebody who has thought deeply about the paradoxical strangeness and familiarity and wonder of life' (Sister Stanislaus Kennedy).

I first met him in Dublin in 1985 when he was recovering from alcoholism. He spent the following summer in hospital in Dublin, fighting his demons and listening to angry abused women, as he wrote in his preface to *Medea* (1988/1991), a reworking fed by that experience. As he rebuilt his life, he felt supported by the many thousands of Irish people who love him and look to him for wisdom as well as by a friendship and editorial marriage which has transformed the way in which his work has been published and received.

He has published 20 titles with Bloodaxe, and over 30 books of poetry altogether, including *Familiar Strangers: New & Selected Poems 1960-2004* (2004). He is best-known for two controversial poetry books: *Cromwell*, published in Ireland in 1983 and in Britain by Bloodaxe in 1987, and his epic poem *The Book of Judas* (1991), which topped the Irish bestsellers list (see page 249). His third epic, *Poetry My Arse* (1995), did much to outdo these in notoriety. His other poetry titles include *Glimpses* (2001), *The Little Book of Judas* (2002), *Martial Art* (2003) and *Now* (2006).

His modern versions of Greek tragedies have been widely performed, and are collected in *When Then Is Now* (2006), a trilogy comprising Sophocles' *Antigone* and Euripides' *Medea* and *The Trojan Women*. His other versions include Lorca's *Blood Wedding* (1996). *Journey into Joy: Selected Prose*, edited by Åke Persson, was published by Bloodaxe in 1994, along with *Dark Fathers into Light*, a critical anthology on his work edited by Richard Pine.

In 2007 he had a fellowship at Boston College. We filmed him on an extraordinarily hot day. He knows hundreds of poems by heart, and wanted to read his selection in one take. 'Raglan Lane' is his response to Patrick Kavanagh's 'On Raglan Road', and has been sung by Mary Black and others (to the tune of 'The Dawning of the Day'). 'Begin' was widely circulated amongst Irish Americans in the immediate aftermath of 9/11.

Love Cry

LOVE CRY 1972

He mounted her, growing between her thighs.
A mile away, the Shannon swelled and thrust
Into the sea, ignoring the gaunt curlew-cries.
Near where the children played in gathering dusk
John Martin Connor cocked his polished gun
And fired at plover over Nolan's hill;
A second late, he shot the dying sun
And swore at such an unrewarding kill.

A quick voice called, one child turned and ran,
Somewhere in Brandon's river a trout leaped,
Infinite circles made nightspirits stare;
The hunter tensed, the birds approached again
As though they had a binding tryst to keep.
Her love-cry thrilled and perished on the air.

I See You Dancing, Father

THE BOATS ARE HOME 1980

No sooner downstairs after the night's rest
And in the door
Than you started to dance a step
In the middle of the kitchen floor.

And as you danced
You whistled.
You made your own music
Always in tune with yourself.

Well, nearly always, anyway.
You're buried now
In Lislaughtin Abbey
And whenever I think of you

I go back beyond the old man
Mind and body broken
To find the unbroken man.
It is the moment before the dance begins,

Your lips are enjoying themselves
Whistling an air.
Whatever happens or cannot happen
In the time I have to spare
I see you dancing, father.

Bread

BREAD 1971

Someone else cut off my head
In a golden field.
Now I am re-created

By her fingers. This
Moulding is more delicate
Than a first kiss,

More deliberate than her own
Rising up
And lying down,

I am fine
As anything in
This legendary garden

Yet I am nothing till
She runs her fingers through me
And shapes me with her skill.

The form that I shall bear
Grows round and white.
It seems I comfort her

Even as she slits my face
And stabs my chest.
Her feeling for perfection is

Absolute.
So I am glad to go through fire
And come out

Shaped like her dream.
In my way
I am all that can happen to men.
I came to life at her finger-ends.
I will go back into her again.

Raglan Lane
(after Patrick Kavanagh)
FAMILIAR STRANGERS 2004

In Raglan Lane, in the gentle rain, I saw dark love again,
Beyond belief, beyond all grief, I felt the ancient pain,
The joyful thrust of holy lust, I stretched on heaven's floor,
One moment burned what the years had learned and I was wild once more.

The years' deep cries in her sad eyes became a source of light,
The heavy gloom and sense of doom changed to pure delight.
And as we walked in joy and talked we knew one thing for sure,
That love is blessed togetherness and loneliness is poor.

Then I grew rich with every touch, we loved the whole night long
Her midnight hair on the pillow there became an angel's song,
Her happy skin, beyond all sin, was heaven opened wide
But as the dawn came shyly on, I slept, and she left my side.

Why did she go? I'll never know, nor will the gentle rain,
Her up and go was a cruel blow, and yet I felt no pain
For I had known her body and soul in my own loving way,
So I lay and thanked the God of love at the dawning of the day.

Begin

GOOD SOULS TO SURVIVE 1967

Begin again to the summoning birds
to the sight of light at the window,
begin to the roar of morning traffic
all along Pembroke Road.
Every beginning is a promise
born in light and dying in dark
determination and exaltation of springtime
flowering the way to work.
Begin to the pageant of queuing girls
the arrogant loneliness of swans in the canal
bridges linking the past and future
old friends passing though with us still.
Begin to the loneliness that cannot end
since it perhaps is what makes us begin,
begin to wonder at unknown faces
at crying birds in the sudden rain
at branches stark in the willing sunlight
at seagulls foraging for bread
at couples sharing a sunny secret
alone together while making good.
Though we live in a world that dreams of ending
that always seems about to give in
something that will not acknowledge conclusion
insists that we forever begin.

GALWAY KINNELL
Filmed in Vermont, 9 September 2007

GALWAY KINNELL's diverse work ranges from odes of kinship with nature to realistic evocations of urban life, from religious quest to political statement, from brief imagistic lyrics to extended, complex meditations. His poetry has always been marked by precise, furious intelligence, by rich aural music, by devotion to the things and creatures of the world, and by transformations of every understanding into singing, universal art. In the citation for the 2003 National Book Award, the judges called Kinnell 'America's preeminent visionary' whose work 'greets each new age with rapture and abundance [and] sets him at the table with his mentors: Rilke, Whitman, Frost'. He is a poet who 'writes about the terror and wonder of human beings: the terror, because we know we must die; the wonder, because we are so capable of love' (Bill Moyers).

Born in Providence, Rhode Island, in 1927, he made his living mostly from teaching from 1949 to 2005, in France, Iran and Australia as well as at colleges and universities across America. In 1982 his *Selected Poems* won a Pulitzer Prize and a National Book Award. An updated and expanded edition was published as *Selected Poems* by Bloodaxe in Britain in 2001. He has also published several translations, including Yves Bonnefoy's *On the Motion and Immobility of Douve* in the Bloodaxe Contemporary French Poets series (1992). His latest collection, *Strong Is Your Hold*, published with an audio CD in 2007 by Bloodaxe, includes his long poem 'When the Towers Fell', a requiem for those who died in the World Trade Center on 9/11 in direct view of his New York apartment. He now lives only in a remote part of northern Vermont, in the house he bought as a wreck in the 60s, where he has written much of his work. The poems he reads on the film are from *Selected Poems* and *Strong Is Your Hold*.

I first saw him read in November 1998 in London, when he began by reciting Keats's 'To Autumn' from memory in a moving tribute to Ted Hughes, who had just died and was to have appeared with him at Poetry International. Afterwards I stood in the signing queue, and had him sign my copies of his books before asking if he'd sign for Bloodaxe. When I was working with Miramax in 2002 on the American adaptation of *Staying Alive*, I asked if he'd help with suggestions of poems to be added. His response, as well as giving his own invaluable feedback, was to invite me to dinner with a group of friends who all pitched in: Russell Banks, Breyten Breytenbach, Philip Levine, Sharon Olds and Chase Twichell. This was also my first meeting with Philip Levine, and led to Bloodaxe's publication of his poetry in 2006.

Saint Francis and the Sow

MORTAL ACTS, MORTAL WORDS 1980

The bud
stands for all things,
even for those things that don't flower,
for everything flowers, from within, of self-blessing;
though sometimes it is necessary
to reteach a thing its loveliness,
to put a hand on its brow
of the flower
and retell it in words and in touch
it is lovely
until it flowers again from within, of self-blessing;
as Saint Francis
put his hand on the creased forehead
of the sow, and told her in words and in touch
blessings of earth on the sow, and the sow
began remembering all down her thick length,
from the earthen snout all the way
through the fodder and slops to the spiritual curl of the tail,
from the hard spininess spiked out from the spine
down through the great broken heart
to the sheer blue milken dreaminess spurting and shuddering
from the fourteen teats into the fourteen mouths sucking and blowing
          beneath them:
the long, perfect loveliness of sow.

Daybreak

MORTAL ACTS, MORTAL WORDS 1980

On the tidal mud, just before sunset,
dozens of starfishes
were creeping. It was
as though the mud were a sky
and enormous, imperfect stars
moved across it as slowly
as the actual stars cross heaven.
All at once they stopped,
and, as if they had simply
increased their receptivity
to gravity, they sank down
into the mud, faded down

into it and lay still, and by the time
pink of sunset broke across them
they were as invisible
as the true stars at daybreak.

Parkinson's Disease

IMPERFECT THIRST 1994

While spoon-feeding him with one hand
she holds his hand with her other hand,
or rather lets it rest on top of his,
which is permanently clenched shut.
When he turns his head away, she reaches
around and puts in the spoonful blind.
He will not accept the next morsel
until he has completely chewed this one.
His bright squint tells her he finds
the shrimp she has just put in delicious.
She strokes his head very slowly, as if
to cheer up each hair sticking up
from its root in his stricken brain.
Standing behind him, she presses
her cheek to his, kisses his jowl,
and his eyes seem to stop seeing
and do nothing but emit light.
Could heaven be a time, after we are dead,
of remembering the knowledge
flesh had from flesh? The flesh
of his face is hard, perhaps
from years spent facing down others
until they fell back, and harder
from years of being himself faced down
and falling back, and harder still
from all the while frowning
and beaming and worrying and shouting
and probably letting go in rages.
His face softens into a kind
of quizzical wince, as if one
of the other animals were working at
getting the knack of the human smile.
When picking up a cookie he uses
both thumbtips to grip it
and push it against an index finger
to secure it so that he can lift it.

She takes him to the bathroom,
and when they come out, she is facing him,
walking backwards in front of him
holding his hands, pulling him
when he stops, reminding him to step
when he forgets and starts to pitch forward.
She is leading her old father into the future
as far as they can go, and she is walking
him back into her childhood, where she stood
in bare feet on the toes of his shoes
and they foxtrotted on this same rug.
I watch them closely: she could be teaching him
the last steps that one day she may teach me.
At this moment, he glints and shines,
as if it will be only a small dislocation
for him to pass from this paradise into the next.

Rapture

IMPERFECT THIRST 1994

I can feel she has got out of bed.
That means it is seven A.M.
I have been lying with eyes shut,
thinking, or possibly dreaming,
of how she might look if, at breakfast,
I spoke about the hidden place in her
which, to me, is like a soprano's tremolo,
and right then, over toast and bramble jelly,
if such things are possible, she came.
I imagine she would show it while trying to conceal it.
I imagine her hair would fall about her face
and she would become apparently downcast,
as she does at a concert when she is moved.
The hypnopompic play passes, and I open my eyes
and there she is, next to the bed,
bending to a low drawer, picking over
various small smooth black, white,
and pink items of underwear. She bends
so low her back runs parallel to the earth,
but there is no sway in it, there is little burden, the day has hardly begun.
The two mounds of muscles for walking, leaping, lovemaking,
lift toward the east – what can I say?
Simile is useless; there is nothing like them on earth.

Her breasts fall full; the nipples
are deep pink in the glare shining up through the iron bars
of the gate under the earth where those who could not love
press, wanting to be born again.
I reach out and take her wrist
and she falls back into bed and at once starts unbuttoning my pajamas.
Later, when I open my eyes, there she is again,
rummaging in the same low drawer.
The clock shows eight. Hmmm.
With huge, silent effort of great,
mounded muscles the earth has been turning.
She takes a piece of silken cloth
from the drawer and stands up. Under the falls
of hair her face has become quiet and downcast,
as if she will be, all day among strangers,
looking down inside herself at our rapture.

Everyone Was in Love
STRONG IS YOUR HOLD 2006/2007

One day, when they were little, Maud and Fergus
appeared in the doorway naked and mirthful,
with a dozen long garter snakes draped over
each of them like brand-new clothes.
Snake tails dangled down their backs,
and snake foreparts in various lengths
fell over their fronts. With heads raised and swaying,
alert as cobras, the snakes writhed their dry skins
upon each other, as snakes like doing
in lovemaking, with the added novelty
of caressing soft, smooth, moist human skin.
Maud and Fergus were deliciously pleased with themselves.
The snakes seemed to be tickled, too.
We were enchanted. Everyone was in love.
Then Maud drew down off Fergus's shoulder,
as off a tie rack, a peculiarly
lumpy snake and told me to look inside.
Inside the double-hinged jaw, a frog's green
webbed hind feet were being drawn,
like a diver's, very slowly as if into deepest waters.
Perhaps thinking I might be considering rescue,
Maud said, 'Don't. Frog is already elsewhere.'

PHILIP LEVINE
Filmed in Brooklyn, 12 December 2006

PHILIP LEVINE is the authentic voice of America's urban poor. Born in 1928, the son of Russian-Jewish immigrants, he spent his early years doing a succession of heavy labouring jobs. Trying to write poetry 'for people for whom there is no poetry', he chronicled the lives of the people he grew up with and worked with in Detroit: 'Their presence seemed utterly lacking in the poetry I inherited at age 20, so I've spent the last 40-some years trying to add to our poetry what wasn't there.'

Much of his poetry addresses the joys and sufferings of industrial life, with radiant feeling as well as painful irony: 'It took me a long time to be able to write about it without snarling or snapping. I had to temper the violence I felt toward those who maimed and cheated me with a tenderness toward those who had touched and blessed me.' Always a poet of memory and invention, he has continually written poems which search for universal truths. His plain-speaking poetry is a testament to the durability of love, the strength of the human spirit and the persistence of life in the face of death.

He taught at Fresno in California for many years, and divides his time between Fresno and Brooklyn. He has received many literary awards, including the National Book Award (1980 & 1991), and the Pulitzer Prize in 1995 for *The Simple Truth*. His memoir *The Bread of Time: Toward an Autobiography* (1994) includes compelling portraits of two of his poetic mentors, John Berryman and Yvor Winters.

All the poems he reads on the film are included in *Stranger to Nothing: Selected Poems*, published by Bloodaxe in 2006. This covers the full range of his American collections, from *On the Edge* (1963) to *Breath* (2004), and was his first UK publication since Secker published an earlier *Selected Poems* in 1984.

I first met him at a dinner held by Galway Kinnell (see page 117), and later heard him read at the Cooper Union launch of the American edition of *Staying Alive* in 2003 (page 261), when Meryl Streep told him she felt honoured to appear on the same stage.

When we filmed him in Brooklyn, we had to contend with a police helicopter buzzing up and down the East River which kept returning to frustrate our endeavours, but in the end were able to get good takes of all five of his poems. His facial expressions during some of the readings register his awareness of possible further intrusions by the helicopter. Before starting the session, we tried to put him at his ease about reading to a camera, but this was quite unnecessary in his case: 'I'm not sitting in front of a camera,' he said. 'I'm sitting in front of two people.'

The Simple Truth

THE SIMPLE TRUTH 1994

I bought a dollar and a half's worth of small red potatoes,
took them home, boiled them in their jackets
and ate them for dinner with a little butter and salt.
Then I walked through the dried fields
on the edge of town. In middle June the light
hung on in the dark furrows at my feet,
and in the mountain oaks overhead the birds
were gathering for the night, the jays and mockers
squawking back and forth, the finches still darting
into the dusty light. The woman who sold me
the potatoes was from Poland; she was someone
out of my childhood in a pink spangled sweater and sunglasses
praising the perfection of all her fruits and vegetables
at the roadside stand and urging me to taste
even the pale, raw sweetcorn trucked all the way,
she swore, from New Jersey. 'Eat, eat,' she said,
'Even if you don't I'll say you did.'
                                    Some things
you know all your life. They are so simple and true
they must be said without elegance, meter and rhyme,
they must be laid on the table beside the salt shaker,
the glass of water, the absence of light gathering
in the shadows of picture frames, they must be
naked and alone, they must stand for themselves.
My friend Henri and I arrived at this together in 1965
before I went away, before he began to kill himself,
and the two of us to betray our love. Can you taste
what I'm saying? It is onions or potatoes, a pinch
of simple salt, the wealth of melting butter, it is obvious,
it stays in the back of your throat like a truth
you never uttered because the time was always wrong,
it stays there for the rest of your life, unspoken,
made of that dirt we call earth, the metal we call salt,
in a form we have no words for, and you live on it.

Starlight

ASHES 1977

My father stands in the warm evening
on the porch of my first house.
I am four years old and growing tired.
I see his head among the stars,
the glow of his cigarette, redder
than the summer moon riding
low over the old neighborhood. We
are alone, and he asks me if I am happy.
'Are you happy?' I cannot answer.
I do not really understand the word,
and the voice, my father's voice, is not
his voice, but somehow thick and choked,
a voice I have not heard before, but
heard often since. He bends and passes
a thumb beneath each of my eyes.
The cigarette is gone, but I can smell
the tiredness that hangs on his breath.
He has found nothing, and he smiles
and holds my head with both his hands.
Then he lifts me to his shoulder,
and now I too am there among the stars
as tall as he. Are you happy? I say.
He nods in answer, Yes! oh yes! oh yes!
And in that new voice he says nothing,
holding my head tight against his head,
his eyes closed up against the starlight,
as though those tiny blinking eyes
of light might find a tall, gaunt child
holding his child against the promises
of autumn, until the boy slept
never to waken in that world again.

What Work Is

WHAT WORK IS 1991

We stand in the rain in a long line
waiting at Ford Highland Park. For work.
You know what work is – if you're
old enough to read this you know what
work is, although you may not do it.
Forget you. This is about waiting,
shifting from one foot to another.
Feeling the light rain falling like mist
into your hair, blurring your vision
until you think you see your own brother
ahead of you, maybe ten places.
You rub your glasses with your fingers,
and of course it's someone else's brother,
narrower across the shoulders than
yours but with the same sad slouch, the grin
that does not hide the stubbornness,
the sad refusal to give in to
rain, to the hours wasted waiting,
to the knowledge that somewhere ahead
a man is waiting who will say, 'No,
we're not hiring today', for any
reason he wants. You love your brother,
now suddenly you can hardly stand
the love flooding you for your brother,
who's not beside you or behind or
ahead because he's home trying to
sleep off a miserable night shift
at Cadillac so he can get up
before noon to study his German.
Works eight hours a night so he can sing
Wagner, the opera you hate most,
the worst music ever invented.
How long has it been since you told him
you loved him, held his wide shoulders,
opened your eyes wide and said those words,
and maybe kissed his cheek? You've never
done something so simple, so obvious,
not because you're too young or too dumb,
not because you're jealous or even mean
or incapable of crying in
the presence of another man, no,
just because you don't know what work is.

Every Blessed Day

WHAT WORK IS 1991

First with a glass of water
tasting of iron and then
with more and colder water
over his head he gasps himself
awake. He hears the *cheep*
of winter birds searching
the snow for crumbs of garbage
and knows exactly how much light
and how much darkness is there
before the dawn, gray and weak,
slips between the buildings.
Closing the door behind him,
he thinks of places he
has never seen but heard
about, of the great desert
his father said was like
no sea he had ever crossed
and how at dusk or dawn
it held all the shades of red
and blue in its merging shadows,
and though his life was then
a prison he had come to live
for these suspended moments.
Waiting at the corner he feels
the cold at his back and stamps
himself awake again. Seven miles
from the frozen, narrow river.
Even before he looks he knows
the faces on the bus, some
going to work and some coming back,
but each sealed in its hunger
for a different life, a lost life.
Where he's going or who he is
he doesn't ask himself, he
doesn't know and doesn't know
it matters. He gets off
at the familiar corner, crosses
the emptying parking lots
toward Chevy Gear & Axle #3.
In a few minutes he will hold
his time card above a clock,
and he can drop it in
and hear the moment crunching

126

down, or he can not, for
either way the day will last
forever. So he lets it fall.
If he feels the elusive calm
his father spoke of and searched
for all his short life, there's
no way of telling, for now he's
laughing among them, older men
and kids. He's saying, 'Damn,
we've got it made.' He's
lighting up or chewing with
the others, thousands of miles
from their forgotten homes, each
and every one his father's son.

The Mercy

THE MERCY 1999

The ship that took my mother to Ellis Island
Eighty-three years ago was named 'The Mercy'.
She remembers trying to eat a banana
without first peeling it and seeing her first orange
in the hands of a young Scot, a seaman
who gave her a bite and wiped her mouth for her
with a red bandana and taught her the word,
'orange', saying it patiently over and over.
A long autumn voyage, the days darkening
with the black waters calming as night came on,
then nothing as far as her eyes could see and space
without limit rushing off to the corners
of creation. She prayed in Russian and Yiddish
to find her family in New York, prayers
unheard or misunderstood or perhaps ignored
by all the powers that swept the waves of darkness
before she woke, that kept 'The Mercy' afloat
while smallpox raged among the passengers
and crew until the dead were buried at sea
with strange prayers in a tongue she could not fathom.
'The Mercy', I read on the yellowing pages of a book
I located in a windowless room of the library
on 42nd Street, sat thirty-one days
offshore in quarantine before the passengers
disembarked. There a story ends. Other ships
arrived, 'Tancred' out of Glasgow, 'The Neptune'
registered as Danish, 'Umberto IV',
the list goes on for pages, November gives
way to winter, the sea pounds this alien shore.
Italian miners from Piemonte dig
under towns in western Pennsylvania
only to rediscover the same nightmare
they left at home. A nine-year-old girl travels
all night by train with one suitcase and an orange.
She learns that mercy is something you can eat
again and again while the juice spills over
your chin, you can wipe it away with the back
of your hands and you can never get enough.

DVD 2

GWYNETH LEWIS
Filmed in Cardiff, 3 July 2007

GWYNETH LEWIS was made National Poet of Wales in 2005, the first writer to be given the Welsh laureateship. She is a bilingual virtuoso, and has published three collections in Welsh as well as three in English, *Parables & Faxes* (1995), *Zero Gravity* (1998) and *Keeping Mum* (2003), all published by Bloodaxe and combined in *Chaotic Angels: Poems in English* (2005). In 2004 she composed the words on the front of the Wales Millennium Centre in Cardiff.

Her work has been widely praised for its formalist style and wit as well as for its music, a combination which can be appreciated much more fully when her poetry is read aloud. All the poems she reads in the film are included in *Chaotic Angels*. Four are sections from *Zero Gravity*, the 16-poem title-sequence of her second English collection. Part space documentary, part requiem, this draws on the experience of watching her American cousin, astronaut Joe Tanner, helping to repair the Hubble Space Telescope. The BBC later made a documentary of *Zero Gravity*.

The first and last two poems relate to her bilingualism, which she discusses in an essay in *Strong Words* (2000): 'If you're truly bilingual it's not that there are two languages in your head, but that not everybody understands the whole of your personal speech. [...] You know that one language will only take you so far along the route of experiential journey. [...] In this sense, being of a dying culture is, paradoxically, of great value to a poet, if you're interested in ultimate questions about language and the nature of reality [...] poetry isn't about being poetical, it's about telling things as they are.'

In 1989 I wrote to Gwyneth to request poems for Carol Rumens to consider for *New Women Poets* (1990), an anthology introducing the work of a new generation of poets who had published in magazines and pamphlets but had not yet published their first books. We kept in touch and she later sent the manuscript of her first collection in English, *Parables & Faxes*. Ten out of the 25 poets included in *New Women Poets* went on to publish first collections with Bloodaxe.

Born in Cardiff in 1959, she studied at Girton College, Cambridge, and at Harvard and Columbia in the States under Derek Walcott and Joseph Brodsky. She later received a D.Phil in English from Oxford for a thesis on 18th-century literary forgery. After working for many years as a documentary producer and director for BBC Wales in Cardiff, she became a freelance writer. Her other books include *Sunbathing in the Rain: A Cheerful Book on Depression* (Flamingo, 2002), and *Two in a Boat: A Marital Voyage* (Fourth Estate, 2005), her account of the voyage she made in small boat from Cardiff to North Africa when her husband became gravely ill.

from Welsh Espionage

PARABLES & FAXES 1995

V

Welsh was the mother tongue, English was his.
He taught her the body by fetishist quiz,
father and daughter on the bottom stair:
'Dy benelin yw *elbow*, dy wallt di yw *hair*,

chin yw dy ên di, *head* yw dy ben.'
She promptly forgot, made him do it again.
Then he folded her *dwrn* and, calling it fist,
held it to show her knuckles and wrist.

'Let's keep it from Mam, as a special surprise.
Lips are *gwefusau, llygaid* are eyes.'
Each part he touched in their secret game
thrilled as she whispered its English name.

The mother was livid when she was told.
'We agreed, no English till four years old!'
She listened upstairs, her head in a whirl.
Was it such a bad thing to be Daddy's girl?

from Zero Gravity: A Space Requiem

ZERO GRAVITY 1998

In memory of my sister-in-law Jacqueline Badham (1944-1997)
and to commemorate the voyage of my cousin Joe Tanner
and the crew of Space Shuttle STS-82 to repair
the Hubble Space Telescope (February 1997)

VI

Last suppers, I fancy, are always wide-screen.
I see this one in snapshot: your brothers are rhymes
with you and each other. John has a shiner
from surfing. Already we've started counting time
backwards to zero. The Shuttle processed
out like an idol to its pagan pad.
It stands by its scaffold, being tended and blessed
by priestly technicians. You refuse to feel sad,

131

can't wait for your coming wedding with speed
out into weightlessness. We watch you dress
in your orange space suit, a Hindu bride,
with wires like henna for your loveliness.
You carry your helmet like a severed head.
We think of you as already dead.

VIII

Thousands arrive when a bird's about to fly,
crowding the causeways. 'Houston. Weather is a go
and counting.' I pray for you as you lie
on your back facing upwards. A placard shows
local, Shuttle and universal time.
Numbers run out. Zero always comes.
'Main engines are gimballed' and I'm
not ready for this, but clouds of steam
billow out sideways and a sudden spark
lifts the rocket on a collective roar
that comes from inside us. With a sonic crack
the spaceship explodes to a flower of fire
on the scaffold's stamen. We sob and swear,
helpless, but we're lifting a sun
with our love's attention, we hear
the Shuttle's death rattle as it overcomes
its own weight with glory, setting car alarms
off in the Keys and then it's gone
out of this time zone, into the calm
of black and we've lost the lemon dawn
your vanishing made. At the viewing site
we pick oranges for your missing light.

XI

The second time the comet swung by
the knife went deeper. It hissed through the sky

like phosphorus on water. It marked a now,
an only-coming-once, a this-ness we knew

we'd keep forgetting. Its vapour trails
mimicked our voyage along ourselves,

our fire with each other, the endless cold
which surrounds that burning. Don't be fooled

by fireworks. It's no accident that *leave*
fails but still tries to rhyme with *love*.

   XIII
What is her vanishing point?
Now that she's dead
but still close by
we assume she's heard

our conversations.
Out of sight? Out of mind?
On her inward journey
she's travelled beyond

the weight of remembering.
The g-force lifts
from her labouring chest.
Forgetting's a gift

of lightness. She's sped
vast distances
already, she's shed
her many bodies –

cancer, hope, regard,
marriage, forgiving.
Get rid of time
and everything's dancing,

forget straight lines,
all's blown away.
Now's honey from the bees of night,
music from the bees of day.

'One day, feeling hungry'

ZERO GRAVITY 1998

One day, feeling hungry, I swallowed the moon.
It stuck, like a wafer, to the top of my mouth,
dry as an aspirin. It slowly went down,

showing the gills of my vocal cords,
the folded wings in my abdomen,
the horrible twitch of my insect blood.

Lit from inside, I stood alone
(dark to myself) but could see from afar
the brightness of others who had swallowed stars.

The Flaggy Shore

(for Nora Nolan)

ZERO GRAVITY 1998

Even before I've left, I long
for this place. For hay brought in before the rain,
its stooks like stanzas, for glossy cormorants
that make metal eyes and dive like hooks,
fastening the bodice of the folding tide
which unravels in gardens of carraigín.
I walk with the ladies who throw stones at the surge
and their problems, don't answer the phone
in the ringing kiosk. Look. In the clouds
hang pewter promontories, long bays
whose wind-indented silent coasts
make me homesick for where I've not been.
Quicksilver headlands shoot into the night
till distance and the dying of day
dull steel and vermilion to simple lead
blown downwind to the dark, then out of sight.

What's in a Name?

Today the wagtail finally forgot
that I once called it *sigl-di-gwt*.

It didn't give a tinker's toss,
kept right on rooting in river moss,

(no longer *mwswgl*) relieved, perhaps,
that someone would be noticing less

about its habits. Magpies' fear of men
lessened, as we'd lost one means

(the word *pioden*) of keeping track
of terrorist birds out in the back.

Lleian wen is not the same as 'smew'
because it's another point of view,

another bird. There's been a cull:
gwylan's gone and we're left with 'gull'

and blunter senses till that day
when 'swallows', like *gwennol*, might stay away.

Mother Tongue

'I started to translate in seventy-three
in the schoolyard. For a bit of fun
to begin with – the occasional "fuck"
for the bite of another language's smoke
at the back of my throat, its bitter chemicals.
Soon I was hooked on whole sentences
behind the shed, and lessons in Welsh
seemed very boring. I started on print,
Jeeves & Wooster, Dick Francis, James Bond,
in Welsh covers. That worked for a while
until Mam discovered Jean Plaidy inside
a Welsh concordance one Sunday night.
There were ructions: a language, she screamed,
should be for a lifetime. Too late for me.
Soon I was snorting Simenon
and Flaubert. Had to read much more
for any effect. One night I OD'd
after reading far too much Proust.
I came to, but it scared me. For a while
I went Welsh-only but it was bland
and my taste was changing. Before too long
I was back on translating, found that three
languages weren't enough. The "ch"
in German was easy, Rilke a buzz...
For a language fetishist like me
sex is part of the problem. Umlauts make me sweat,
so I need a multilingual man
but they're rare in West Wales and tend to be
married already. If only I'd kept
myself much purer, with simpler tastes,
the Welsh might be living...
                              Detective, you speak
Russian, I hear, and Japanese.
Could you whisper some softly?
I'm begging you. Please...'

JOAN MARGARIT
Filmed with Anna Crowe in Aldeburgh, 5 November 2006

Joan Margarit is one of Spain's major modern writers. Born in 1938, he worked as an architect and first published his work in Spanish, but for the past three decades has become known for his mastery of the Catalan language. The melancholy and candour of his poetry show his affinity with Thomas Hardy, whose work he has translated. In poems evoking the Spanish Civil War and its aftermath, the harshness of life in Barcelona under Franco, and grief at the death of a beloved handicapped daughter, he reminds us that it is not death we have to understand but life. His poetry confronts the worst that life can throw at us, yet what lingers in the mind is its warmth and humanity.

His daughter Joana suffered from Rubinstein-Taybe syndrome, a mental condition also involving severe physical problems which compelled her to use crutches or a wheelchair. She understood that her well-being depended on the affection of those around her and quickly learned that affection breeds more affection. But he took many years to appreciate this. The first poem he reads in the film, 'Dark Night in Balmes Street', set around the time of Joana's birth in 1970, reveals how badly prepared he was for this grief. 'The eyes in the rear-view mirror' celebrates his daughter's shining qualities.

Born in 1938 in Sanaüja, La Segarra region, in Catalonia, he was Professor of Structural Calculations at Barcelona's Technical School of Architecture from 1968 until his retirement. A continuing project for much of this time was his work on Gaudí's unfinished church of the Sagrada Familia in Barcelona.

I first heard him read in 2005 at StAnza, Scotland's poetry festival in St Andrews, where his translator Anna Crowe was Artistic Director for seven years. I immediately asked them both if they would produce a selection of his poems in translation for Bloodaxe. Naomi Jaffa was also at the reading, and said that if the book could be ready for the following year, Aldeburgh Poetry Festival would be delighted to launch it. *Tugs in the Fog: Selected Poems*, launched by Bloodaxe at Aldeburgh in 2006, was his first English publication.

Introducing *Tugs in the Fog*, he describes 'the linguistic circumstances affecting many people who, like me, were born into a Catalan family during or at the end of the Spanish Civil War, when the fascist dictatorship banned my language and ruled that all teaching should be in Castilian. This is why I began writing in Castilian, since I had no culture in any other language. Years later I moved over to writing in Catalan, searching for that which goes deeper in all of us than literary culture.'

Nit fosca al carrer Balmes

ESTACIÓ DE FRANÇA 1999

Acomplerts amenaces i temors,
– tots els carrers duen ja a la vellesa –
passo davant la clínica on vas néixer,
ja fa vint-i-sis anys, una nit fosca
ferida per la llum d'un passadís.
Aquí vas arribar, petita i indefensa,
a la platja suau del teu somriure,
a les dificultats de la paraula,
a les escoles que no et van voler,
als cansaments dels ossos, a la calma
aparent i cruel dels passadissos
que vigilen callades bates blanques
amb freda remor d'àngels.
Polzes torçats, el nas com bec d'ocell,
les ratlles de les mans desordenades:
la nostra fesomia i també la de la síndrome,
com si hi hagués hagut una altra mare
desconeguda oculta en el jardí.
Lluny de la intel·ligència, de la bellesa;
ara només importa la bondat,
la resta són qüestions d'un món inhòspit
del qual ens és difícil ocultar-nos
en rars trajectes de felicitat.

Torno a aquell jardí fosc que contemplava
des de la màquina de fer cafè,
única companyia d'aquelles matinades.
Torno a la culpa i al remordiment,
vells camps de runes que travesso encara:
les mans es van negar
a fer el que jo volia. Com respecto
la lucidesa de les meves mans, que es tornen contra mi
i m'agafen pel coll a la vellesa,
obligant-me a mirar cap al matí
on just et vas salvar
amb la teva tendresa fent-me front.
Vell malentès de la felicitat,
i el món a l'entorn, ni amic ni enemic:
concemplo la gencada pels carrers,
les obres, els despatxos, indagant
sobre les llàgrimes perdudes.

138

Dark Night in Balmes Street

ESTACIÓ DE FRANÇA 1999

Threats and fears fulfilled –
all streets lead to old age –
I go past the clinic where you were born,
twenty-six years ago now, on a dark night
wounded by the light of a corridor.
Here you came, small and defenceless,
to the gentle beach of your smile,
to the difficulties with speech,
to the schools that did not want you,
to the bones' weariness, to the cruel
and obvious calm of the corridors
watched over by silent white coats
with the cold murmur of angels.
Twisted thumbs, a nose like a bird's beak,
the lines in your hand confused:
our own features and those too of the syndrome,
as though you had had another, unknown
mother hidden in the garden.
A far cry from intelligence, from beauty;
now only goodness matters,
the rest are questions of an inhospitable world
from which it is hard to hide ourselves
in rare flights of happiness.

I go back to that dark garden that I was gazing at
from the coffee-machine,
sole companion of those early mornings.
I go back to the blame and the remorse,
old fields of rubble I am still crossing:
my hands refused
to do what I wanted. How I respect
the wisdom of my hands,
that turned against me
and dragged me by my neck towards old age,
forcing me to look at the morning
on which, facing me squarely,
your tenderness just saved you.
Old misunderstanding of what happiness is,
and the world around me, neither friend nor foe:
I gaze at the crowds in the streets,
the building-works, the offices, enquiring
into tears that are lost.

Tu eres la flor, nosaltres el brancatge,
per això el cop de vent, en desfullar-te,
ens feia quedar nus, oscil·lant de dolor.
Encara et protegeixo i, en passar
vora el jardí, tan fosc, d'aquell estiu,
m'hi aboco i torno a veure aquella feble
llum de la màquina de fer cafè.
Vint-i-sis anys. I sé que sóc feliç
i que he tingut la vida que em mereixo.
Mai no podria ser res més
que fos diferent d'ella, atzar i foc.
Atzar per a la vida, foc
per a la mort, per no tenir ni tomba.

Els ulls del retrovisor
AGUAFUERTES 1995

Ja estem acostumats els dos, Joana,
que aquesta lentitud,
quan recolzes les crosses i vas baixant del cotxe,
desperti les botzines i el seu insult abstracte.
Em fa feliç la teva companyia
i el somriure d'un cos que està molt lluny
del que sempre s'ha dit de la bellesa,
la penosa bellesa, tan distant.
L'he canviat per la seducció
de la tendresa que il·lumina
el buit deixat per la raó al teu rostre.
I, quan em miro en el retrovisor,
no veig uns ulls senzills de reconèixer,
perquè hi brilla l'amor que hi han deixat
tantes mirades, i la llum, i l'ombra
del que he vist, i la pau que reflecteix
la teva lentitud, que és dins de mi.
És tan gran la riquesa que no sembla
que aquests ulls del mirall puguin ser els meus.

You are the flower, we the branches,
and the gust of wind, stripping your petals,
left us naked, shaking with grief.
I still protect you and passing so close
to the garden, so dark, that summer,
I lean out and see once more that feeble
light from the coffee-machine.
Twenty-six years. And I know that I am happy
and that I've had the life I deserve.
Never could I be something
different from her, chance and fire.
A chance for life, fire
for death, for not even having a tomb.

The eyes in the rear-view mirror
ETCHINGS 1995

We have both grown accustomed, Joana,
for this slowness,
when you lean on your crutches, and climb out of the car,
to start off a sally of car-horns and their abstract abuse.
Your company makes me happy,
and the smile of a body so far
from what was always called beauty,
that tedious beauty, so far-off.
I have exchanged it for the seductiveness
of tenderness that lights up the gap
that reason left in your face.
And, if I look at myself in the rear-view mirror,
I see a pair of eyes I do not easily recognise,
for in them there shines the love left
by looks, and light, the shadow
of everything I have seen,
and the peace your slowness reflects back to me.
So great is their wealth
that the eyes in the rear-view mirror don't seem to be mine.

Perdiu jove

CÀLCUL D'ESTRUCTURES 2005

S'arraulia en un solc i, en agafar-la,
he sentit com si fos la teva mà en la meva.
Duia taques de sang seca en una ala:
els petits ossos, com barnilles,
eren trencats per la perdigonada.
Ha provat de volar, però amb prou feines,
l'ala penjant, s'ha arrossegat per terra
fins a amagar-se rere d'una pedra.
Encara sento l'escalfor a la mà,
perquè un ser fràgil va donar sentit
a cada un dels meus dies. Un ser fràgil
que ara també és darrere d'una pedra.

Young partridge

STRUCTURAL CALCULATIONS 2005

It was crouching in a furrow, and when I picked it up,
it felt as though your hand was in mine.
There were patches of dried blood on one wing:
the tiny bones, like ribs,
were shattered by buckshot.
It tried to fly but, trailing the wing,
could scarcely drag itself along the ground
before hiding beneath a stone.
I still feel that warmth in my hand,
because a fragile creature gave meaning
to each of my days. A fragile creature
likewise now beneath a stone.

ADRIAN MITCHELL
Filmed in London, 25 January 2008

Adrian Mitchell is a prolific poet, playwright and children's writer. His poetry's simplicity, clarity, passion and humour show his allegiance to a vital, popular tradition embracing William Blake as well as the Border Ballads and the blues. His most nakedly political poems – about nuclear war, Vietnam, prisons and racism – have become part of the folklore of the Left, sung and recited at demonstrations and mass rallies. His childlike questioning has been a constant reminder since the 60s that poetry is first and foremost an assertion of the human spirit. His short poem stating *'Most people ignore most poetry / because / most poetry ignores most people'* summed up what was wrong with poetry before Mitchell and others rescued it from the deadening clutches of the university old boys' network.

An idealist who has remained true to his heartfelt beliefs, he has reported back for the past half-century from a world blighted by war, compromise, double-talk and pragmatism without losing his innocence, integrity and impish sense of humour. Kenneth Tynan called him 'the British Mayakovsky' and Angela Carter described him as 'joyous, acrid and demotic tumbling lyricist Pied Piper determinedly singing us away from catastrophe'.

After Allison & Busby stopped publishing poetry, he brought his work to Bloodaxe. The cover picture of *Adrian Mitchell's Greatest Hits* (1991) was Ralph Steadman's outlandish portrait of him, which hangs in his house and is seen at the start of the film. This was followed by four books covering 50 years of his work: *Heart on the Left: Poems 1953-1984* (1997), *Blue Coffee: Poems 1985-1996* (1996), *All Shook Up: Poems 1997-2000* (2000) and *The Shadow Knows: Poems 2000-2004* (2004).

Born in London in 1932, he worked as a journalist from 1955 to 1966, when he became a full-time writer. He has given many hundreds of readings throughout the world in theatres, colleges, pubs, prisons, streets, public transport, cellars, clubs and schools of all kinds. Many of his plays and stage adaptations have been performed at the National Theatre as well as by the Royal Shakespeare Company and other theatre companies.

He first read 'To Whom It May Concern' at an anti-Vietnam War protest in Trafalgar Square in 1964, and keeps changing the last verse. In 2002, the socialist magazine *Red Pepper* dubbed him Shadow Poet Laureate and asked him to write regular republican poems for their columns. In a National Poetry Day poll in 2005, 'Human Beings' was voted the poem that most people would like to see launched into space, and an arts project is now in hand which may see that happen.

What Is Poetry?

ON THE BEACH AT CAMBRIDGE 1984

Look at those naked words dancing together!
Everyone's very embarrassed.
Only one thing to do about it –
Off with your clothes
And join in the dance.
Naked words and people dancing together.
There's going to be trouble.
Here come the Poetry Police!

Keep dancing.

Human Beings

THE SHADOW KNOWS 2004

look at your hands
your beautiful useful hands
you're not an ape
you're not a parrot
you're not a slow loris
or a smart missile
you're human

not british
not american
not israeli
not palestinian
you're human

not catholic
not protestant
not muslim
not hindu
you're human

we all start human
　　we end up human
　　　human first
　　　　human last
　　　we're human
　　or we're nothing

nothing but bombs
　　and poison gas
nothing but guns
　　and torturers
nothing but slaves
of Greed and War
if we're not human

　　　look at your body
with its amazing systems
of nerve-wires and blood canals
　　think about your mind
which can think about itself
　　and the whole universe
　　　look at your face
which can freeze into horror
　　　or melt into love
　　look at all that life
　　　all that beauty
　　　you're human
　　they are human
　　we are human
let's try to be human

　　　dance!

A Puppy Called Puberty

BLUE COFFEE 1996

It was like keeping a puppy in your underpants
A secret puppy you weren't allowed to show to anyone
Not even your best friend or your worst enemy

You wanted to pat him stroke him cuddle him
All the time but you weren't supposed to touch him

He only slept for five minutes at a time
Then he'd suddenly perk up his head
In the middle of school medical inspection
And always on bus rides
So you had to climb down from the upper deck
All bent double to smuggle the puppy off the bus
Without the buxom conductress spotting
Your wicked and ticketless stowaway.

Jumping up, wet-nosed, eagerly wagging –
He only stopped being a nuisance
When you were alone together
Pretending to be doing your homework
But really gazing at each other
Through hot and hazy daydreams

Of those beautiful schoolgirls on the bus
With kittens bouncing in their sweaters.

Back in the Playground Blues

FOR BEAUTY DOUGLAS 1982

I dreamed I was back in the playground, I was about four feet high
Yes dreamed I was back in the playground, standing about four feet high
Well the playground was three miles long and the playground was five miles wide

It was broken black tarmac with a high wire fence all around
Broken black dusty tarmac with a high fence running all around
And it had a special name to it, they called it The Killing Ground

Got a mother and a father, they're one thousand years away
The rulers of The Killing Ground are coming out to play
Everybody thinking: 'Who they going to play with today?'

    Well you get it for being Jewish
    And you get it for being black
    Get it for being chicken
    And you get it for fighting back
    You get it for being big and fat
    Get it for being small
    Oh those who get it get it and get it
    For any damn thing at all

Sometimes they take a beetle, tear off its six legs one by one
Beetle on its black back, rocking in the lunchtime sun
But a beetle can't beg for mercy, a beetle's not half the fun

I heard a deep voice talking, it had that iceberg sound
'It prepares them for Life' – but I have never found
Any place in my life worse than The Killing Ground.

Beattie Is Three

THE APEMAN COMETH 1975

At the top of the stairs
I ask for her hand. O.K.
She gives it to me.
How her fist fits my palm,
A bunch of consolation.
We take our time
Down the steep carpetway
As I wish silently
That the stairs were endless.

To Whom It May Concern (Tell Me Lies about Vietnam)

OUT LOUD 1968

I was run over by the truth one day.
Ever since the accident I've walked this way
   So stick my legs in plaster
   Tell me lies about Vietnam.

Heard the alarm clock screaming with pain,
Couldn't find myself so I went back to sleep again
   So fill my ears with silver
   Stick my legs in plaster
   Tell me lies about Vietnam.

Every time I shut my eyes all I see is flames.
Made a marble phone book and I carved all the names
   So coat my eyes with butter
   Fill my ears with silver
   Stick my legs in plaster
   Tell me lies about Vietnam.

I smell something burning, hope it's just my brains.
They're only dropping peppermints and daisy-chains
    So stuff my nose with garlic
    Coat my eyes with butter
    Fill my ears with silver
    Stick my legs in plaster
    Tell me lies about Vietnam.

Where were you at the time of the crime?
Down by the Cenotaph drinking slime
    So chain my tongue with whisky
    Stuff my nose with garlic
    Coat my eyes with butter
    Fill my ears with silver
    Stick my legs in plaster
    Tell me lies about Vietnam.

You put your bombers in, you put your conscience out,
You take the human being and you twist it all about
    So scrub my skin with women
    Chain my tongue with whisky
    Stuff my nose with garlic
    Coat my eyes with butter
    Fill my ears with silver
    Stick my legs in plaster
    Tell me lies, tell me lies about Aghanistan.
    Tell me lies about Israel.
    Tell me lies about Congo.
    Tell me, tell me lies Mr Bush.
    Tell me lies Mr B-B-Blair, Brown, Blair-Brown.
    Tell me lies about Vietnam.

Death Is Smaller Than I Thought

(NEW POEM 2006)

My Mother and Father died some years ago
I loved them very much.
When they died my love for them
Did not vanish or fade away.
It stayed just about the same,
Only a sadder colour.
And I can feel their love for me,
Same as it ever was.

Nowadays, in good times or bad,
I sometimes ask my Mother and Father
To walk beside me or to sit with me
So we can talk together
Or be silent.

They always come to me.
I talk to them and listen to them
And think I hear them talk to me.
It's very simple –
Nothing to do with spiritualism
Or religion or mumbo jumbo.

It is imaginary.
It is real.
It is love.

Telephone

BLUE COFFEE 1996

Telephone told me that you were dead
Now I hate every telephone's stupid head
I'd rather sit here turning to a block of stone
Than pick up any snake of a telephone

Especially When It Snows

(for Boty)

BLUE COFFEE 1996

especially when it snows
and every tree
has its dark arms and widespread hands
full of that shining angelfood

especially when it snows
and every footprint
makes a dark lake
among the frozen grass

especially when it snows darling
and tough little robins
beg for crumbs
at golden-spangled windows

ever since we said goodbye to you
in that memorial garden
where nothing grew
except the beautiful blank-eyed snow

and little Caitlin crouched to wave goodbye to you
down in the shadows

especially when it snows
and keeps on snowing

especially when it snows
and down the purple pathways of the sky
the planet staggers like King Lear
with his dead darling in his arms

especially when it snows
and keeps on snowing

TAHA MUHAMMAD ALI
Filmed with Peter Cole in Aldeburgh, 3 November 2007

TAHA MUHAMMAD ALI is a celebrated Palestinian poet whose work is driven by a storyteller's vivid imagination, disarming humour and unflinching honesty. Born in 1931 in Saffuriyya in rural Galilee, he was left without a home when his village was destroyed during the Arab-Israeli war of 1948, forcing his family to flee to Lebanon. Out of this history of shared loss and survival, he has created art of the first order. His poems portray experiences ranging from catastrophe to splendour, all the while preserving an essential human dignity.

His family later slipped back across the border and settled in Nazareth, where he has lived ever since. An autodidact, he owns a souvenir shop now run by his sons near Nazareth's Church of the Annunciation. In Israel, in the West Bank and Gaza, and in Europe and in America, audiences have been powerfully moved by his poetry of political complexity and humanity. He has published several collections of poetry and one volume of short stories. His bilingual edition *So What: New & Selected Poems 1971-2005*, translated by Peter Cole, Yahya Hijazi and Gabriel Levin, was his first book to be published in the US (by Copper Canyon in 2006) and Britain (by Bloodaxe in 2007). I first met him, with Peter Cole, when they came to Aldeburgh Poetry Festival in 2007 to launch the book in Britain.

In his introduction to *So What*, Gabriel Levin writes: 'Muhammad Ali writes a literary Arabic that occasionally incorporates or, as he puts it, "grafts" onto the classical forms certain elements of a quasi-colloquial and often idiosyncratic Arabic, along with – in some instances – full-fledged dialect when his characters speak. In contrast to the stylised, heightened diction of most of his contemporaries, Muhammad Ali's lower register anchors the poetry to a sense of place without ever sounding merely like dialect. [...] Arabic poets and critics have pointed out that Muhammad Ali's originality (and even his relevance to the Palestinian cause) lies precisely in his blending of registers and employment of natural, homespun imagery – both of which contribute to the poetry's apparent simplicity while belying all along its complex sensibility. Saffuriyya may have been razed to the ground, but its *mores*, language, and landscape remain paradigms of durable hope in the poet's imagination. In effect the rhetoric and technique of Muhammad Ali's poetry constitute yet another means of clinging to his home and land, and of being a *samid* – a term coined by Palestinians in the late 70s and meaning one who holds on tenaciously to his land and its culture and perseveres in adverse times.'

عَبْد الهادي يُصارِعُ دَوْلَةً عُظْمى

في حَياتِهِ
ما قَرَأَ وَلا كَتَبَ.
في حَياتِهِ
ما قَطَعَ شَجَرَةً،
وَلا طَعَنَ بَقَرَةً.
في حَياتِهِ، ما جابَ سِيرَةَ النِّيويورْك تايْمز؛
بِغيابِها.
في حَياتِهِ،
ما رَفَعَ صَوْتَهُ على أَحَدٍ
إلّا بِقَوْلِه:
« تْفَضَّلْ...
وَاللهِ العَظيمْ غيرْ تْتْفَضَّلْ! »

—

وَمَعَ ذلِكَ،
فَهُوَ يَحْيا قَضِيَّةً خاسِرَةً.
حالَتُهُ، مَيْؤوسٌ مِنْها،
وَحَقُّهُ ذَرَّةُ مِلْحٍ،
سَقَطَتْ في المُحيطِ.

أَيُّها السَّادَةُ!
إنَّ مُوَكَّلي، لا يَعْرِفُ شَيْئًا عَنْ عَدُوِّه.

وَأُؤَكِّدُ لَكُمْ،
أَنَّهُ لَوْ رَأَى بَحَّارَةَ الإنْتِرْبْرايْز
لَقَدَّمَ لَهُمُ البَيْضَ المَقْلِيَّ،
وَلَبَنَ الكيس!

154

Abd el-Hadi Fights a Superpower

(VII 1973)

In his life
he neither wrote nor read.
In his life he
didn't cut down a single tree,
didn't slit the throat
of a single calf.
In his life he did not speak
of the *New York Times*
behind its back,
didn't raise
his voice to a soul
except in his saying:
'Come in, please,
by God, you can't refuse.'

*

Nevertheless –
his case is hopeless,
his situation
desperate.
His God-given rights are a grain of salt
tossed into the sea.
Ladies and gentlemen of the jury:
about his enemies
my client knows not a thing.

And I can assure you,
were he to encounter
the entire crew
of the aircraft carrier *Enterprise*,
he'd serve them eggs
sunny-side up,
and labneh
fresh from the bag.

تَحْذِير

إلى هُواةِ الصَّيْدِ
وَشُداةِ القَنْصِ!
لا تُصَوِّبوا غَدَّاراتِكُمْ
إلى فَرحي!
فَهُوَ لا يُساوي ثَمَنَ الخَرْطوشَة
(تُبَدِّدُ باتِّجاهِه)
فَمَا تَرَوْنَهُ
أنيقًا وَسَريعًا
كَغَزالٍ،
وَيَفِرُّ في كُلِّ اتِّجاهٍ
كَديكِ حَجَلٍ:
لَيْسَ فَرَحًا.
صَدِّقوني –
فَرَحي
لا عَلاقَةَ لَهُ بالفَرَحِ!

أماليد

لا الموسيقَى...
ولا الشهرةُ والثَّرْوَة
ولا حَتى الشِعْرُ نَفْسُه
بِمُستطيع أَن يعزِّيني
عن قِصَرِ عمرِ الإنسان
وعن أن «الملك لير»
ثَمانون صَفْحة (وتنتهي)
وعن محض التَصَوُّر:
أنَّ المرء قد يُرْزَأُ
بِإبنٍ عاقٍّ!

‒

156

Warning
(12 ix 1988)

Lovers of hunting,
and beginners seeking your prey:
Don't aim your rifles
at my happiness,
which isn't worth
the price of the bullet
(you'd waste on it).
What seems to you
so nimble and fine,
like a fawn,
and flees
every which way,
like a partridge,
isn't happiness.
Trust me:
my happiness bears
no relation to happiness.

from Twigs
(1989–91)

Neither music,
fame, nor wealth,
not even poetry itself,
could provide consolation
for life's brevity,
or the fact that *King Lear*
is a mere eighty pages long and comes to an end,
and for the thought that one might suffer greatly
on account of a rebellious child.

*

حُبِّي لكِ
هو العَظيم!
أما أنا وأنتِ والآخرون
فأغلبُ الظنِ أنَّنا أُناسٌ عاديونْ!

ــ

وهكذا...
إِسْتَغْرَقْتُ
السِتين سنةً كاملةً
حتى أدركتُ:
أن الماءَ ألذُّ الأشربةِ
وأنَّ الخُبزَ من الأَطعمةِ أَشْهاها
وأَنَّ لا قيمة حقيقية لأي فنٍ
إلا إذا أَدْخَلَ البَهْجَةَ
إلى قَلْبِ الإِنْسَان!

ــ

بَعْدَ أَن نموتْ
وَيُسْدِل القلبُ المُتْعَبُ
أجفانَه الأَخيرةَ
على كُلِ ما فَعَلْناه
على كُلِ ما تَمَنَّيْناه
وعلى كُلِ ما حَلِمْنا به...
تَشَوَّقْنا إليه
أو أَحْسَسْناه ــ
سَتكونُ الكراهيةُ
أولَ ما يَتَعَفَّنُ
فِينا!

158

My love for you
is what's magnificent,
but I, you, and the others,
most likely,
are ordinary people.

*

And so
it has taken me
all of sixty years
to understand
that water is the finest drink,
and bread the most delicious food,
and that art is worthless
unless it plants
a measure of splendor in people's hearts.

*

After we die,
and the weary heart
has lowered its final eyelid
on all that we've done,
and on all that we've longed for,
on all that we've dreamt of,
all we've desired
or felt,
hate will be
the first thing
to putrefy
within us.

ريتِك مَا تْصَرّفِيهَا

ها أَنَذا في المَوْقِع ذاتِه
لكِنَّ المَكانَ لَيْسَ تُرابًا وَفَضاءُ
وَلَيْسَ حِجارَة.
أَيْنَ اللَّوْزُ الأَخْضَرُ؟
أَيْنَ الشَّحِيتيّاتُ وَالثُّغاءُ؟
أَيْنَ رُمَّانُ الأُمْسِيات
وَرائِحَةُ الخُبْز؟
أَيْنَ القُطا وَالشَّبابيك؟
أَيْنَ رَفَّةُ جَديلَة أَميرَة؟
أَيْنَ السُّمّانُ
وَصَهيلُ المُحَجَّلات
مَطْلوقاتِ اليَمين؟
أَيْنَ أَعْراسُ السُّنونو؟
أَيْنَ أَعْيادُ الزَّيْتون؟
وَفَرَحُ السَّنابِل؟
أَيْنَ أَهْدابُ الزَّعْفَران
وَمَلاعِبُ العُمَيْضَة؟
أَيْنَ قاسِم؟
أَيْنَ الزَّعْتَرُ؟
أَيْنَ الشُّوحَةُ؟
تَنْقَضُّ عَلى الدّجاجاتِ
مِنْ عاشِر سَما...

فَتَصْرُخُ خَلْفَها الجَدَّةُ:
«أَخَذْتِ الرُّزَّيْه
يا فاجِري!
ريتِك مَا تْصَرّفِيها
يا بُعيدي...
ريتِك مَا تْصَرّفِيها!»

160

The Place Itself, or I Hope You Can't Digest It

(16 IV 2004)

And so I come to the place itself,
but the place is not
its dust and stones and open space.
For where are the red-tailed birds
and the almonds' green?
Where are the bleating lambs
and pomegranates of evening –
the smell of bread
and the grouse?
Where are the windows,
and where is the ease of Amira's braid?
Where are the quails
and white-footed fettered horses whinnying,
their right leg alone set free?
Where are the wedding
parties of swallows –
the rites and feasts of the olives?
The joy of the branching spikes of wheat?
And where is the crocus's eyelash?
Where are the fields we played
our games of hide-and-seek in?
And where is Qasim?
Where are the hyssop and thyme?
Where is the kite descending on chicks
from the heaven's heights,
as the old woman shouts at it:
'You took our speckled hen,
you whore!
I hope you can't digest it!
You there, in the distance:
I hope you can't digest it!'

لَيْسَ إِلَّا

اَلتَّغَيُّرَاتُ الَّتِي تَعَرَّضْتُ لَها
في جَسَدِي
بَعْدَ أَنْ وَضَعْتُ قَدَمي
في السِّتِّينَاتِ
مِنْ عُمْرِي
كَانَتْ مَعْدُودَةً وَعَادِيَّةً .
بِضْعُ تَغَيُّرَاتٍ، لَيْسَ إِلَّا :
ضَغْطٌ يُضاغِطُ « سُكَّرِيَ »
اِلْتِهَابٌ مُقِيمٌ في المَفاصِلِ .
اِضْطِرَابٌ مُزْمِنٌ
في عُصارَاتٍ كَوْكَبَةٍ
مِنَ الغُدَدِ الأَساسِيَّةِ .
فُضَّ فَمِي
ثَقُلَ سَمَعِي
خَلَلٌ جَذْرِيٌّ
في رُؤْيَتِي عَبْرَ نَظَّارَاتٍ سَميكَةٍ .
اَلاِعْتِمَادُ الكُلِّيُّ عَلى العُكَّازِ
حَتَّى، عِنْدَما أَسْعُلُ .
أَرَقٌّ مَجُوسِيٌّ لا يَخْمَدُ
في لَيْلٍ أَسْوَدَ أَسْوَدَ
أَطْوَلَ مِنْ شَعْرِ سِتِّينَ غُولَةً .

بِضْعَةُ « تَغَيُّرَاتٍ »، كَما تَرى،
إِلى جانِبِ وَهْنٍ دائِمٍ
في عَضَلَةِ الفَرَحِ مِنْ قَلْبِي .

أَيْضًا، مُلاحَظَةُ حالاتٍ عامِّيَةٍ لافِتَةٍ :
مِنْ فِئَةِ اللُّجوءِ إِلى اسْتِعْمالِ التَّعْبِيرِ :
« فُضَّ فَمِي »
بَدَلَ القَوْلِ :
« سَقَطَتْ أَسْناني . »

162

Nothing More

(1 v 2004)

The changes facing my body
when I first set foot in my sixties
were normal.
There were only a handful, nothing more:
a battle between my sugar and blood,
persistent inflammation in joints,
and chronic trouble
with the fluids flowing
from the principal cluster of glands.
I held my tongue
as my hearing worsened,
and a serious flaw developed
in my vision, even through thick glasses,
along with a total dependence
on my cane, even when coughing.
An unrelenting,
Zoroastrian insomnia pursued me
on the blackest of nights –
longer than the hair of sixty ghouls.

As you see, there were only a few –
apart from those involving
ceaseless fatigue in the muscle
charged with joy in my heart.

An interesting general condition
was also observed –
along the lines of my resorting
to using the expression
'I held my tongue,'
instead of saying:
'My teeth fell out.'

Translations by Peter Cole, Yahya Hijazi & Gabriel Levin

NAOMI SHIHAB NYE
Filmed in Aldeburgh, 4 November 2006

Naomi Shihab Nye is a wandering poet. For over 30 years she has travelled America and the world to read and teach. Born in 1952 in St Louis, Missouri to a Palestinian father and an American mother, she grew up in St Louis, Jerusalem and San Antonio. Drawing on her Palestinian-American background, the cultural diversity of Texas, and her experiences in Asia, Europe, Canada, Mexico, Central and South America and the Middle East, her poetry 'reflects this textured heritage, which endowed her with an openness to the experiences of others and a sense of continuity across borders' (Bill Moyers). As well as her father's bedtime stories of life in Palestine, her formative influences included books by Margaret Wise Brown, Louisa May Alcott, Carl Sandburg, Langston Hughes and William Blake (*Songs of Innocence*): 'Reading gave us voices of friends speaking from everywhere, so it followed that one might write down messages too.'

Through her empathetic use of poetic language, she reveals the shining nature of our daily lives, whether writing about local life in her inner-city Texan neighbourhood or the daily rituals of Jews and Palestinians in the war-torn Middle East. Probing the fragile connection between language and meaning, she shows how lives are marked by tragedy, inequity and misunderstanding, and that our best chance of surviving losses and shortcomings is to be acutely aware of the sacred in all things.

She has published more than 25 books, including poetry, essays, picture books, novels and anthologies for younger readers. Her latest book of essays is *I'll Ask You Three Times, Are You Okay? Tales of Driving and Being Driven* (2007).

She has received many literary awards, and has been a Lannan Fellow, a Guggenheim Fellow, and a Witter Bynner Fellow (Library of Congress). Her work has been presented on National Public Radio on *A Prairie Home Companion* and *The Writer's Almanac*, and she has been featured on two of Bill Moyers' PBS poetry specials on American television networks. She lives in San Antonio, Texas.

After including her poems in *Being Alive: the sequel to 'Staying Alive'* (2004), I contacted her and her US publishers in the hope that we could publish a selection of her work in the Bloodaxe World Poets series, and arranged to meet to discuss the book in November 2006 at Aldeburgh, where she was giving a reading at the festival. The following day we filmed her reading four poems which would later appear in her first UK poetry publication, *Tender Spot: Selected Poems*, published by Bloodaxe in 2008.

So Much Happiness

(for Michael)

HUGGING THE JUKEBOX 1982

It is difficult to know what to do with so much happiness.
With sadness there is something to rub against,
a wound to tend with lotion and cloth.
When the world falls in around you, you have pieces to pick up,
something to hold in your hands, like ticket stubs or change.

But happiness floats.
It doesn't need you to hold it down.
It doesn't need anything.
Happiness lands on the roof of the next house, singing,
and disappears when it wants to.
You are happy either way.
Even the fact that you once lived in a peaceful tree house
and now live over a quarry of noise and dust
cannot make you unhappy.
Everything has a life of its own,
it too could wake up filled with possibilities
of coffee cake and ripe peaches,
and love even the floor which needs to be swept,
the soiled linens and scratched records...

Since there is no place large enough
to contain so much happiness,
you shrug, you raise your hands, and it flows out of you
into everything you touch. You are not responsible.
You take no credit, as the night sky takes no credit
for the moon, but continues to hold it, and share it,
and in that way, be known.

Kindness

DIFFERENT WORDS TO PRAY 1980

Before you know what kindness really is
you must lose things,
feel the future dissolve in a moment
like salt in a weakened broth.
What you held in your hand,
what you counted and carefully saved,
all this must go so you know

165

how desolate the landscape can be
between the regions of kindness.
How you ride and ride
thinking the bus will never stop,
the passengers eating maize and chicken
will stare out the window forever.

Before you learn the tender gravity of kindness,
you must travel where the Indian in a white poncho
lies dead by the side of the road.
You must see how this could be you,
how he too was someone
who journeyed through the night with plans
and the simple breath that kept him alive.

Before you know kindness as the deepest thing inside,
you must know sorrow as the other deepest thing.
You must wake up with sorrow.
You must speak to it till your voice
catches the thread of all sorrows
and you see the size of the cloth.

Then it is only kindness that makes sense anymore,
only kindness that ties your shoes
and sends you out into the day to mail letters and purchase bread,
only kindness that raises its head
from the crowd of the world to say
It is I you have been looking for,
and then goes with you everywhere
like a shadow or a friend.

Colombia

The Day
YOU AND YOURS 2005

I missed the day
on which it was said
others should not have
certain weapons, but we could.
Not only could, but should,
        and do.
I missed that day.

Was I sleeping?
I might have been digging
in the yard,
doing something small and slow
as usual.
Or maybe I wasn't born yet.
What about all the other people
who aren't born?
Who will tell them?

For Mohammed Zeid of Gaza, Age 15

YOU AND YOURS 2005

There is no *stray* bullet, sirs.
No bullet like a worried cat
crouching under a bush,
no half-hairless puppy bullet
dodging midnight streets.
The bullet could not be a pecan
plunking tin roof,
not hardly, no fluff of pollen
on October's breath,
no humble pebble at our feet.

So don't gentle it, please.

We live among stray thoughts,
tasks abandoned midstream.
Our fickle hearts are fat
with stray devotions, we feel at home
among bits and pieces,
all the wandering ways of words.

But this bullet had no innocence, did not
wish anyone well, you can't tell us otherwise
by naming it mildly, this bullet was never the friend
of life, should not be granted immunity
by soft saying – friendly fire, straying death-eye,
why have we given the wrong weight to what we do?

Mohammed, Mohammed, deserves the truth.
This bullet had no secret happy hopes,
it was not singing to itself with eyes closed
under the bridge.

MICHEAL O'SIADHAIL

Filmed in Booterstown, Co. Dublin, 11 January 2007

MICHEAL O'SIADHAIL [pronounced *Mee-hall Oh Sheel*] is a prolific Irish poet and linguist whose work sets the intensities of a life against the background of worlds shaken by change. He has published eight books of poetry with Bloodaxe, including *Our Double Time* (1998), *Poems 1975-1995* (1999), *The Gossamer Wall: poems in witness to the Holocaust* (2002) and *Love Life* (2005). He translated his first three collections – originally written in Irish – into English for *Hail! Madam Jazz: New and Selected Poems* (1992).

In his most recent collection, *Globe* (2007), he explores how a world is shaped; how the past and memories bear on the present; how to face the open wounds of tragedies and loss. He constantly seeks new dimensions through his poetry: examining the passions of friendship, marriage, trust and betrayal in an urban culture, tracing the intricacies of music and science as he tries to shape an understanding of the shifts and transformations of late modernity. In *Musics of Belonging: The Poetry of Micheal O'Siadhail* (Carysfort Press, 2007), the book's co-editor David F. Ford lists O'Siadhail's characteristic themes as 'despair, women, love, friendship, language, school, vocation, music, city life, science and other cultures and histories. There is a wrestle for meaning, with no easy resolution – both the form and the content are hard-won.' Jazz is *leitmotiv* throughout his work.

Born in 1947, he was educated at Clongowes Wood College, Trinity College Dublin and the University of Oslo. He has been a lecturer at Trinity College Dublin and a professor at the Dublin Institute for Advanced Studies. Among his many academic works are *Learning Irish* (Yale University Press, 1988) and *Modern Irish* (Cambridge University Press, 1989). He is a fluent speaker of a surprising number and range of languages, including Norwegian, Icelandic, German, Welsh and Japanese. As well as some of the great English-language writers (Donne, Milton, Yeats, Kavanagh), his main influences include much literature in other languages, read and assimilated in the original (Irish monastic and folk poetry, Dante, Rilke, Paul Valéry, Karin Boye, the Eddas and the Sagas).

In 1987 he resigned his professorship order to write poetry full-time, supported by giving numerous readings in many parts of the world. He lives in Booterstown, on the edge of Dublin Bay.

We filmed him on his 60th birthday, before the party. It was a blustery day in January. In the film, the mid-afternoon light fades in his attic study as the sky darkens over Dublin; then driving rain lashes the skylight as he reads the last poem, 'Only End'. The storm made filming impossible after that, but we were happy to keep that final poem with its atmospheric accompaniment.

Cosmos

THE MIDDLE VOICE 1982

'All right?' booms the saxophone man,
'everybody feeling chameleon?' The combo
expands the tune of a well-battered song.
An opulence of sound, clash and flow
as a spotlight tunnels dust in its beam,
glints the trumpet's bell and the hall
turns hot and hybrid, beery listeners
swaying and bobbing the mood of a theme.

From rainbows of timbre a strand of colour
floats into the air: the trumpet solo
burping one phrase of a melody, ripe
and brassy and buttoned down as though
a song is breathing over its origins,
those four hot-blooded notes weeping
their pleasure again on an old civil war
bugle. A sleazy backroom in New Orleans.

Sax and rhythm. The brightness of a reed,
winding tube and crook are working on
another hue of the tune that moves
into its own discourse: *Bud Freeman,
Johnny Hodges, Charlie Parker.* 'All right?'
he drawls, then scats a little as we clap
a tradition of subversions. But he's off again.
I watch swarms of dust in the spotlight,

swirls of galaxies, and imagine he's blowing
a huge balloon of space that's opening
our world of order. In a waft of creation
his being becomes a music's happening.
A red-shirted pianist now leans to seize
a gene of the song which seems to veer
and improvise, somehow catching a moment's
shifts and humours. Hail! Madam Jazz.

Let the theme return, its mutants echoing
as a tune balances against its freedom.
One key – so open-toned and open-stitched.
A beat poised, a crossgrained rhythm,
interplays, imbrications of voice over voice,
mutinies of living are rocking the steady
state of a theme; these riffs and overlappings
a love of deviance, our genesis in noise.

Between

THE MIDDLE VOICE 1982

As we fall into step I ask a penny for your thoughts.
'Oh, nothing,' you say, 'well, nothing so easily bought.'

Sliding into the rhythm of your silence, I almost forget
how lonely I'd been until that autumn morning we met.

At bedtime up along my childhood's stairway, tongues
of fire cast shadows. Too earnest, too highstrung.

My desire is endless: others ended when I'd only started.
Then, there was you: so whole-hog, so wholehearted.

Think of the thousands of nights and the shadows fought.
And the mornings of light. I try to read your thought.

In the strange openness of your face, I'm powerless.
Always this love. Always this infinity between us.

Transit

A FRAGILE CITY 1995

Urgencies of language: check-in, stand-by, take-off.
Everything apace, businesslike. But I'm happy here
Gazing at all the meetings and farewells. I love
To see those strangers' faces quickened and bare.
A lost arrival is wandering. A moment on edge,
He pans a lounge for his countersign of welcome.
A flash of greeting, sudden lightening of baggage,
As though he journeyed out only to journey home.
I watch a parting couple in their embrace and freeing.
The woman turns, a Veronica with her handkerchief
Absorbing into herself a last stain of a countenance.
She dissolves in crowds. An aura of her leaving glance
Travels through the yearning air. Tell me we live
For those faces wiped into the folds of our being.

from Our Double Time

OUR DOUBLE TIME 1998

1

A morning leaving hospital, suddenly the height,
The breadth, the depth. Autumn of my overhaul
When senses seemed to double. Rilke was right:
Some fruit in me keeps ripening for a mellow fall.
Scalpel and needle of growth. A wound's suture.
Etched wonder of what's both brittle and finite:
Two girls linking arms and so full of the future;
The unbearable joy of a sumac's crimson light.
Had I been too busy to notice all this before,
Too concerned to catch the obvious rhyme?
Everything vibrates. A voice. A scent. A colour.
Charged and marvellous. Everything in double time.
To have been to the edge, just to be allowed return
To moments of utter in-loveness, utter unconcern.

Only End

GLOBE 2007

Music of a given globe,
Off-chance jazz forever bringing
More being into being
Out of history's tangled knots and loops
Spirituals and flophouse bands
In hymns and charismatic whoops,
In night-clubs' vibe and strobe,
Nothing buts now *everything ands.*

Our heads are ancient Greeks
Who think just because they think
A body's out of sync
With thought but maybe we relearn the way
Our mind can pulse to intransigent
Musics of once broken to play
Beyond perfect techniques
The livelong midrash of a moment.

171

Given a globe of profusion,
We players are no legislators
More like mediators,
Who extemporising seem to up the ante
To find the nit and grit that has
A universal image for a Dante,
An aim without conclusion
To play mein host to Madam Jazz

Playing without end.
Growling, wailing, singing Madam
In anguish and joys we jam
As Davis's almost vibratoless horn
Wraps around *Embraceable You*
Somehow original and still reborn
Swooping back to mend,
Resolving just to clash again.

All time to understand
Infinite blues of what ifs,
Breaks and tragic riffs
As traditions wander into other spaces
Zigzagging and boundary crossing
In clustered face-to-faces
Commonplace and grand,
Sweet nuisances of our being

On song and off-beam,
Hanging loose, hanging tough,
Offbeat, off the cuff,
Made, broken and remade in love,
Lived-in boneshaking pizzazz
Of interwoven polyphony above
An understated theme.
The only end of jazz is jazz.

PETER READING

Filmed in Ludlow, Shropshire, 24 June 2007

PETER READING is one of Britain's most original and controversial poets: angry, uncompromising, gruesomely ironic, hilarious and heartbreaking – as funny as he is disconcerting. He is probably the most skilful and technically inventive poet writing today, mixing the matter and speech of the gutter with highly sophisticated metrical and syllabic patterns to produce scathing and grotesque accounts of lives blighted by greed, meanness, ignorance, political ineptness and cultural impoverishment.

Born in Liverpool in 1946, he studied at Liverpool College of Art, then worked for 22 years as a weighbridge operator at an animal feedmill in Shropshire, a job which left him free to think, until he was sacked for refusing to wear a uniform introduced by new owners of the business. His only break was a two-year residency at Sunderland Polytechnic, where I first heard him read in 1983.

The benevolence of America's Lannan Foundation rescued him from poverty. He is the only British poet to have won the Lannan Award for Poetry twice, in 1990 and 2004, and the only poet to read an entire life's work for the Lannan Foundation's DVD archive, which involved a week's filming at Highgreen Manor in 2001.

His books are typographically complex, so the accuracy of proofs from Bloodaxe for his work in *The New Poetry* (1993) surprised and delighted him. By then he was so exasperated with successive publishers Secker and Chatto that he was organising his own typesetting and submitting books camera-ready for printing. Moving to Bloodaxe removed the necessity for this. Bloodaxe published the first two parts of his *Collected Poems* in 1995 and 1996, followed by five collections later reprinted in the third volume of *Collected Poems* (2003); another collection, *-273.15* (2005); and a critical study of his work, *Reading Peter Reading* by Isabel Martin (2000).

Each of his collections has been self-contained, as carefully constructed and plotted as a novel, interweaving voices, narrative strands and artwork. We filmed him reading sections from two of his poetry narratives, *Going On* (1985) and *Evagatory* (1992), from *Collected Poems: 2: Poems 1985-1996* (1996). The two extracts from *Going On* are examples of Alcmanic verse, a metre used in Greek drama consisting of catalectic dactylic hexameters, adapted with remarkable incantatory effect to catalogue more modern horrors: 'These are the days of the horrible headlines' $| - \smile \smile | - \smile \smile | - \smile \smile | - - |$. In *Evagatory* he uses 'dispersed Alcaics', an Aeolic verse metre combining dactyls and trochees. Few poets since Tennyson have written quantitative verse, and the musical effectiveness of Reading's use of forms traditionally associated with the beautiful and heroic for his grim subject-matter comes across in his reading.

These are the days of the horrible headlines,
**Bomb Blast Atrocity, Leak From Reactor,
Soccer Fans Run Amok, Middle East Blood Bath,
PC Knocks Prisoner's Eye Out In Charge Room.**
Outside, the newsvendors ululate. Inside,
lovers seek refuge in succulent plump flesh,
booze themselves innocent of the whole shit-works.
Why has the gentleman fallen face-forward
into his buttered asparagus, Garçon?
He and his girlfriend have already drunk two
bottles of Bollinger and they were half-tight
when they arrived at the place half-an-hour since.
Waiters man-handle the gentleman upright,
aim him (with smirks at the lady) towards his
quails (which he misses and slumps in the gravy –
baying, the while, for 'Encore du Savigny').
He is supplied with the Beaune, which he noses,
quaffs deeply, relishes… sinks to the gingham
where he reposes susurrantly. There is
'63 Sandeman fetched to revive him.
Chin on the Pont l'Evêque, elbow in ash-tray,
as from the *Book of the Dead*, he produces
incomprehensible hieroglyphs, bidding
Access surrender the price of his coma
unto the restaurateur, kindly and patient.
These are the days of the **National Health Cuts**,
days of the end of the innocent liver;
they have to pay for it privately, who would seek anaesthetic.

[…]

This is unclean: to eat turbots on Tuesdays,
tying the turban unclockwise at cockcrow,
cutting the beard in a south-facing mirror,
wearing the mitre whilst sipping the Bovril,
chawing the pig and the hen and the ox-tail,
kissing of crosses with peckers erected,
pinching of bottoms (except in a yashmak),
flapping of cocks at the star-spangled-banner,
snatching the claret-pot off of the vicar,
munching the wafer without genuflexion,
facing the East with the arse pointing backwards,
thinking of something a little bit risqué,

174

raising the cassock to show off the Y-fronts,
holding a Homburg without proper licence,
chewing the cud with another man's cattle,
groping the ladies – or gentry – o'Sundays,
leaving the tip on the old-plum-tree-shaker,
speaking in physics instead of the Claptrap,
failing to pay due obeisance to monkeys,
loving the platypus more than the True Duck,
death without Afterlife, smirking in Mecca,
laughing at funny hats, holding the tenet
how that the Word be but fucking baloney,
failing to laud the Accipiter which Our Lord saith is Wisdom.

Started by *Australopithecus*, these are
time-honoured Creeds (and all unHoly doubters
shall be enlightened by Pious Devices:
mayhems of tinytots, low-flying hardwares,
kneecappings, letterbombs, deaths of the firstborns,
total extinctions of infidel unclean wrong-godded others).

from **Evagatory**
EVAGATORY 1992

Came to an island farctate with feculence:
chip-papers, Diet-Pepsi cans clattering,
prams, supermarket trolleys, spent mattresses,

bus-rank of steel and rank uriniferous
concrete, a footbridge richly enlivened with
   aerosol squirtings, daubed graffiti,

      pustular simian sub-teenagers
hurling abuse and empty bottles
      over the parapet into crowds of
      pensioners waiting for **X-PRESS SERVISS**,

      xylophone tinkle of smashed glass, crackle
under a tyre, a hapless old fart
stanching the flow from freshly sliced flesh.

Avian botulism thriving
(black plastic bin-bags/scavenging *Laridae*);
   sand-eels depleted (over-fishing):

sanitised quondam herring gull colony,
sanitised quondam kittiwake colony –
   all that remains, their last year's shit's stink.

53 bus approaching the terminus;
     dapper sartorial English elder
   suited in Manx tweed, close-clipped grey tash:

Too much is wrong, Gibbonian undertones,
   schooling and bread and dress and manners,
era's decline, Elgarian sadnesses;

too much is wrong, duff ticker, insomnia,
   ulcer and thyrotoxicosis,
     end of the world in one's lifetime likely,
flight of a sparrow brief through the feasting hall.

Perilous trek, unarmed, unaccompanied:
     set out from Cranium, through uncharted
   swamp, to arrive at Lingua Franca,
thence to this Logaoedic Dependency.

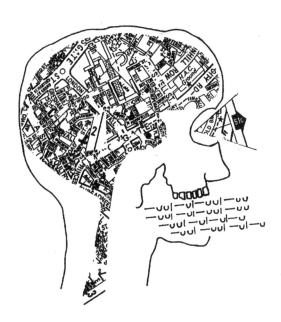

Cranial voice loquacious/inadequate
   (translationese from life to lingo):

Only a troubled idyll now possible,
pastoral picnic under an ozone hole,
England, *The Times* screwed up in a trash-bucket,
   gliding astern, the Thames, the old prides,
   end of an era, nation, notion,
      Albion urban, devenustated
   (one of those routine periodic
faunal extinctions [cf. the Permian]),
arthropod aberration (posterity).

a dreadful, bloody, civil insurrection among the poor mad islanders brought about because their automobiles, which they had revered above all else, and which had helped boost their weak, inferior egos, had been confiscated by their (suddenly aware and panic-stricken) government. For it seems that, whereas the manifest absurdity of mayhem on congested tarmac and the lowering mantle of ferruginous fog had somehow failed to awaken authoritarian sensibility, this abrupt (albeit long-prognosticated) termination of a fundamental, unrenewable

Newspapers there (the sumps of society,
draining off, holding up for inspection a
    corporate concentrated slurry)
retail, with relish, mayhem and muck of a
        clapped-out, subliterate, scrap-stuffed fake state:
    23.3 million vehicles,
    29.8 million drivers,
300 000 maimed on their ludicrous
    tarmac p.a., 5000 flenched dead –
        fortunate, then, that it doesn't matter
(for they are far too philoprogenitive).

    Snow-haired, an elder, dulled eyes gum-filled,
tuning a sweet-toned curious instrument,
        gulps from a goblet of local merlot,
    sings on a theme whose fame was fabled,
that of a sad realm farctate with feculence
        (patois and translationese alternately):

Gobschighte damapetty,   Wonderful little Madam,
   gobby Fer-dama,   self-mocking Iron Lady,
   getspeeke baggsy,   who some said was a windbag,
   getspeeke parly   some said talked
   comma cul, comma   like an arsehole, like
   malbicker-bicker,   a termagant – why,
porky getspeeke?, porky?   why did some say that?

Pascoz vots clobberjoli,   Because your pretty frocks,
   vots chevvy-dur dur,   your permed-stiff hair,
   vots baggsymain chic,   your smart handbag, your
   vots collier-prick,   tight-sharp necklace,
   cuntyvach twitnit,   satrapess so marvellous,
   iscst pukkerjoli –   were so beautiful –
illos jalouz dats porky!   they were envious, that's it!

Ni iscst vots marrypappa   Nor was your spouse
   grignaleto, ne.   a pipsqueak – far from it!
   Mas vots pollytiq   But your many wise policies
   saggio sauvay   were saving your islet,
   vots salinsula,   your filthy isle, and
   insulapetty,   made all equal with nil.
et fair tutts egal mit-nochts.

PENELOPE SHUTTLE
Filmed in York, 16 November 2006

PENELOPE SHUTTLE's first collection with Bloodaxe, *Redgrove's Wife* (2006), is a book of lament and celebration. Its focus is the life and death of her husband, the poet Peter Redgrove, coupled with the loss of her father. Here grief, depression and ageing are confronted with painful directness, but transformed into life-affirming and redemptive poetry, most powerfully in the long 24-part poem 'Missing You', which she reads in the film.

In a note to the book, she writes: 'Despite Peter's worsening health, many of the poems take as their task the search for a renewal of life during difficult circumstances. How to go on loving the world, which is what a poet is for, when it deals you severe blows, forcing you to give up much of what gives life its energy and delight. My years as a carer for Peter and the sadness of witnessing his decline into frailty due to a combination of Parkinson's, arthritis and diabetes, were a time when I fought off depression and anger, not always successfully, but turned to poetry as channel for and transformer of such emotions. After Peter died it was poetry that provided me with "the proper consolations of human loneliness".'

Other poems written over the same five-year period were inspired by a wide variety of subjects, from Cornish history and landscape to time, weather, spiders and postal regulations. Some draw on myth and dream to reinvent reality, while others take surprising liberties with language itself. *Redgrove's Wife* offers an extraordinary range of different kinds of poetry characteristic of all her collections: sensous and ceremonial, elegiac and erotic, visionary and playful.

Her first collection, *The Orchard Upstairs* (1981) was followed by six other books from Oxford University Press, including *Selected Poems 1980-1996* (1998). Following the closure of the OUP poetry list, *A Leaf Out of His Book* (1999) was published by Oxford Poets/ Carcanet. *Redgrove's Wife* was shortlisted for both the Forward Prize and the T.S. Eliot Prize in 2006. Her fiction includes *All the Usual Hours of Sleeping* (1969), *Wailing Monkey Embracing a Tree* (1973) and *Rainsplitter in the Zodiac Garden* (1977). With Peter Redgrove, she is co-author of *The Wise Wound: Menstruation and Everywoman* (1978) and *Alchemy for Women: Personal Transformation Through Dreams and the Female Cycle* (1995), as well as a book of poems, *The Hermaphrodite Album* (1973), and two novels, *The Terrors of Dr Treviles* (1974) and *The Glass Cottage: A Nautical Romance* (1976).

Born in 1947 in Middlesex, she has lived in Cornwall since 1970. We filmed her before a Riverlines event in York at which she and I presented and talked about poems from *Staying Alive*, a set text at York St John University, before her reading from *Redgrove's Wife*.

179

Missing You

REDGROVE'S WIFE 2006

1

This year no one will ask how you voted,
or if you know the way to town

No one will call you as an eye-witness
or teach you how to train a bird of prey

No one will bring you your *New Scientist*,
try to sell you double-glazing
or tell you their secrets

People will write to you
but you won't answer their letters

The high sheriff of mistletoe
will never catch your eye again

No one will peel apples for you,
or love you more than you can bear

No one will forget you

2

I wept in Tesco,
Sainsburys
and in Boots

where they gave me
medicine for grief

But I wept in Asda,
in Woolworths
and in the library

where they gave me
books on grief

I wept in Clarks
looking in vain for shoes
that would stop me weeping

I wept on the peace march
and all through the war

I wept in Superdrug
where they gave me
a free box of tissues

I wept in the churches,
the empty empty churches,

and in the House of Commons –
they voted me out of office

3

I can't cry anyone's tears except my own,
can't teach anything but my own ignorance

I can only fall from my own mountain,
ledge by ledge

I can't rival the wasp's sting
or sew except with my needle

Like a saltwater wife,
I prise open the oyster of my loss,

hoick out the pearl of your death

4

The rainbow is not enough,
nor the flood

My eye can't see enough,
nor my ear absorb sufficient silence

January is not enough,
nor June

Books are not enough,
nor the El Grecos

Christianity is not enough,
nor Judaism

China is not enough,
nor India

Good luck is not enough,
nor absolution from the bad

Jasmine is not enough,
nor the rose

Kingdoms are not enough,
nor the oldest city in the world,

without you

   5
I used to be a planet,
you discovered me

I used to be a river,
you travelled to my source

I used to be a forest,
you ran away to me

I used to be the sky,
you traipsed up mountains to touch me

I used to be a moon,
you saw by my light

I was hot coals,
you held me

I used to be an atom,
you split me

I was music,
you often sang me

   6
Like a tough Polish soldier
you put your clean shirt on wet

Like a rainbow without red,
you troubled the sky

You were my sower sowing wide,
my queue dans la bouche

You loved top-knotted Islamic angels
with their steep wings of gold and blue

You preferred astronomer's weather,
sciences of the birds

You were a prayer across the Orinoco,
a Tiber fitting me to perfection

7

The sky knows everything about you
but won't tell

My questions vanish to the south-west

The sea knows something about you
but keeps silent,

my enquiries turned back on the tide

The moon knows all about you
but won't speak for a thousand years

The world, knowing all about you,
swings away on its axis,

not beating about the beautiful bush

I bide my time,
just as you warned me I would

8

I've forgotten everything
the sun and moon taught me

Perhaps they were not so wise

The world was so small
I hid it in my heart

like a woman pregnant
before she was born

I've forgotten what a painter of portraits
does with a brush,

what a musician does with tone and semi-tone,
what a gardener does with a seed,

forgotten that fire burns,
grief's disbelief never ends

9

Don't bring me the sea,
or clouds, or those packs of trees,
don't bring me night, or stars
or forthright moons, or the solitude
of the river; take away
that farmyard of cyclamen,
your flooded side-street, don't bring me
the sun, leave it where it is,
don't offer me operas or banknotes,
spider-webs peppered with dew –
I don't want a bullfight
or a cushion you've worked yourself –
I don't want anything except the past,
bring me five years ago, last winter,
the week before last, yesterday

10

I make my home in your absence,
take your smallest hope

and make it grow

I wake to the dusk of everywhere
as if assisting at my own birth

or arriving in a country
where all the rivers settle down to be ice

11

World was one word
I could not guess it

World was one gesture
I could not copy it

World was one question
I couldn't answer it

World was one song
How could I sing it?

World was one forest
I couldn't fell it

World was one bridge
How was I to cross it?

12

You're a tree's guess,
a cloud's confidence,

the continent of January,
the solitude of a comet,

a world without a wren

You're the heart of when,
the pulse of where,

sleepy as a motorway,
eager as an earthquake,

elusive as an elegy,
daring as dusk

You invent your own exit
via the black economy of poetry

13

My tamer of doves,
my alphabet of the moon,
fool of night,
harvest's welcome, the grief

of day, my blind man
and my seer,
dreamer against his will,
my furious saint,
warrior of peace

14

I won't find you in the featherbed of thought
or in the blip of the city

To find you I must be the bloodhound of love,
block capitals of the rain,

swift and slow at once,
because you'll be everywhere I'm not

Suddenly I'll be there beside you
as if all the time you'd been only four streets away

15

I'm the leopard changing my spots,
the horse led to water I must drink,

the elephant who forgets,
a silk purse sewn from the sow's ear

I'm the long long road with no turning,
the cloud without a silver lining

Mine is the last straw
that mends the camel's back,

sails us both
through the needle's effortless eye

16

Think of me
as a small backward country
appealing for aid from the far-off first world

Imagine the dirt of my shrines,
the riddle of my dry rivers,
the jinx of my cities

When you hold the full purse of autumn
or celebrate the nativity of a pear,

picture me as the hawk of spring,
a one-pupil school,
the safe-keeper of sunrise

Think of me without you,
stuck here forever between rainless May
and the drought of June

17

Your name didn't change
after your death –
many others also answered to it

After your death
the climate didn't change,
the government stayed calm

Waterfalls
remembered you forever,
remaining loyal,
looking for you everywhere,
storm after storm, teacup after teacup

18

Autumn fans its tail without you
and spring bears its burden alone

Summer, that small supernatural being,
manages without you

and winter closes your many doors

Like an interval between kings,
the year is a confusion of reds and golds,

but in the gulag of August
days are where you left them,

nights,
the same

19

Are you visiting the harems of April?
Travelling the great world of May?

Are you researching the archives of June?
Do the rains of July grieve you?

Are you saluting the landslides of August,
the independence of September?

Are you in unarmed combat with October?
Does November please you?

Is December your new best friend?
Are you hunting that grail, January?

Do you still have time for February?
Have you seen March,
celebrating the marriage of green and blue?

20

We were our own seraphs –
hours came and went
in the name of the east

All trees were the product of our love,
every bit of woodland listened to us

Ours was the tabernacle of light,
the sun our sphinx of the air

We signed the electoral register
of our hearts,

voting ourselves into office
again and again

21

I've lived with your death for a year,
that despot death, that realist,

stunned,
as if I've just given birth to a foal,
or made an enemy of the rain

All at once
you had more important things to do
than to live

Death is the feather in your cap,
the source of your fame,
my darkest lesson

This dropout year closes,
I begin my second year without you,
just me and the paper-thin world

    22

The TV asks me,
how long after being widowed
before you start dating?

When China tours the world
by rowing boat,

when India is small as Ireland,

when that unbeliever water
turns to wine

    23

I'm letting go of you
year by year

Today it was 1970,
tomorrow it may be 1977

There is so much of you,
you will never completely cease,

but slowly
I'm releasing some of you from me,

there's no rush, no deadline,
time doesn't matter,

its just that I can't despair forever

so I pour you away from me,
libation by libation,

as if discarding the water
from the font at Manaccan
in which an infant has just been baptised.

24

A world's daylight was not enough to keep you here,
nor the night's secret of success

Summer will never forget you,
nor friendly autumn

They'd stop at nothing
to keep you where you belong

Every afternoon reads between the lines
for news of you

and on the spur of the moment
evening welcomes you, who are never there

Next week knows his fatherland is too small for you,
and next year knows it too

No city working till late at night could keep you,
nor the happy endings of the sea

The theatre sold-out every night couldn't hold you,
nor the long disobedience of the truth

Today,
who is a shadow of his former self,
lets you go,

and so do I,
all my schools closed for summer,
silent for weeks

ANNE STEVENSON
Filmed at Highgreen, Tarset, 23 February 2008

ANNE STEVENSON is both an American and a British poet. Born in 1933 in Cambridge, England of American parents, she grew up in New England and Michigan. Her father, Charles L. Stevenson, wrote the philosophy classic, *Ethics and Language* (1944). She studied music, European literature and history at the University of Michigan, returning later to read English and publishing the first critical study of Elizabeth Bishop. After several transatlantic switches, she settled in Britain in 1964, and has since lived in Cambridge, Scotland, Oxford, the Welsh Borders and latterly in North Wales and Durham.

Rooted in close observation of the world and acute psychological insight, her poems continually question how we see and think about the world. They are incisive as well as entertaining, marrying critical rigour with personal feeling, and a sharp wit with an original brand of serious humour. After publishing nine books with Oxford University Press, she took her work to Bloodaxe in 1999 following the closure of the OUP poetry list: our publishing connections go back to 1977 (see page 240). *Granny Scarecrow* (2000), her first collection with Bloodaxe, was followed by *Poems 1955-2005* in 2005, a remaking of her earlier OUP edition *Poems 1955-1995*, drawing on over a dozen previous collections as well as new poems, with this book's new thematic arrangements emphasising the craft, coherence and architecture of her life's work. Her latest collection, *Stone Milk*, was published by Bloodaxe in 2007.

Since moving to Bloodaxe she has achieved much wider recognition for her work in Britain and America, which she believes was no coincidence. She was the inaugural winner of Britain's biggest literary prize, the Northern Rock Foundation Writer's Award, in 2002. Her second critical study of Elizabeth Bishop's work, *Five Looks at Elizabeth Bishop*, had been unavailable for many years, and Bloodaxe's reissue of the book in 2006 was very important to her. In 2007 she received three major American awards: the Lannan Lifetime Achievement Award for Poetry, the Poetry Foundation's Neglected Masters Award and the Aiken Taylor Award in Modern Poetry. With the Neglected Masters Award came publication of her *Selected Poems* in 2008 in the Library of America series devoted to the major figures in American literature.

She has also published a landmark biography, *Bitter Fame: A Life of Sylvia Plath* (Viking, 1989), and *Between the Iceberg and the Ship: Selected Essays* (University of Michigan Press, 1998). John Lucas and Matt Simpson's *The Way You Say the World: A Celebration for Anne Stevenson*, published by Shoestring Press on her 70th birthday in 2003, offers an invaluable guide to her life and work.

as you still have me, Caroline.
Why does a mother need a daughter?
Heart's needle, hostage to fortune,
freedom's end. Yet nothing's more perfect
than that bleating, razor-shaped cry
that delivers a mother to her baby.
The bloodcord snaps that held
their sphere together. The child,
tiny and alone, creates the mother.

A woman's life is her own
until it is taken away
by a first particular cry.
Then she is not alone
but part of the premises
of everything there is:
a time, a tribe, a war.
When we belong to the world
we become what we are.

A Marriage
REPORT FROM THE BORDER 2003

When my mother knew why her treatment wasn't working,
She said to my father, trying not to detonate her news,
'Steve, you must marry again. When I'm gone, who's going
To tell you to put your trousers on before your shoes?'

My father opened his mouth to – couldn't – refuse.
Instead, he threw her a look; a man just shot
Gazing at the arm or leg he was about to lose.
His cigarette burned him, but he didn't stub it out.

Later, on the porch, alive in the dark together,
How solid the house must have felt, how sanely familiar
The night-lit leaves, their shadows patterning the street.
The house is still there. The elms and the people, not.

It was now, and it never was now. Like every experience
Of being entirely here, yet really not being.
They couldn't imagine the future that I am seeing,
For all his philosophy and all her common sense.

Arioso Dolente
(for my grandchildren when they become grandparents)
GRANNY SCARECROW 2000

A mother, who read and thought and poured herself into me;
she was the jug and I was the two-eared cup.
How she would scorn today's 'show-biz inanity,
democracy twisted, its high ideals sold up!'
          Cancer filched her voice, then cut her throat.
                    Why is it
          none of the faces in this family snapshot
                    looks upset?

A father, who ran downstairs as I practised the piano;
barefooted, buttoning his shirt, he shouted 'G,
D-natural, C-*flat*! *Dolente, arioso.*
Put all the griefs of the world in that change of key.'
          Who then could lay a finger on his sleeve
                    to distress him with
          'One day, Steve, two of your well-taught daughters
                    will be deaf.'

Mother must be sitting, left, on the porch-set,
you can just see her. My sister's on her lap.
And that's Steve confiding to his cigarette
something my mother's mother has to laugh at.
          The screened door twangs, slamming
                    on its sprung hinge.
          Paint blisters on the steps; iced tea, grasscuttings,
                    elm flowers, mock orange...

A grand June evening, like this one, not too buggy,
unselfquestioning midwestern, maybe 1951.
And, of course, there in my grandmother's memory
lives just such another summer – 1890 or 91.
          Though it's not on her mind now/then.
                    No, she's thinking of
          the yeast-ring rising in the oven. Or how *any* shoes
                    irritate her bunion.

Paper gestures, pictures, newsprint laughter.
And after the camera winks and makes its catch,
the decibels drain away *for ever and ever.*
No need to say 'Look!' to these smilers on the porch,
          'Grandmother will have her stroke,
                    and you, mother, will nurse her.'
Or to myself, this woman died paralysed-dumb, and that one
                    dumb from cancer.

194

Sufficient unto the day... Grandmother, poor and liturgical,
whose days were duties, stitches in the tea-brown blanket
she for years crocheted, its zigzag of yellow wool,
her grateful offering, her proof of goodness to present,
      gift-wrapped, to Our Father in Heaven. 'Accept,
          O Lord, this best-I-can-make-it soul.'
And He: 'Thou good and faithful servant, lose thyself
             and be whole.'

Consciousness walks on tiptoe through what happens.
So much is felt, so little of it said.
But ours is the breath on which the past depends.
'What happened' is what the living teach the dead,
      who, smilingly lost to their lost concerns,
          in grey on grey,
     are all of them deaf, blind, unburdened
          by today.

As if our recording selves, our mortal identities,
could be cupped in a concave universe or lens,
ageless at all ages, cleansed of memories,
not minding that meaningful genealogy extends
      no further than mind's flash images reach back.
        As for what happens next,
       let all the griefs of the world
        find keys for that.

Arioso dolente: from Beethoven's piano sonata, opus 110,
third movement; introduction to the fugue.

The Minister

ENOUGH OF GREEN 1977

We're going to need the minister
to help this heavy body into the ground.

But he won't dig the hole;
others who are stronger and weaker will have to do that.
And he won't wipe his nose and his eyes;
others who are weaker and stronger will have to do that.
And he won't bake cakes or take care of the kids –
women's work. Anyway,
what would they do at a time like this
if they didn't do that?

No, we'll get the minister to come
and take care of the words.

He doesn't have to make them up,
he doesn't have to say them well,
he doesn't have to like them
so long as they agree to obey him.

We have to have the minister
so the words will know where to go.

Imagine them circling and circling
the confusing cemetery.
Imagine them roving the earth
without anywhere to rest.

Beach Kites

STONE MILK 2007

Is this a new way of being born?
To feel some huge crescent personality
burgeoning out of your shoulders,
winging you over the sand, the sluggish sea?
Mile upon mile of contaminated Wash is
tucking a cold March sky into the horizon.

You can drive no further.
Look down at the thrashing water,
the upfalls of its reach
failing, failing again to take the cliff –
sandpipers hunch on the geomorphic ledge –
rock face and wave force, story without speech.

But it's one thing to pause at the cutting edge,
another to face the evolving beach, the gap
where the road stops and the dunes heap
and the wind blows fiercely in the wrong direction.

One gaudy comma ascends... another... another...
the air is rocking alert with punctuation.

Grey sickle cells cluster under a microscope.

A jumbo wasp, a pterodactyl, a peacock feather
jockey for space against moon-parings, rainbow zeppelins,
prayer flags – imagination battling with imagination,
spotted species chasing the plain – as out they float,
strong men steering their wild umbilical toys

away from the girlfriends in the car park, who
leathered from heel to neck in steel-studded black,
headscarfed against the wind, seem coolly resigned
to an old dispensation, a ritual of mating
that puts up again with the cliff-hanging habits of boys.
Is this a new way of writing?
The heroes off flying or fighting, the women waiting?

Small Philosophical Poem

MINUTE BY GLASS MINUTE 1982

Dr Animus, whose philosophy is a table,
sits down contentedly to a square meal.
The plates lie there, and there,
just where they should lie.
His feet stay just where they should stay,
between legs and the floor.
His eyes believe the clean waxed surfaces
are what they are.

But while he's eating his un-
exceptional propositions, his wise
wife, Anima, sweeping a haze-gold decanter
from a metaphysical salver,
pours him a small glass of doubt.
Just what he needs.
He smacks his lips and cracks his knuckles.
The world is the pleasure of thought.

He'd like to stay awake all night
(elbows on the table)
talking of how the table might not be there.
But Anima, whose philosophy is hunger,
perceives the plates are void in empty air.
The floor is void beneath his trusting feet.
Peeling her glass from its slender cone of fire,
she fills the room with love. And fear. And fear.

GEORGE SZIRTES

Filmed in Wymondham, Norfolk, 5 November 2007

GEORGE SZIRTES was born in Budapest in 1948, and came to Britain with his family as an eight-year-old refugee after the Hungarian uprising in 1956. Educated in England, he trained as a painter, and has always written in English. In recent years he has worked as a translator of Hungarian literature. He is married to artist Clarissa Upchurch, and teaches at the University of East Anglia.

Haunted by his family's knowledge and experience of war, occupation and the Holocaust, as well as by loss, danger and exile, his poetry covers universal themes: love, desire and illusion; loyalty and betrayal; history, art and memory; humanity and truth. Throughout his work there is a conflict between two states of mind, the possibility of happiness and apprehension of disaster. These are played out especially in his celebrated long poems and extended sequences, *The Photographer in Winter*, *Metro*, *The Courtyards*, *An English Apocalypse* and *Reel*.

The extracts he reads from *Metro* in the film are from part of the sequence where he tries to make sense of his mother's betrayal and removal to the Nazi concentration camp at Ravensbrück. 'My father carries me across a field' reconstructs his memory of crossing the border into Austria by night. 'Death by Deluge' is from *An English Apocalypse*, which imagines England's destruction in five apocalypses. 'Water' was written in response to a photograph by Sebastião Salgado in an exhibition at the Barbican Art Gallery.

After four collections with Secker and five with Oxford University Press, he brought his work to Bloodaxe following the closure of the OUP poetry list in 1999, and like other ex-OUP authors he believes the forced move has been enormously beneficial. I had known him for many years. We'd worked on three earlier Bloodaxe titles: two books of poetry in translation, Ottó Orbán's *The Blood of the Walsungs: Selected Poems* (1993) and the landmark anthology *The Colonnade of Teeth: Modern Hungarian Poetry* (1996), co-edited with George Gömöri; and his posthumous edition of Freda Downie's *Collected Poems* (1995). The frontispiece etching of Martin Bell's *Complete Poems* (1988) was his portrait of Bell, an early influence on his work, and 'one of the most important and underrated poets of the post-war period'.

Bloodaxe has since published his Hungarian selection *The Budapest File* (2000); *An English Apocalypse* (2001); his translation of Ágnes Nemes Nagy's poetry, *The Night of Akhenaton* (2004); and *Reel* (2004), winner of the T.S. Eliot Prize. His *New & Collected Poems* is published on his 60th birthday in 2008 at the same time as the first critical study of his work, *Reading George Szirtes* by John Sears.

FROM 4 *Flying backwards*

She worked as a photographer. The war had started
But you'd hardly know it. She met my father late,
When he returned from camp in Proskyrov.
It was February, 1944.
Next month the Germans entered Budapest
And he was recalled to unit. The date,
Nineteenth of March. Facts, bare bones, the rest
Are silences. A 'safe house' in August
With father's family two floors above.
September, October, the Arrow Cross, the raid.
Her feet are clattering in the gallery,
His family are hiding or departed
And only she remains to be betrayed.

*

5 *Betrayals*

Betrayed? She felt and thought she was. But who
Betrayed her (if it was betrayal) and how?
Betrayal by omission was the way,
Betrayal by those she trusted. Down below,
The soldiers in the yard, the quasi-military.
They called her down. It was a minute's work.
But why was she out on the gallery
When it was far more sensible to hide?
And why did no one tell her? Who were they
Who should have done so? Why did they shirk
Their human duty? The wound was always fresh:
Even at fifty-one, the year she died,
It bored and tunnelled deep into her flesh,

*

Katona József Street. The Swedish house.
My father's family came from the North,
Moravia and Bohemia, tailors, painters,
Vendors of musical instruments, a broker,
And father's father was a shoemaker.
How much is all this information worth?
The list is endless and monotonous,
Their season's over, summers, autumns, winters:
Few made the final spring of '45.
My father had been brought up by the aunts
Who coddled me in my turn. To survive
Was an achievement, but my grandparents
Were under-achievers all of them, bar one.

*

My father's mother. Large-eyed, beaky-nosed.
We must have met but I've no recollection,
Except of something owl-like, something scented.
Her absence gave her little enough protection
From mother's fury. The matter was closed,
No letters exchanged. In '56 she went
To Argentina, wrote, sent messages,
But his replies were censored or forbidden.
Her case was settled. Sometimes she sent me presents,
Pale useless things, the kind my mother resented
And fanned her hatred for her. It was the hidden
Secret of my childhood, what she'd done.
Even now I don't know what the truth is.

*

My aunts (or great-aunts to be precise)
Brought father up. His home was there. The owl
Had farmed him out. When evidence
Was weighed at home this counted much against her
And nobody replied in her defence.
Numerus clausus, numerus nullus: twice
Father was hit by laws against the Jews,
His education stopped, he worked in knit-wear,
Was twice promoted then forced out. A friend
Advised him, trained him, offered him a place
He couldn't decently refuse:
Apprentice plumber, master of the bowl.
For both of them it was an hour of grace.

*

Inevitably, labour camps. How many
Perished here: the artists, writers,
Musicians, plumbers, brothers? Escapades,
Adventures, tragedies, the company
Reduced, disbanded then recalled.
The dark-eyed girl in February, back home.
Road building, retreat, escape. The waters
Close about my grandfather and fold
Over him in Auschwitz. Brief episodes
Of dire intensity, each trivial sum
A fortune lost. The dark-eyed girl moves in
With father's mother, sister, baby niece.
It's lists and rosters, jigsaws piece by piece.

*

They fall together, stand and fall together.
The day the soldiers came she was alone
And heard them shouting. On another floor
The female threesome. She looks for them. The door
Is open. She calls their names, the mother,
Sister, niece. They do not answer. Where have they gone?
Where are they hiding? Nothing. Not a sound.
She wanders out, is spotted. It is fear:
Fear of discovery, fear of strangers. It's done.
They have not answered. Someone shouts, Come down!
And who is it pretended not to hear?
The rough voice rises. I speak for another
And buy my ticket for the underground.

*

My father carries me across a field

(FROM *Flesh: An Early Family History*)
REEL 2004

My father carries me across a field.
It's night and there are trenches filled with snow.
Thick mud. We're careful to remain concealed

From something frightening I don't yet know.
And then I walk and there is space between
The four of us. We go where we have to go.

Did I dream it all, this ghostly scene,
The hundred-acre wood where the owl blinked
And the ass spoke? Where I am cosy and clean

In bed, but we are floating, our arms linked
Over the landscape? My father moves ahead
Of me, like some strange, almost extinct

Species, and I follow him in dread
Across the field towards my own extinction.
Spirits everywhere are drifting over blasted

Terrain. The winter cold makes no distinction
Between them and us. My father looks round
And smiles then turns away. We have no function

In this place but keep moving, without sound,
Lost figures who leave only a blank page
Behind them, and the dark and frozen ground

They pass across as they might cross a stage.

Death by Deluge

AN ENGLISH APOCALYPSE 2001

I have seen roads come to a full stop in mid-
sentence as if their meaning had fallen off
the world. And this is what happened, what meaning did

that day in August. The North Sea had been rough
and rising and the bells of Dunwich rang
through all of Suffolk. One wipe of its cuff

down cliffs and in they went, leaving birds to hang
puzzled in the air, their nests gone. Enormous
tides ran from Southend to Cromer. They swung

north and south at once, as if with a clear purpose,
thrusting through Lincolnshire, and at a rush
drowning Sleaford, Newark, leaving no house

uncovered. Nothing remained of The Wash
but water. Peterborough, Ely, March, and Cambridge
were followed by Royston, Stevenage, the lush

grass of Shaw's Corner. Not a single ridge
remained. The Thames Valley filled to the brim
and London Clay swallowed Wapping and Greenwich.

Then west, roaring and boiling. A rapid skim
of Hampshire and Dorset, then the peninsula:
Paignton, Plymouth, Lyme, Land's End. A slim

line of high hills held out but all was water-colour,
the pure English medium, intended for sky, cloud,
and sea. Less earth than you could shift with a spatula.

Water

(FROM *Three Poems for Sebastião Salgado*)
REEL 2004

The hard beautiful rules of water are these:
That it shall rise with displacement as a man
does not, nor his family. That it shall have no plan
or subterfuge. That in the cold, it shall freeze;
in the heat, turn to steam. That it shall carry disease
and bright brilliant fish in river and ocean.
That it shall roar or meander through metropolitan
districts whilst reflecting skies, buildings and trees.

And it shall clean and refresh us even as we slave
over stone tubs or cower in a shelter or run
into the arms of a loved one in some desperate quarter
where the rats too are running. That it shall have
dominion. That it shall arch its back in the sun
only according to the hard rules of water.

C.K. WILLIAMS
Filmed in London, 8 October 2007

C.K. WILLIAMS is an American writer noted for his discursive poems of psychological insight, most of which use his characteristic long line to tease meaning from the chaos of everyday life. They are startlingly intensive narratives on love, death, secrets and wayward thought which examine the inner life with unflinching candour in precise, daring language.

Chase Twichell has called him 'A voice that has become utterly distinctive: restless, passionate, dogged, and uncompromising in its quest to find and speak the truth...an intelligence both compassionate and fierce. The result is four decades of poems that delve into everything from the most joyous and private matters of the heart (he is one of our greatest love poets) to the chaos and horror of politics, warfare, and our species' seemingly innate penchant for cruelty and self-destruction. Like Whitman's, his world view is simultaneously micro- and macrocosmic. Williams' rangy, elastic lines are measures of thought, and his syntax enacts the ways in which the mind moves through mood and memory, speculation and logic. Because the voice is both cerebral and muscular in its reflexes, the music it makes feels spontaneous, individual, and directly representative of the experience of which it sings. The poems are wholly American in this regard; their simultaneous tenderness and outrage bring to mind the music of Charles Ives.'

He was born in New Jersey in 1936, and lives for part of the year in France, latterly in Normandy, and part in Princeton. He won the Pulitzer Prize for his 1999 collection, *Repair*, which was shortlisted for the T.S. Eliot Prize in Britain. His many books include *Poetry and Consciousness: Selected Essays* (1998), a memoir, *Misgivings: My Mother, My Father, Myself* (2000), and translations of Sophocles, Euripides, Adam Zagajewski and Francis Ponge.

I was introduced to his work by Tony Harrison, who gave me a copy of *Tar* (1983) after returning from a trip to New York. This was the second collection in which Williams uses his signature long line. His next collection, *Flesh and Blood*, was published in Britain by Bloodaxe, simultaneously with his *Poems 1963-1983*, and launched at Bloodaxe's 10th birthday reading in Newcastle in October 1988 (when he read with Miroslav Holub, Brendan Kennelly, Marin Sorescu and Tomas Tranströmer). Bloodaxe has since published all his poetry books: *A Dream of Mind* (1992), *New & Selected Poems* (1995), *The Vigil* (1997), *Repair* (1999), *The Singing* (2003), and *Collected Poems*, which includes over 20 new poems, and was published by Bloodaxe in Britain and Farrar, Straus & Giroux in the States on his 70th birthday in November 2006.

The Dog

TAR 1983

Except for the dog, that she wouldn't have him put away, wouldn't let him die,
    I'd have liked her.

She was handsome, busty, chunky, early middle-aged, very black, with a stiff,
    exotic dignity

that flurried up in me a mix of warmth and sexual apprehension neither of
    which, to tell the truth,

I tried very hard to nail down: she was that much older and in those days there
    was still the race thing.

This was just at the time of civil rights: the neighborhood I was living in was
    mixed.

In the narrow streets, the tiny three-floored houses they called father-son-holy-
    ghosts

which had been servants' quarters first, workers' tenements, then slums, still
    were, but enclaves of us,

beatniks and young artists, squatted there and commerce between everyone was
    fairly easy.

Her dog, a grinning mongrel, rib and knob, gristle and grizzle, wasn't terribly
    offensive.

The trouble was that he was ill, or the trouble more exactly was that I had to
    know about it.

She used to walk him on a lot I overlooked, he must have had a tumor or a
    blockage of some sort

because every time he moved his bowels, he shrieked, a chilling, almost human
    scream of anguish.

It nearly always caught me unawares, but even when I'd see them first, it wasn't
    better.

The limp leash coiled in her hand, the woman would be profiled to the dog,
    staring into the distance,

apparently oblivious, those breasts of hers like stone, while he, not a step away,
    laboring,

trying to eject the feeble, mucus-coated, blood-flecked chains that finally spurted
    from him,

would set himself on tiptoe and hump into a question mark, one quivering back
    leg grotesquely lifted.

Every other moment he'd turn his head, as though he wanted her, to no avail,
    to look at him,

then his eyes would dim and he'd drive his wounded anus in the dirt, keening
    uncontrollably,

lurching forward in a hideous, electric dance as though someone were at him
    with a club.

When at last he'd finish, she'd wipe him with a tissue like a child; he'd lick
    her hand.

It was horrifying; I was always going to call the police; once I actually went
      out to chastise her –
didn't she know how selfish she was, how the animal was suffering? – she scared
      me off, though.
She was older than I'd thought, for one thing, her flesh was loosening, pouches
      of fat beneath the eyes,
and poorer, too, shabby, tarnished: I imagined smelling something faintly acrid
      as I passed.
Had I ever really mooned for such a creature? I slunk around the block, chag-
      rined, abashed.
I don't recall them too long after that. Maybe the dog died, maybe I was just
      less sensitive.
Maybe one year when the cold came and I closed my windows, I forgot them
      ...then I moved.
Everything was complicated now, so many tensions, so much bothersome self-
      consciousness.
Anyway, those back streets, especially in bad weather when the ginkgos lost
      their leaves, were bleak.
It's restored there now, ivy, pointed brick, garden walls with broken bottles
      mortared on them,
but you'd get sick and tired then: the rubbish in the gutter, the general sense
      of dereliction.
Also, I'd found a girl to be in love with: all we wanted was to live together, so
      we did.

Love: Beginnings
FLESH AND BLOOD 1987/1988

They're at that stage where so much desire streams between them, so much
      frank need and want,
so much absorption in the other and the self and the self-admiring entity and
      unity they make –
her mouth so full, breast so lifted, head thrown back so far in her laughter at
      his laughter,
he so solid, planted, oaky, firm, so resonantly factual in the headiness of being
      craved so,
she almost wreathed upon him as they intertwine again, touch again, cheek,
      lip, shoulder, brow,
every glance moving toward the sexual, every glance away soaring back in flame
      into the sexual –
that just to watch them is to feel again that hitching in the groin, that filling
      of the heart,
the old, sore heart, the battered, foundered, faithful heart, snorting again, stamp-
      ing in its stall.

The Singing
THE SINGING 2003

I was walking home down a hill near our house on a balmy afternoon under
the blossoms
Of the pear trees that go flamboyantly mad here every spring with their bur-
geoning forth

When a young man turned in from a corner singing no it was more of a cad-
enced shouting
Most of which I couldn't catch I thought because the young man was black
speaking black

It didn't matter I could tell he was making his song up which pleased me he
was nice-looking
Husky dressed in some style of big pants obviously full of himself hence his
lyrical flowing over

We went along in the same direction then he noticed me there almost beside
him and 'Big'
He shouted-sang 'Big' and I thought how droll to have my height incorporated
in his song

So I smiled but the face of the young man showed nothing he looked in fact
pointedly away
And his song changed 'I'm not a nice person' he chanted 'I'm not I'm not a
nice person'

No menace was meant I gathered no particular threat but he did want to be
certain I knew
That if my smile implied I conceived of anything like concord between us I
should forget it

That's all nothing else happened his song became indecipherable to me again
he arrived
Where he was going a house where a girl in braids waited for him on the porch
that was all

No one saw no one heard all the unasked and unanswered questions were left
where they were
It occurred to me to sing back 'I'm not a nice person either' but I couldn't
come up with a tune

Besides I wouldn't have meant it nor he have believed it both of us knew just
where we were
In the duet we composed the equation we made the conventions to which we
were condemned

Sometimes it feels even when no one is there that someone something is watch-
    ing and listening
Someone to rectify redo remake this time again though no one saw nor heard
    no one was there

The World
THE SINGING 2003

Splendid that I'd revel even more in the butterflies harvesting pollen
from the lavender in my father-in-law's garden in Normandy
when I bring to mind Francis Ponge's poem where he transfigures them
to levitating matches, and the flowers they dip into to unwashed cups;
it doesn't work with lavender, but still, so lovely, matches, cups,
and lovely, too, to be here in the fragrant summer sunlight reading.

Just now an essay in *Le Monde*, on Fragonard, his oval oil sketch
of a mother opening the bodice of her rosily blushing daughter
to demonstrate to a young artist that the girl would be suitable as a "model";
the snide quotation marks insinuate she might be other than she seems,
but to me she seems entirely enchanting, even without her top
and with the painter's cane casually lifting her skirt from her ankle.

Fragonard needs so little for his plot; the girl's disarranged underslips
a few quick swirls, the mother's compliant mouth a blur, her eyes
two dots of black, yet you can see how crucial this transaction is to her,
how accommodating she'd be in working through potential complications.
In the shadows behind, a smear of fabric spills from a drawer,
a symbol surely, though when one starts thinking symbol, what isn't?

Each sprig of lavender lifting jauntily as its sated butterfly departs,
Catherine beneath the beech tree with her father and sisters, me watching,
everything and everyone might stand for something else, *be* something else.
Though in truth I can't imagine what; reality has put itself so solidly before me
there's little need for mystery... Except for us, for how we take the world
to us, and make it more, more than we are, more even than itself.

The Gaffe

COLLECTED POEMS (NEW POEMS) 2006

1

If that someone who's me yet not me yet who judges me is always with me,
as he is, shouldn't he have been there when I said so long ago that thing I said?

If he who rakes me with such not trivial shame for minor sins now were there
       then,
shouldn't he have warned me he'd even now devastate me for my unpardonable
      affront?

I'm a child then, yet already I've composed this conscience-beast, who harries
      me:
is there anything else I can say with certainty about who I was, except that I,
      that he,

could already draw from infinitesimal transgressions complex chords of remorse,
and orchestrate ever undiminishing retribution from the hapless rest of myself?

2

The son of some friends of my parents has died, and my parents, paying their
      call,
take me along, and I'm sent out with the dead boy's brother and some others
      to play.

We're joking around, and words come to my mind, which to my amazement
      are said.
How do you know when you can laugh when somebody dies, your brother dies?

is what's said, and the others go quiet, the backyard goes quiet, everyone stares,
and I want to know now why that someone in me who's me yet not me let me
      say it.

Shouldn't he have told me the contrition cycle would from then be ever upon
      me,
it didn't matter that I'd really only wanted to know how grief ends, and when?

3

I could hear the boy's mother sobbing inside, then stopping, sobbing then
      stopping.
Was the end of her grief already there? Had her someone in her told her it
      would end?

Was her someone in her kinder to her, not tearing at her, as mine did, still does,
    me,
for guessing grief someday ends? Is that why her sobbing stopped sometimes?

She didn't laugh, though, or I never heard her. *How do you know when you can
    laugh?*
Why couldn't someone have been there in me not just to accuse me, but to
    explain?

The kids were playing again, I was playing, I didn't hear anything more from
    inside.
The way now sometimes what's in me is silent, too, and sometimes, though
    never really, forgets.

Cassandra: Iraq

COLLECTED POEMS (NEW POEMS) 2006

1

She's magnificent, as we imagine women must be
who foresee and foretell and are right and disdained.

This is the difference between us who are like her
in having been right and disdained, and us as we are.

Because we, in our foreseeings, our having been right,
are repulsive to ourselves, fat and immobile, like toads.

Not toads in the garden, who after all are what they are,
but toads in the tale of death in the desert of sludge.

2

In this tale of lies, of treachery, of superfluous dead,
were there ever so many who were right and disdained?

With no notion what to do next? If we were true seers,
as prescient as she, as frenzied, we'd know what to do next.

We'd twitter, as she did, like birds; we'd warble, we'd trill.
But what would it be really, to *twitter*, to *warble*, to *trill*?

Is it *ee-ee-ee*, like having a child? Is it uh-uh-uh, like a wound?
Or is it inside, like a blow, silent to everyone but yourself?

   3

Yes, inside, I remember, *oh-oh-oh*: it's where grief
is just about to be spoken, but all at once can't be: *oh*.

When you no longer can "think" of what things like lies,
like superfluous dead, so many, might mean: *oh*.

Cassandra will be abducted at the end of her tale, and die.
Even she can't predict how. Stabbed? Shot? Blown to bits?

Her abductor dies, too, though, in a gush of gore, in a net.
That we know; she foresaw that – in a gush of gore, in a net.

C.D. WRIGHT
Filmed in New York City, 8 December 2006

C.D. WRIGHT's work is enormously varied: she is an experimental writer, a Southern writer, and a socially committed writer, yet she continuously reinvents herself with each new volume. Much of her poetry is rooted in the landscape and people of her childhood in the Ozark Mountains of Arkansas. Long admired for the honed ferocity of her vision, she writes with a distinctive Southern accent and a cinematic eye. The resulting poems offer what she calls 'a once-and-for-all thing, opaque and revelatory, ceaselessly burning'.

Bloodaxe published the first UK edition of her work in 2007: *Like Something Flying Backwards: New & Selected Poems*, which presents a wide range of her lyrics, narratives, prose poems and odes. Based on *Steal Away: Selected and New Poems* (2003), a finalist for the Griffin Poetry Prize, its selection was expanded to include more later work, and the complete text of her book-length poem *Deepstep Come Shining* (1998).

She had just finished working on the final proofs of her Bloodaxe edition when we met for the first time on a wintry day in New York to film her reading for *In Person*. My first sight of CD (as everyone calls her) was a slight figure tightly wrapped against the snow, huddled in the street below, peering into the intercom monitor.

Born in 1949, she has published twelve volumes of poetry, including two book-length poems, *Deepstep Come Shining* (1998) and *Just Whistle* (1993), as well as *Cooling Time* (2005), a book comprised of poetry, memoir and essay. She has collaborated on many projects with photographer Deborah Luster, most recently *One Big Self: Prisoners of Louisiana* (2003). She was State Poet of Rhode Island from 1995 to 1999. Her many honours include a Lannan Literary Award and a MacArthur Fellowship. She is a professor of English at Brown University, and edited Lost Roads Publishers for nearly 30 years with her husband, poet Forrest Gander.

The Griffin judges described her work as 'plain gorgeous; it is clean-wrought, rich, rambunctious, and pure-thrown, like a perfect game. This is the generous art of a graceful outlaw troubadour, singing to us as if from within ourselves. The poems...are dense with a sense of substance and absence, love and grief and humor and horror.' She has described *Just Whistle* as a '*about* something as vague as the horrors inside me and as concrete and physical as the birth of my only child and none of that had to be apparent as subject. I didn't have to tell a story per se: I could fracture it, I could dump a whole lot of stuff into it and it would still be there. The telling itself stays partly in my head, but the poetry evidences a trace of a tale.'

Our Dust

STRING LIGHT 1991

I am your ancestor. You know next to nothing
about me.
There is no reason for you to imagine
the rooms I occupied or my heavy hair.
Not the faint vinegar smell of me. Or
the rubbered damp
of Forrest and I coupling on the landing
en route to our detached day.

You didn't know my weariness, error, incapacity,
I was the poet
of shadow work and towns with quarter-inch
phone books, of failed
roadside zoos. The poet of yard eggs and
sharpening shops,
jobs at the weapons plant and the Maybelline
factory on the penitentiary road.

A poet of spiderwort and jacks-in-the-pulpit,
hollyhocks against the toolshed.
An unsmiling dark blond.
The one with the trowel in her handbag.
I dug up protected and private things.
That sort, I was.
My graves went undecorated and my churches
abandoned. This wasn't planned, but practice.

I was the poet of short-tailed cats and yellow
line paint.
Of satellite dishes and Peterbilt trucks. Red Man
Chewing Tobacco, Triple Hit
Creme Soda. Also of dirt daubers, nightcrawlers,
martin houses, honey, and whetstones
from the Novaculite Uplift.

I had registered dogs 4 sale; rocks, dung
and straw.
I was a poet of hummingbird hives along with
redheaded stepbrothers.

The poet of good walking shoes – a necessity
in vernacular parts – and push mowers.
The rumor that I was once seen sleeping

215

in a refrigerator box is false (he was a brother
who hated me).
Nor was I the one lunching at the Governor's
mansion.

I didn't work off a grid. Or prime the surface
if I could get off without it. I made
simple music
out of sticks and string. On side B of me,
experimental guitar, night repairs, and suppers
such as this.
You could count on me to make a bad situation
worse like putting liquid makeup over
a passion mark.

I never raised your rent. Or anyone else's by God.
Never said I loved you. The future gave me chills.
I used the medium to say: Arise arise and
come together.
Free your children. Come on everybody. Let's start
with Baltimore.

Believe me I am not being modest when I
admit my life doesn't bear repeating. I
agreed to be the poet of one life,
one death alone. I have seen myself
in the black car. I have seen the retreat
of the black car.

'Mack trapped a spider...'
ONE BIG SELF: PRISONERS OF LOUISIANA 2003

Mack trapped a spider
Kept in a pepper jar
He named her Iris
Caught roaches to feed her
He loved Iris
When Iris died
He wrote her a letter

Floating Trees

TREMBLE 1996

a bed is left open to a mirror
a mirror gazes long and hard at a bed

light fingers the house with its own acoustics

one of them writes this down
one has paper

bed of swollen creeks and theories and coils
bed of eyes and leaky pens

much of the night the air touches arms
arms extend themselves to air

their torsos turning toward a roll
of sound: thunder

night of coon scat and vandalized headstones
night of deep kisses and catamenia

his face by this light: saurian
hers: ash like the tissue of a hornets' nest

one scans the aisle of firs
the faint blue line of them
one looks out: sans serif

'Didn't I hear you tell them you were born
on a train'

what begins with a sough and ends with a groan
groan in which the tongue's true color is revealed

the comb's sough and the denim's undeniable rub
the chair's stripped back and muddied rung

color of stone soup and garden gloves
color of meal and treacle and sphagnum

hangers clinging to their coat
a soft-white bulb to its string

217

the footprints inside us
iterate the footprints outside

the scratched words return to their sleeves

the dresses of monday through friday
swallow the long hips of weekends

a face is studied like a key
for the mystery of what it once opened

'I didn't mean to wake you
angel brains'

ink of eyes and veins and phonemes
the ink completes the feeling

a mirror silently facing a door
door with no lock no lock

the room he brings into you
the room befalls you

like the fir trees he trues her
she nears him like the firs

if one vanishes one stays
if one stays the other will or will not vanish

otherwise my beautiful green fly
otherwise not a leaf stirs

Song of the Gourd

TREMBLE 1996

In gardening I continued to sit on my side of the car: to
drive whenever possible at the usual level of distraction:
in gardening I shat nails glass contaminated dirt and
threw up on the new shoots: in gardening I learned to
praise things I had dreaded: I pushed the hair out of my
face: I felt less responsible for one man's death one
woman's long-term isolation: my bones softened: in
gardening I lost nickels and ring settings I uncovered
buttons and marbles: I laid half the worm aside and
sought the rest: I sought myself in the bucket and won-
dered why I came into being in the first place: in gar-
dening I turned away from the television and went
around smelling of offal the inedible parts of the
chicken: in gardening I said excelsior: in gardening I re-
quired no company I had to forgive my own failure to
perceive how things were: I went out barelegged at
dusk and dug and dug and dug: I hit rock my ovaries
softened: in gardening I was protean as in no other
realm before or since: I longed to torch my old belong-
ings and belch a little flame of satisfaction: in gardening
I longed to stroll farther into soundlessness: I could al-
most forget what happened many swift years ago in
arkansas: I felt like a god from down under: chthonian:
in gardening I thought this is it body and soul I am
home at last: excelsior: praise the grass: in gardening I
fled the fold that supported the war: only in gardening
could I stop shrieking: stop: stop the slaughter: only in
gardening could I press my ear to the ground to hear
my soul let out an unyielding noise: my lines softened: I
turned the water onto the joy-filled boychild: only in
gardening did I feel fit to partake to go on trembling in
the last light: I confess the abject urge to weed your
beds while the bittersweet overwhelmed my daylilies: I
summoned the courage to grin: I climbed the hill with
my bucket and slept like a dipper in the cool of your
body: besotted with growth; shot through by green

Key Episodes from an Earthly Life

TREMBLE 1996

As surely as there are crumbs on the lips
of the blind   I came for a reason

I remember when the fields were no taller
than a pencil   do you remember that

I told him   I've got socks older than her
but he would not listen

You will starve out girl   they told her
but she did not listen

As surely as there is rice in the cuffs
of the priest   sex is a factor   not a fact

Everything I do is leaning   toward
what we came for   is that perfectly clear

I like your shoes your uncut hair
I like your use of space too

I wanted to knock her lights out
the air cut in and did us some good

One thing about my television set it has
a knob on it enabling me to switch channels

Now it is your turn   to shake or
provoke   or heal me   I won't say it again

Do you like your beets well-cooked and chilled
even if they make your gums itch

Those dark arkansas roads   that is the sound
I am after   the choiring of crickets

Around this time of year   especially evening
I love everything   I sold enough eggs

To buy a new dress   I watched him drink the juice
of our beets   And render the light liquid

I came to talk you into physical splendor
I do not wish to speak to your machine

220

YANG LIAN
Filmed in London, 28 June 2007

YANG LIAN was one of the original Misty Poets who reacted against the strictures of the Cultural Revolution. He has been one of the most innovative and influential poets in China, both before and since his exile. Widely hailed in America and Europe as a highly individual voice in world literature, he has been translated into many languages. Unlike his contemporaries from the heady days of the Beijing Spring in the late 1970s – most of whom have either retreated into a very private poetry or stopped writing altogether – Yang Lian has gone on to forge a mature and complex poetry whose themes are the search for a Yeatsian mature wisdom, the accommodation of modernity within the ancient and book-haunted Chinese tradition, and a *rapprochement* between the literatures of East and West. His poems can be disturbing and strange, haunted by the eerie ordinariness of life and death. But in the end it is a triumphant poetry, wholly engaged with the struggle to be alert to life, in daily renewal, the search for that 'shore / where we see ourselves set sail'.

Born in 1955 in Switzerland, the son of a diplomat, he grew up in Beijing and began writing when he was sent to the countryside in the 1970s. On his return he co-founded the influential literary magazine *Jintian* (*Today* – now published in exile in Scandinavia). His work was banned in China in 1983, and he has lived in exile since 1989, when he organised memorial services for the dead of Tiananmen while in New Zealand. After spells in Australia, Germany and the USA, he settled in London, the setting of *Lee Valley Poems*, due from Bloodaxe in 2009. He is currently co-editing a substantial anthology of contemporary Chinese poetry with W.N. Herbert.

The connection with Bloodaxe came via Brian Holton who, when I first met him, was teaching Chinese at Newcastle University and translating Yang Lian's most recent work, as well as living next-door to Bill Herbert. Two editions followed: *Where the Sea Stands Still* in 1999, a bilingual edition also including Brian's memoir explaining how he 'came to find an English voice for Yang Lian'; and then *Concentric Circles* in 2005.

Yang Lian has written that *Concentric Circles* is 'the most important piece since I came out from China', and that it is emphatically not a political work, but instead a work focused on 'deep reality' and the nature of how humans understand that reality through the medium of language. The book, like the sections of which it is comprised, uses a kind of collage, where many small fragments, each complete in itself, are aligned together in a series of patterns to form a grander mosaic: from line to line, poem to poem, cycle to cycle, in ever-widening concentric structures.

大海停止之处

某个地址上　孩子切开一只石榴
某个地址把孩子想象成
眼睛　肉里白色的核
血　凝固成玻璃的吱吱叫的鸟儿
一半躯体在手中看不见地扭动
而牙齿上沾满被咬破的淡红色果冻
死　孩子看到了

那忘记我们的与被忘记无情复原的
一座入夜城市中抽象的灯火
是再次　却决非最后一次

剥夺我们方向的与被太多方向剥夺的
蓝　总弥漫于头颅的高度
　　　　　　　　在凝视里变黑
总得有一个地点让妄想突围
让构成地址的辞　习惯人群的溃烂

空虚　在眼眶里
　　　　　　　仅仅对称于
大海　在瞎子们触摸下没有形状

某个地址指定种植银色幽香的骨头
剥开我们深处
孩子被四季烘烤的杏仁
成为每个
　　　　　　想象　被看到否定的
　　　　　　被毁灭鼓舞的
石榴　裹紧蓝色钙化的颗粒
大海从未拍击到孤独之外
从未有别人在悬崖下粉身碎骨
我们听见　自己都摔在别处粉身碎骨
没有海不滑入诗的空白
用早已死亡的光切过孩子们　停止
这是从岸边眺望自己出海之处

[4TH PART]: 3

at some address   kids slice open a pomegranate
         some address   imagines kids as
               eyes   white nuts in flesh
         blood   chirping bird congealed into glass
    half a body twisting invisibly in the hands
    and chewed-up pink jelly smeared on the teeth
               death   kids have seen

    what forgets us and what is pitilessly restored by forgetting
         lamplight abstracted from a city at dusk
              is again   but never for the last time

   what strips us of direction and what is stripped by too many directions
         blue   always unfurled in the heights of the head
                             blackening in a stare
         must always have somewhere for vain hope to sortie out
to let the words that make addresses   get used to the pustulence of the crowd

              blank   in the eye-socket
                             only in symmetry with
         the sea   shapeless beneath blind men's hands
    some address is assigned to plant silvery perfumed bones
                   to strip away our depths
         kids   almonds roasted by the seasons
                   become every
                   imagination   denied by being seen
                   inspired by destruction
    the pomegranate   is wrapped in blue calcified pips
         the sea never yet slapped beyond solitude
    never yet had another   shatter below the cliff
    we hear ourselves   fall elsewhere and shatter
     no sea that doesn't slip into the void of the poem
kids sliced by long-dead light   stand still   this shore
              is where we see ourselves set sail

Translated by Brian Holton

223

同心圆

怕冷被寒冷剩下
岩石惨白的高度被岩石的盲目剩下
刺耳的秋天　被肌肉萎缩的树
从树干之间减去

风　就不在枯枝间只在骸骨间
不是果皮只是烂掉的听觉
不擦亮翅膀只擦亮金属千百年的合唱声

死者们射穿大雾　把死亡剩下
旷野　犁沟间炖出肉味的黑色视野
一只只冻僵的核桃被拧下
一杯杯酒的地址间　冷酷鲜艳的大海
每分钟空出一座储存我们恐惧的大教堂

减去　直到毁灭的总和

那总是一条幽暗走廊里隐约听到的
耳鸣　在耳朵之外远远移动

石头海拔上
声音　拆散一只鸟骨骼的和弦
逆向追逐会疼痛的肉体
我们用一对粉红色器官反复诞生的肉体

那总被加剧的现实　涌出风的隧道
一千棵仙人掌嫁给作曲家的夜色
山羊居高临下的空眼窝逾越我们的天气

声音移开耳朵就摔得粉碎

from Concentric Circles

CONCENTRIC CIRCLES 2005

[FIRST CIRCLE]: CHAPTER ONE

1

fear of cold left behind by the cold
pale height of rocks left behind by blindness of rocks
ear-piercing autumn   by atrophied trees
subtracted from between the tree-trunks

then wind   not among withered branches but human bones only
not fruit skin but decayed hearing only
not to scour wings but to scour bright the age-old chorus of metals only

the dead fire through dense fog   leaving death behind
empty fields   dark vision where furrows emit the smell of stew
frozen stiff walnuts twisted off one by one
among addresses of wine by the glass   an ocean colourful and cruel
every minute empties out a cathedral where our fears are stored

subtracted   down to the sum of destruction

2

there is always what's heard vaguely in a dim corridor
buzzing in the ears   moves far away outside the ears

at the sea-level of stone
sound   breaking up the chord of bird bone
chases in reverse a body that can feel pain
our bodies born again and again by a pair of pink organs

reality always intensified   gushes out from a tunnel of wind
a thousand cacti married to a composer's night
from high above goats' empty orbits exceed our air

sound moves away   ears smashed to pieces

Translated by Brian Holton & Agnes Hung-Chong Chan

BENJAMIN ZEPHANIAH

Filmed in Lincolnshire, 5 November 2007

BENJAMIN ZEPHANIAH is an oral poet, novelist, playwright, children's writer and reggae artist. Born in 1958 in Birmingham, he grew up in Jamaica and in Handsworth, where he was sent to an approved school for being uncontrollable, rebellious and 'a born failure', ending up in jail for burglary. After prison he turned from crime to music and poetry. In 1989 he was nominated for Oxford Professor of Poetry, and has since received honorary doctorates from several English universities, but famously refused to accept a nomination for an OBE in 2003. He has appeared in a number of television programmes, including *Eastenders, The Bill, Live and Kicking, Blue Peter* and *Wise Up*, and played Gower in a BBC Radio 3 production of Shakespeare's *Pericles* in 2005.

Best known for his performance poetry with a political edge for adults – and his poetry with attitude for children – he has his own rap/reggae band. He has produced numerous recordings, including *Dub Ranting* (1982), *Rasta* (1983), *Us and Dem* (1990), *Back to Roots* (1995), *Belly of de Beast* (1996) and *Naked* (2004). He was the first person to record with the Wailers after the death of Bob Marley, in a musical tribute to Nelson Mandela, which Mandela heard while in prison on Robben Island. Their later meetings led to Zephaniah working with children in South African townships and hosting the President's Two Nations Concert at the Royal Albert Hall in 1996.

His first book of poems, *Pen Rhythm*, was produced in 1980 by a small East London publishing cooperative, Page One Books. His second collection, *The Dread Affair*, was published by Hutchinson's short-lived Arena imprint in 1985, but out of print by the time I first saw him perform his work at Newcastle Arts Centre in the early 90s. He has since published three collections with Bloodaxe, *City Psalms* (1992), *Propa Propaganda* (1996) and *Too Black Too Strong* (2001), the latter including poems written while working with Michael Mansfield QC and other Tooks barristers on the Stephen Lawrence case.

His other titles include his poetry books for children, *Talking Turkeys* (1994), *Funky Chickens* (1996) and *Wicked World* (2000), all from Puffin/Penguin; his novels for teenagers, *Face* (1999), *Refugee Boy* (2001), *Gangsta Rap* (2004) and *Teacher's Dead* (2007), all from Bloomsbury; *The Bloomsbury Book of Love Poems* (1999); *Schools Out: Poems Not for School* (1997) and *The Little Book of Vegan Poems* (2001) from AK Press; and *We Are Britain* (Frances Lincoln, 2003).

No Problem

PROPA PROPAGANDA 1996

I am not de problem
But I bare de brunt
Of silly playground taunts
An racist stunts,
I am not de problem
I am a born academic
But dey got me on de run
Now I am branded athletic,
I am not de problem
If yu give I a chance
I can teach yu of Timbuktu
I can do more dan dance,
I am not de problem
I greet yu wid a smile
Yu put me in a pigeon hole
But I am versatile.

These conditions may affect me
As I get older,
An I am positively sure
I hav no chips on me shoulders,
Black is not de problem
Mother country get it right,
An juss fe de record,
Sum of me best friends are white.

Man to Man

CITY PSALMS 1992

Macho man
Can't cook
Macho man
Can't sew
Macho man
Eats plenty Red Meat,
At home him is King,
From front garden to back garden
From de lift to de balcony
Him a supreme Master,
Controller.

Food mus ready
On time,
Cloth mus ready
On time,
Woman mus ready
On time,
How Macho can yu go?

Cum
Talk to me bout sexuality,
Cum meditate,
Cum Save de Whale,
Dose bulging muscles need Tai Chi
Yu drunken eyes need herb tea,
Cum, Relax.

Macho man
Can't cook, sew or wash him pants,
But Macho Man is in full control.

Meditate and Communicate
PROPA PROPAGANDA 1996

A Sadhu
Like a lotus
Sits on India,
Waiting for the truth
To take him home,
And India
Is busy
Getting busier,
Trying to repay its World Bank Loan.

The Sadhu
Takes his ganja
Like a Rastaman,
He blesses it
And burns it
For the nation,
And as the smoke arrives
In central Pakistan,
The Sadhu talks to God
In meditation.

One day
They say
Gods will return to India,
And all our mixed up lives
Will fall in place,
But first the Gods
Must deal with Bombay's Mafia,
And the Mafia
Control a lot of space.

A Sadhu
Like a lotus
Sits on India,
Waiting for the truth
To take him home,
He's a pure
And dedicated
Meditator,
He's just meditating
With his mobile phone.

To Do Wid Me

TOO BLACK TOO STRONG 2001

There's a man beating his wife
De woman juss lost her life
Dem called dat domestic strife?
Wot has dat gotta do wid me?

Babies are buried under floors
In a church behind closed doors
I don't know de bloody cause
Wot has dat gotta do wid me?

I've seen all de documentaries
An there's nothing I can do
I've listened to de commentaries
Why should I listen to you?
If I am told to I go vote
If I need more money I strike
If I'm told not to then I won't
I want de best deal out of life

De fit cannot go jogging
Coz there's someone out there mugging
When they should be spreading luving
Wot has dat gotta do wid me?

You an me must juss stand back
Coz they're gonna bomb Iraq
It's a surgical attack so
Wot has dat gotta do wid me?

I juss wanna live my life mate
So juss leave me alone
Why should I fight de state?
When I'm trying to buy my home,
I juss wanna earn my bread guy
An feed my family
You may starve and you may die
But wot has dat gotta do wid me?

Poets are dying in Nigeria
Or forced to leave de area
Multinationals are superior
Wot has dat gotta do wid me?

An in somewhcrestan I've heard
Dat she can't say a word
An he must grow a beard
Wot has dat gotta do wid me?

Wot has dis gotta do wid me
I'm juss dis guy from Birmingham
An all I want to do is live good in de hood,
It's got nothing to do wid me
I'm juss your average football fan
An hey sum foreign teams are very, very good,
Why should you worry yourself?
You cannot change a single thing
All you gotta do is tek wot you can get,
Why should you worry yourself?
Try hard an you will die trying
Wot can any of us do about Tibet?

I see a million refugees
On twenty million TVs
An I think who de fuck are these?
Wot has dat gotta do wid me?

Hurry up I've got no time
Don't you mess wid wot is mine
Yes I signed de dotted line but
Wot has dat gotta do wid me?

Your school has juss been closed down
Your tax is buying bombs
An although you come from downtown
You don't know where you're coming from,
You don't know wot you are eating
Your food has a terrible taste
An you can be sure dat you are drinking
Sum kinda chemical waste

There's a price upon your head
Even though you're newly wed
A police juss shot you dead
Wot has dat gotta do wid me?

An down in de police station
They are killing de black nation
But dat's normal race relations
Wot has dat gotta do wid me?

Wot has dat gotta do wid
De man upon de corner dat is selling guns
So we can kill each other as we rave,
Or de crackhead who is trying to crack up everyone
Teking all your cash as you become a slave,
Or de mother in de gutter who is begging bread
Where de man dressed in de Gucci hails a cab,
All I am trying to do is praise de Lord it must be said
Wot has dis to do wid anything I've had

A baby in Pakistan
Is making footballs for de man
Or is she an Indian?
Wot has dat gotta do wid me?

There's no propa propaganda
About Malawi or Rwanda
An all dis makes me wonder
Wot has dat gotta do wid me?

I used to go on demonstrations
Now me feet can't tek de pace,
I've tried be a vegan
But there's egg upon me face,
My last stand was de Miners Strike
I did de cop patrol,
Now it's central heating dat I like
An I juss don't need no coal

Indonesia needs more
British arms for East Timor
More western bombs to bomb de poor
Wot has dat gotta do wid me?

An over in Algeria
They say there's another massacre
Isn't dat a part of Africa
Wot has dat gotta do wid me?

An I don't plan to go
To an American death row
There's no compassion there I know but
Wot has dat gotta do wid me?

My God, I can see you have been tortured
An your wife has been drawn an quartered
An your children have been slaughtered
But wot has dat gotta do wid me?

BONUS TRACK

FILM BY IVOR BOWEN

KEN SMITH

(1938-2003)

KEN SMITH
Filmed by Ivor Bowen in London, January 2002

KEN SMITH was the first poet to be published by Bloodaxe Books, 30 years ago in 1978 (see page 240), and we wanted to honour his work and memory by adding a reading by him after the 30 *In Person* films. His lifelong friend Ivor Bowen filmed him reading 'Three Docklands fragments', firstly while wandering the Docklands, and afterwards at Ken's home in East Ham (the section on the DVD).

Ken Smith was a major figure in world poetry. Once dubbed 'the godfather of the new poetry', his politically edgy, cuttingly collo-quial, muscular poetry influenced a whole generation of younger British poets, from Simon Armitage to Carol Ann Duffy. His work shifted territory with time, from rural Yorkshire, America and London to the war-ravaged Balkans and Eastern Europe (before and after Communism). His early books span a transition from a pre-occupation with land and myth to his later engagement with urban Britain and the politics of radical disaffection. 'Three Docklands fragments' are representative of just one vein of his later poetry.

He published 15 books with Bloodaxe, and collected his poetry from four decades in two volumes: *The Poet Reclining: Selected Poems 1962-1980* (1982), which included work from *The Pity* (1967), *Work, distances* (1972), *Tristan Crazy* (1978) and *Fox Running* (1980); and *Shed: Poems 1980-2001* (2002), which houses his later collections *Terra* (1986), *Wormwood* (1987), *The heart, the border* (1990), *Tender to the Queen of Spain* (1993) and *Wild Root* (1998), along with new poems. *Wild Root* was a Poetry Book Society Choice and shortlisted for the T.S. Eliot Prize. The posthumous *You Again: last poems & other words* followed in 2004. His earlier prose was collected in *A Book of Chinese Whispers*, published by Bloodaxe in 1987.

Born in 1938 in the North Riding of Yorkshire, the son of an itinerant farm labourer, he grew up on various farms and later in Hull. He lived in Leeds during the 60s, moving to America in 1969, where his work was better-known until Bloodaxe's publication of *The Poet Reclining* in 1982. After a period in Exeter in the mid-70s, he endured a difficult time in London, an experience charted in his long poem *Fox Running*, until he met American writer Judi Benson and moved with her to East Ham. The major work collected in *Shed* was written in London, or on the hoof in Berlin and Eastern Europe. He also wrote books on Berlin and on his time as writer-in-residence at Wormwood Scrubs prison (1985-87). He received America's prestigious Lannan Literary Award for Poetry in 1997, which gave him much needed financial support.

He contracted Legionnaire's Disease in Cuba, and later died in London in 2003 after contracting an infection in hospital.

Three Docklands fragments

THE HEART, THE BORDER 1990

1 *The Enterprise Zone*

On my birthday the snow wind
bringing feathery rain, a fine dust
falling on the edge of crystal.

I take the grey road along the river
where pass lives sadder than yours, mine,
slow death in the tower blocks.

These are the Silvertown Blues,
Fight the Rich ghosting out
in concrete, by the flyover.

No one ever gets straight here.
The ego's tale of itself is miserable,
nothing much happens but murder.

Yet that these wastes be repeopled
and the rich inherit, everyone's
moving downriver. This is *the zone*,

carved from the sour and floury air
of London's residuary body,
filling with cranes and dust

and the racket of money being made,
and there's nothing to say but to say
to myself *Thou bone, brother bone. You old bone.*

2 *Of things to come*

Down the Bendy Road to Cyprus and Custom House
where the new cities rise from the drawing-boards
and the ghosts-to-be of George in his Capri,
JoJo in her birthday suit drinking white wine with soda
fly in from Paris for the weekend. Later
they'll gather with friends by the marina.
Later they'll appreciate the view of the river.
Later they'll jive to the mean mad dance of money
between the tower blocks over the runway
amongst the yachts already moored in the development.

3 *Yuppy love*

What he calls her: my little pocket calculator
my fully portable my VDU my organiser my mouse
oh my filofax my cellnet my daisywheel.

What he dreams driving home at the wheel
on the brimming motorway: her electronics
the green screen of her underwear her digital display.

Oh my spreadsheet he groans in the night:
my modem my cursor lusting after her floppies
wanting her printout her linkup her entire database.

NEIL ASTLEY
The Story of Bloodaxe: 1978-2008

THE POETRY REVOLUTION

Adrian Mitchell prefaced his first collection *Poems* in 1964 with this now famous declaration:

> Most people ignore most poetry
> because
> most poetry ignores most people.

When I set up Bloodaxe Books in 1978, I wanted to change all that. I saw myself as a representative reader who was just one of a wide readership hungry for a much broader range of poetry; people who had been starved of the best poetry being written *because not all the best poetry was being published.*

I wanted to publish poets who had a strong following at grassroots level, appreciated by audiences at readings and by the readers of the poetry magazines, but not recognised by the main publishers of poetry, many of whom seemed to think that only poetry by middle-class Oxbridge-educated men from the Home Counties was worth printing. I had been part of that grassroots poetry culture for some time, working for *Stand* magazine in Newcastle for three years as well as producing small press pamphlets and organising readings.

What it took to change this situation was, in poetry terms, a revolution. The seeds of this one were sown in Newcastle, a place which has always harboured revolutionaries, from Garibaldi and Marat to the latter-day poetry rebels who inspired me, including Basil Bunting, Tony Harrison, and the crew of Morden Tower, the medieval turret on the city walls where Tom and Connie Pickard started their reading series in 1964. Bunting gave one of the first Morden Tower readings that year after Pickard had discovered him living in obscurity in Wylam, Northumberland.

Bunting's meeting with Pickard was the catalyst which transformed his life and reputation. Poets such as Robert Creeley, Allen Ginsberg, Hugh MacDiarmid and J.H. Prynne came to Newcastle both to read at the Tower and to meet Bunting. Stimulated by his contact with Pickard and the Tower's highly receptive young audience of poets (including Tony Jackson and Barry MacSweeney) and poetry enthusiasts, Bunting laboured over the next year on his master work, *Briggflatts*, buoyed up by Pickard's enthusiasm and wanting to show him how to write a long poem, giving its first reading at Morden Tower in December 1965. By the time I arrived in Newcastle ten years later, in 1975, it had become one of the liveliest centres for poetry in Britain. Bloodaxe's eclectic, democratic style of publishing was inspired by Newcastle's energetic, internationally-minded poetry culture.

My first taste of Newcastle had been in 1971, when I experienced the wild excesses of the city's nightlife in the company of an escaped prisoner called Mick. I had wanted to see something of Scotland during a half-term break from my college journalism course. After hitching from Portsmouth to Inverness, I was on my way home when Mick picked me up outside Edinburgh in a car he'd just stolen. I didn't know he'd broken out of jail two days earlier and was giving me a lift to help keep him awake. After several bottles of Brown Ale in pubs from Berwick to Newcastle – where we had an especially good time – it became clear that we weren't going to reach Birmingham that night, and were finally arrested in a lay-by just off the A1 near Darlington. A police patrol had spotted the car parked off the road with two men slumped asleep inside, and checked the number plate.

After college I spent six months in post-'68 Paris (where I worked as an *homme au pair*, studied French and was radicalised); then did various jobs around Britain in journalism and press relations, and was briefly secretary to the managing director of Yale University Press in London; there I became interested in editing, but lacked the university degree needed to pursue that. Three years after my first visit to Newcastle, working as a journalist in Australia's Northern Territory in Darwin, I was thinking of returning to England to take an English degree, with a view to getting an editorial job in publishing. Seeing *Get Carter* one night at a drive-in, I remembered how much I'd liked Newcastle, and sent off my application to Newcastle University the next day. A month later, on Christmas Day, 1974, Darwin was destroyed by Cyclone Tracy. I was trapped under a collapsed house. This brush with death was enough to send me post haste to Newcastle, where I was soon working as a bus conductor while waiting to start my course.

In those days the poet Jon Silkin used to sell his literary magazine *Stand* to people waiting in theatre queues. With his dishevelled hair, white beard and earnest manner, he looked every bit the impoverished poet, and sold hundreds of copies hand-to-hand by playing this part. In the course of helping me part with 50p for the latest issue, he learned that I was an ex-journalist with experience of newspaper production work. A week later I had a part-time job as production editor for the magazine. It paid very little, but I could supplement my earnings by hawking the magazine not just to theatre queues – both in Newcastle and in Edinburgh – but also around student unions and door-to-door in halls of residence, first in Newcastle and Durham and later in Oxford and other university towns and cities, partnered by a succession of young English graduates with literary aspirations whom Silkin was able to exploit as co-editors until they'd had enough. We kept 50p from every pound we earned, and after three days selling in Oxford would have covered our petrol costs; keep going for another couple of days and we might make ourselves £50.

Yet the experience gained in helping to edit the magazine for three years was invaluable. The work introduced me to some extraordinary British, European and American poets, including Geoffrey Hill, Roy Fisher, Hans Magnus Enzensberger and Zbigniew Herbert. I was reading batches of poems by new poets whose work I greatly admired, including David Constantine, Helen Dunmore and Nigel Wells, whom I later approached to ask if my new press could publish their first collections. Another influence on Bloodaxe was the poetry published in *Stand* by exiled or persecuted writers from Eastern Europe. I discovered the work of poets such as Osip Mandelstam, Miroslav Holub, Marina Tsvetayeva and Tomas Venclova, and got to know translators who later produced editions for Bloodaxe, notably David McDuff (who also worked on *Stand*), Adam Czerniawski, Michael Hamburger and Ewald Osers. I met Ken Smith and other poets who had worked on the magazine before me, and read and absorbed back numbers going back to the early 1950s, including the remarkable new Czech writing issue edited by Tony Harrison in 1969.

There was also a long-running spat between Jon Silkin, Donald Davie and Michael Schmidt which culminated in a fiery exchange of letters in the *Times Literary Supplement*. I was involved in editing and commissioning work for the *Stand* symposium on poetry and politics which followed this: in one corner, the left-wing 'socially committed' credentials of *Stand*; in the other, what Silkin presented as the reactionary conservatism of Schmidt, Davie, C.H. Sisson and their *Poetry Nation Review*. This prefigured later disagreements I would have with Schmidt not just in our StAnza Poetry Festival lectures in St Andrews, but when Bloodaxe's various initiatives to broaden the readership of contemporary poetry were subjected to repeated attacks in *PN Review* by Schmidt or one or other of his associates.

By the time I started studying English at Newcastle University, I was not only working on *Stand* but going to Friday night readings at Morden Tower, where I was introduced to a still wider range of contemporary poets, from agitprop, avant-garde and pop poets to lively new poets and highly respected literary elders. The late Gordon Brown's anthology *High on the Walls* (1990) gives a flavour of the vibrant mix of poets reading at the Tower in its first 25 years. I also came into contact with editors of other magazines and presses active in the North-East at that time, including Black Suede Boot Press, Ceolfrith Press, Galloping Dog Press, *Iron*, *Ostrich*, Pig Press, *Poetry Information* and *Poetry North-East*, each with its own distinctive editorial style and particular areas of literary interest. It wasn't long before I was designing and producing pamphlets myself, both for *Stand*'s own pamphlet imprint, Northern House (the prototype of Bloodaxe's first pamphlets), and for Morden Tower.

Poets appearing at the Tower would post me a batch of new poems they intended to read, and I typed them up on a golf-ball typewriter with a carbon ribbon, then did an old-fashioned paste-up job with

scalpel and Cow Gum. After the sheets had been printed at Tyneside Free Press Workshop, I cut up the sheets, put them through the folding machine, stapled and trimmed them, and finally took them round to the Tower in the carrying-rack of my butcher's bike. They sold for 20p. The 1977 series included Fleur Adcock, Gavin Ewart, Michael Hamburger and Anne Stevenson, and there was also a magazine anthology with work by all the poets published that year called *Thoth* after the Egyptian god of writing and wisdom (the title suggested by Douglas Dunn after his reading at the Tower).

Anne Stevenson especially liked the pamphlets, and asked if I would produce a series for the Old Fire Station Poets readings she organised in Oxford, and soon I was working at Tyneside Free Press on her publications, including a striking debut collection called *31 Poems* by Scottish poet and scientist G.F. Dutton, who was later published by Bloodaxe. When Anne's publishing energies switched to a new imprint, Mid-Day Publications, I produced some of their books also. It was through Anne that I met Stephen Dunstan, one of her husband's students of Chinese, who was to have been published by Mid-Day; his *Tarot Poems* was the first paperback book from Bloodaxe, in 1980.

BIRTH OF BLOODAXE

Bloodaxe was born in the summer of 1978, when I thought I'd finished my studies at Newcastle University. Morden Tower Publications had folded, leaving me with the typescript of Ken Smith's *Tristan Crazy*. If I could set up my own press, this would be its first publication. I knew I had to start small, with pamphlets, but planned to produce books as soon as I could fund them. My bank manager, however, was unimpressed by my 'speculative venture', refusing my request for an overdraft of £60. I closed my account and went ahead anyway.

A mysterious bale of paper turned up on the doorstep, sent by a well-wisher. It wasn't the right kind, but I sold it to a printer who could use it, putting the proceeds towards the £230 bill for 750 copies of *Tristan Crazy*. Bloodaxe Books was launched at Ken Smith's reading of *Tristan Crazy* at Morden Tower on 26 October 1978. The pamphlet was priced at 65p. I started hawking it around the bookshops and sold copies to people at readings. Ken also was selling copies at other readings he was giving. Then Yorkshire Arts put in a bulk order for a small press distribution scheme servicing bookshops with titles by Yorkshire writers, and Bloodaxe was on its way.

Poetry publishers at that time tended to have names which were either innocuous (often flowers or animals) or obscure. I wanted a name which was both memorable and distinctively northern, but not from the North-East's much plundered ecclesiastical history (with Bede, Caedmon, Ceolfrith and Lindisfarne appropriated by petrol stations, arts centres and folk rock bands). The Viking king Eric Bloodaxe was the last ruler of the independent kingdom of Northumbria, stretching

from the Humber to the Twecd. I first came across him in Basil Bunting's *Briggflatts*, which features Bloodaxe, 'King of Orkney, King of Dublin, twice King of York' along with the saint Cuthbert as two opposing aspects of the Northumbrian – and Bunting's – character. I met him again in *Egil's Saga*, which tells how Eric ordered Egil Skallagrimsson to write him a praise-poem overnight on pain of death, and how Egil's brilliant (but disingenuous) song pleased the king so much that the hero's life was spared. The thought that this made Eric Bloodaxe possibly our first patron of poetry clinched the choice of name, along with the memorable pararhyme of *Bloodaxe Books*.

The axe-head of the first Bloodaxe logo (1978-80) was formed from Eric's name in Anglo-Saxon script taken from the account of the year 954 AD in the *Anglo-Saxon Chronicle*, when the North became part of England for the first time after Eric's expulsion and murder. This was replaced by lettering designed in 1981 by New Zealand artist Gretchen Albrecht for Fleur Adcock's *Hotspur* when that was to have been an elaborate poet-artist-composer publication. Her font was a melding of the lettering of the Bayeux Tapestry with Times Roman. The Eric Bloodaxe title-page logo was designed by Charlotte Cory and used in books from 1987.

I started working full-time for *Stand* in the summer of 1978 as co-editor, production editor and travelling salesman, but by the autumn I was out of a job, after the usual catalysmic row the magazine's so-called co-editors always had with Jon Silkin.

My university tutor came to the rescue: Dr Robert Woof was also director of the Wordsworth Trust, and needed a new assistant to work on publications and fund-raising in the trust's administration office in Newcastle University. Nourished by his great love of English poetry, and especially Wordsworth and the Romantics, Robert was an inspirational person to work for, totally dedicated to his vision of establishing Dove Cottage in Cumbria as the world centre for Wordsworth studies. His enthusiasm was infectious, and if the work was sometimes chaotic and the hours demanding, that didn't matter. He was a driven, thoroughly good man, and you did whatever you could to help him, which could mean agreeing, with no notice, to take his undergraduate seminars on the Romantics when he was suddenly called away on Wordsworth business. Having also started postgraduate research in medieval literature, I was already giving tutorials on Chaucer and Malory, so I didn't quite feel thrown in at the deep end, but it was valuable experience nonetheless, and I know I gained a great deal from working for Robert. And when the day spent working in the cause of William Wordsworth was over, my evenings belonged to the living poets as the Dove Cottage office became the administrative base of Bloodaxe Books.

The second Bloodaxe title, in spring 1979, was *Below Loughrigg* by Fleur Adcock, a sequence written the year before in Cumbria when she had been writer-in-residence at a college in Ambleside; the third

was *The Season of Comfort*, a first collection by Vincent Morrison, a young poet from Sunderland whose work I had admired in *Stand*. Two pamphlets followed by John Cassidy – another poet from *Stand* – and then, in 1980, an LP record of Basil Bunting reading *Briggflatts*, and the first six paperback books, including first collections by two more poets I'd first read in *Stand*, David Constantine (then living in Durham) and Nigel Wells, and a debut volume by Tony Flynn (recommended by Douglas Dunn).

These paperbacks set the production standards which Bloodaxe has always maintained, using high quality acid-free paper which will not discolour, rip or break up after a few years. Thirty years later, the importance of these standards will be clear to anyone who handles an early Bloodaxe title. All printers used by Bloodaxe buy their paper from mills with FSC and PEFC chain of custody certification, which means the wood comes from a properly managed forest. This goes further than replanting schemes to cover also the impact of forestry on the environment. For binding we've always used a chemically-based glue, not derived from any animal product, which only contains waxes and polymers. This is pliable and non-brittle, allowing the book to be opened repeatedly without the spine splitting; because the signatures are sewn as well as glued, the pages will not drop out.

As well as the new poets I wanted to publish, there were other fine writers, such as Ken Smith and John Cassidy, who'd been dropped by London publishers after changes of editor. This was something else I felt Bloodaxe could offer: the encouragement brought by continuing support for a poet's work. However, for such a press to work effectively on behalf of its writers and readers, a stronger business base was needed.

For the first four years my poetry revolution was a shoestring affair run by a volunteer force of one. The Tyneside Free Press let me use their typesetting machine at night. Some days I'd set off with my rep's sample bag of poetry pamphlets and books, hitchhiking to northern cities or London where I'd stay with friends or in B&Bs. Northern Arts had begun to support the programme with one-off grants, and I had a postgraduate research grant to keep the wolf from the door, but because Bloodaxe was taking up most of my energies, I was neglecting the academic work. I couldn't continue to do both. Finally, I had to decide whether to convert my masters thesis into a Ph.D: either I would spend three more years substantiating my quite possibly flawed theories on Anglo-Saxon versification, or I would embark upon the even more risky scenario of trying to turn my struggling small press into an effective poetry imprint.

However, the press's prospects were not good: in 1981 I managed to produce five strong titles – two pamphlets by Tony Harrison, a poet-artist collaboration by Tom Paulin and Noel Connor, and a pamphlet and a book by Ken Smith – but I was running up debts with the printers, and not selling enough books to cover their costs.

Grant aid was sporadic and tied to particular publications, with West Midlands Arts and the Welsh Arts Council subsidising titles by Tony Flynn and Nigel Wells.

Northern Arts had been impressed by the first Bloodaxe publications and wanted to offer more help, but only if the press could be put on a firmer business footing. After much discussion, Roger Garfitt, then chair of the literature panel, proposed a marriage between Bloodaxe Books and Ceolfrith Press, the poetry and art imprint of Sunderland Arts Centre, which had lost its editor as well as its editorial direction. The Bloodaxe list would be absorbed by Ceolfrith; I would be editor of both imprints; and the Arts Centre would get a funding increase to assist what was called 'stabilisation'. It sounded like a good idea, but a visit to Sunderland persuaded me otherwise; I hadn't spent three years working for Jon Silkin not to know when the wool was being pulled over my eyes. Northern Arts were horrified when I turned down the offer, but later said I'd been quite right to do so after discovering that much of Ceolfrith's sales income hadn't been used to fund new publications but to cover losses made on the exhibitions. This wasn't the firmer business footing they'd had in mind.

Determined to keep Bloodaxe going, even on a limited basis, I needed a part-time job. This time my rescuer was a bookseller, Iris Penny, who was opening an arts bookshop called The Bookhouse. She wanted staff who were passionate about books, and in the course of the three years I worked there, I was able to give Newcastle the best poetry section of any bookshop in the North of England, a resource which was no less helpful to me in my Bloodaxe work.

I learned a great deal about how books sold in the bookshops, what worked and what didn't in areas such as design and pricing. Ordering books by American authors via importers, I became aware of which poets or books were popular with readers, and which editions were hard to get hold of. I was also working as an organiser of Newcastle Literary Festival, which launched some of the early Bloodaxe titles with readings to large audiences by poets including Ken Smith and Miroslav Holub. Through the festival I met other authors, such as Angela Carter, whose poetry Bloodaxe would have published had she not abandoned that project; *Come unto These Yellow Sands*, her book of radio plays, followed instead in 1985.

Influenced by the designs of the latest novels I was selling in the shop – and by 80s record covers – I started trying out different ideas in designing the Bloodaxe covers of the time. I believed that poetry books needed to have strong visual covers to project an exciting sense of their content, so what worked for literary novels, trade paperbacks, magazine covers and album sleeves should also work for poetry, which meant using colourful designs with paintings or photographs to complement or act as a kind of visual image of the poetry. There was a sometimes punk element, including Neville Brody's typography and iconoclastic *Face* layouts, as the poet-scientist Holub was to discover

when he found his first Bloodaxe cover had him posed inside the gut of one of his own laboratory mice.

The Bookhouse was one of a number of independent bookshops which flourished until the mid-80s because they stocked the kinds of books you'd never find in W.H. Smith's or an antiquated university bookshop like Thorne's in Newcastle, and that was all the city had then, along with some second-hand bookshops. The shop specialised in areas such as literary fiction, women's literature (Virago and Women's Press especially), politics, poetry and children's books, ran Newcastle Literary Festival's bookstalls and hosted its own readings by writers and actors. When the chain bookstores opened branches in Newcastle, the Bookhouse couldn't survive. My next job was actually working full-time for Bloodaxe, but that didn't happen until 1984.

BLOODAXE THE BUSINESS

Bloodaxe achieved its 'firmer business footing' when my friend Simon Thirsk agreed to help turn round what he called my 'kitchen-table operation'. But there never *was* any kitchen-table: the centre of operations was usually a box-filled bedroom, the first of these being my room in Simon and Nansi Thirsk's house in Heaton, which became Bloodaxe's administrative base after my Wordsworth year.

When we first met, Simon had just returned to journalism after finishing a philosophy degree at Newcastle University, and was working for the *Shields Gazette*; he later switched to Newcastle's *Evening Chronicle*. We talked a lot about poetry and philosophy, and soon he was offering advice and support. Transporting the Bunting records from a factory in Wales jiggered the suspension of his car; afterwards we drove to Bunting's with a record-player to enable him to hear the Bloodaxe LP, and Simon was able to share the experience of hearing Bunting telling tales from his exotic earlier years in the dismal modern house in Washington New Town which was his home at that time.

My own homes were no more permanent, a fact disguised by Bloodaxe's long-term Newcastle address of PO Box 1SN, which offered continuity in areas such as correspondence and orders. From Heaton I moved to Gateshead, then Elswick; the next move, to Fenham, was to a ground-floor flat which quickly filled up with bindery packets of books, stacked in every available space, including under the bed (books whose covers acquired circular indentations from the bed-springs had to be thrown out). I wasn't too popular with the neighbours when a massive articulated lorry backed down the tiny street one day with a load of Paraquat poison sufficient to kill half of Newcastle; squeezed between the barrels was a printer's pallet with copies of Paul Hyland's collection *The Stubborn Forest*. As well as towers of boxes, my bedroom housed a huge drawing-board I'd acquired from the Workers' Educational Association, and this enabled me to shift the design and production work from the Tyneside Free Press into the flat. If a book had to be produced for a deadline, I could now work all through the

night on the paste-up to have it ready for printing in time. Because of my design skills and printing knowledge, the books were better produced than anything the commercial publishers had to offer, which helped when it came to getting orders from bookshops and review coverage in newspapers and poetry magazines. But the operation was still a small press in the way everything else was done, and it needed a sounder business base to get any kind of funding increase. Northern Arts had limited funds for literature, with the lion's share of that budget going to *Stand* magazine. My refusal to play ball with them over the Ceolfrith merger idea didn't help my cause.

The Arts Council, however, had noted that Bloodaxe's publications were not only better designed than the books from most of the presses they funded from London, but were often by the kinds of poets not well represented on those other lists. With new arts funding devolved to the regional arts associations, Northern Arts was responsible for Bloodaxe, but the Arts Council could increase its literature provision to enable Northern Arts to grant annual revenue funding, as long as Bloodaxe was re-formed into a non-profit limited company with a similar constitution and company structure to that of the Arts Council's own literature clients.

Simon joined as co-director when Bloodaxe Books Ltd was constituted in 1982, with a brief to develop the business and marketing side of the company. As part of the business plan submitted to Northern Arts, I would be paid a small wage. Two years later I was able to give up my part-time bookselling job and work full-time for Bloodaxe for the first time, but with Simon needing to guarantee the overdraft, we agreed that he should become chairman, which gave him financial control of the company (eventually his skills would enable Bloodaxe to dispense with risky overdrafts altogether), while I would be editor and managing director with total editorial control. Nansi Thirsk, a solicitor, became the company secretary, and her involvement was to be invaluable in some of the legal battles which lay ahead.

Under Simon's direction, every book was properly costed. The decision as to what books or authors we published was always mine, but I had to produce a balanced publication programme in which deficits from slower selling or higher costing titles were covered by income from books with higher sales. Simon's sound business judgement has been the right foil for my editorial vision ever since. His pessimism has balanced my optimism, and his pragmatism has kept my idealistic excesses in check, but because my hunches have often been right, he's also been willing to let us take risks, taking on trust what is often only an intuitive sense I have that a particular poet or idea for a book has real potential.

Without our strong working partnership, with Simon at the helm, Bloodaxe would not have grown into an international poetry publishing house. This is something overlooked by people who only know about my own contribution as editor. Bloodaxe has changed poetry

publishing in Britain not because it has a single-minded editor but because the whole business has been managed creatively and effectively by the Astley/Thirsk double-act. In particular we have both always viewed marketing – Simon's specialisation – not as something "bolted on" afterwards to sell the books but as an integral part of our thinking as publishers.

The financial assistance of Northern Arts – and later Arts Council England – has been the other key factor in Bloodaxe's growth. Their consistent help has made it possible to publish books by new poets which often take several years to break even. You have to take risks to break new ground. But Simon has made sure that such risks have always been kept within our control.

With an annual revenue grant awarded from 1982, Bloodaxe was able to strengthen its publishing programme and run a much more effective business. A trade distributor, Noonan Hurst in Greenwich, took over the warehousing and sales of the books, and a sales agency called Umbrella gave us professional bookshop repping. In 1984 we moved into our first office, in the old Exchange Buildings on Newcastle Quayside, and employed our first publishing assistant, Brendan Cleary, a young Irish poet who'd worked for *Stand*. When Brendan had to leave, we already had Caroline Burns, a graduate from New Zealand, who'd worked in Thorne's Bookshop and was helping Bloodaxe as a volunteer. Our first publicist was Karen Geary, publicity manager of Michael Joseph in London before moving to Newcastle with her husband. Her main job was with the Northern Sinfonia. We could only afford to pay her for half a day, but she was such a whirlwind that she raised Bloodaxe's national profile in a couple of months. They were succeeded by Stephanie Brown, Brigeen Clafferty and Diane Jamieson (publicity), Sara-Jane Palmer (marketing), Cheryl Stevens and Kate Donovan (administration) and Karen Buchan (bookkeeping); other staff included Sean Dotchin, Lynn Godfrey, Christina Lambert and Matthew Taylor. The typesetting was done by Janet Hall of True North in Milburn House just up the road (later we switched to Bryan Williamson, Ed Skelly and David Stephenson).

Simon has been behind many of the initiatives which have taken Bloodaxe forward, and often I've been the one who's had to do the catching up. He was an early convert to home computers when I was still something of a Luddite; but once we had a chunky Tandy for accounts and administration, and an Amstrad for editorial work, there was no looking back. A huge daisywheel printer churned out budgets and cashflows on long swathes of hole-punched printouts, and I was producing ASCII-coded text files for conversion to typesetting. This was a transitional stage between using outside typesetters and doing all our setting in-house (from 1991).

Simon's full-time job was with the *Evening Chronicle*, but he would trot down the hill to the Quayside at lunchtimes or meet after work, and one of the benefits of his job on the paper was that he was able

to set up the *Evening Chronicle* Poetry Competition. Every year we had full-page spreads of a high circulation broadsheet newspaper filled with poems from the main and children's shortlists; as well as money prizes we sent four promising poets from the region on Arvon courses each year as part of our sponsorship. Winners included several poets who went on to publish books with Bloodaxe or other national publishers.

There was also a brief period of diversification into other kinds of books, including literary fiction, and later local and photography books (including some remarkable titles by Shirley Baker, Jimmy Forsyth and Sirkka-Liisa Konttinen which sold several thousand copies each), following a Arts Council appraisal recommending this. This was discontinued after 1990, when we decided instead to concentrate on developing a stronger specialist poetry publishing operation aimed at broadening the readership of contemporary poetry as well as offering more choice to existing poetry readers.

POETRY IN THE 80s & 90s

During the 1960s, the commercial publishers of poetry had flirted with elements of popular culture, featuring experimental writing, American poets and even translations on their lists, but by the mid-70s most of the mainstream poetry lists had become narrow and out of touch with readers and writers at grassroots level. The small presses were publishing most of the significant new poets as well as a lively mix of innovative writing inspired by American and European writing, but their output had limited distribution and wasn't widely known.

Many of the poets published by the main poetry houses had come out of or been associated with the Movement or the Group during the 50s and 60s. They had studied at Oxford or Cambridge, as had their editors. In sharp contrast with other areas of publishing, notably fiction, 95% of the writers published were men. Black and Asian poets were virtually unknown, except on the lists of American or Commonwealth publishers. The books looked unexciting, were poorly produced and overpriced, and some publishers, believing that the audience for poetry was small, only did tiny print runs of boring-looking expensive hardbacks or shoddy paperbacks which sold mostly to libraries.

It was not just the new poets who were excluded, but some major British and Irish writers, and numerous American and European poets. Women poets were notoriously absent from mainstream poetry lists and anthologies produced by male editors.

The poets who began to break this mould were the beneficiaries of the Butler Education Act, mostly from working-class backgrounds: the generation of Douglas Dunn, Tony Harrison, Seamus Heaney, Geoffrey Hill, Ted Hughes, Derek Mahon and Ken Smith, outsiders from Scotland, Belfast, the Midlands and the North, whose first collections appeared in the 60s when only a handful of women poets were published.

Their work influenced the next generation of poets, including many new writers from northern England first published by Bloodaxe during the 1980s when Bloodaxe generally thought of as a 'northern publisher'. Two of the early anthologies, my *Ten North-East Poets* (1980) and Douglas Dunn's *A Rumoured City: new poets from Hull* (1982), introduced some of these writers, and there were strong first collections from Bloodaxe by poets including David Constantine (1980), Peter Didsbury (1982), Helen Dunmore (1983), Sean O'Brien (1983), David Scott (1984) and Maura Dooley (1986). The launch of *A Rumoured City* at Hull University was especially memorable, with many of the ten poets reading for much too long as the audience and other writers grew steadily more impatient and more intoxicated. Sensing that the curry supper afterwards might best be avoided, Philip Larkin made his excuses and left, so missing the punch-up which wrecked Douglas Dunn's favourite Indian restaurant and left one poet in hospital.

The northern focus was already shifting by then, this broadening of Bloodaxe's coverage marked by other notable debuts, including those of Paul Hyland (1982), Pamela Gillilan (1986), Kathleen Jamie (1987) and Jo Shapcott (1988), as well as by the publication of established British poets such as Frances Horovitz (1983), Jenny Joseph (1986) and Stewart Conn (1987), and of Irish, European and American poets.

The growth of Bloodaxe and other specialist poetry publishers coincided with the emergence of the new generation of British and Irish poets, mostly born in the 50s and early 60s, many first published by these imprints. Twenty of these writers were later tagged 'New Generation Poets' in a promotion organised by the Poetry Society in 1994, but this particular grouping was artificial and should not be taken as a critical guide, for it excluded several key figures from that generation, including Jackie Kay (first published by Bloodaxe in 1991), Ian McMillan, Sean O'Brien, Jo Shapcott and Matthew Sweeney. The first anthology to represent this new generation was Bloodaxe's *The New Poetry* (1993), edited by Michael Hulse, David Kennedy and David Morley, which became a school set text, selling over 50,000 copies. Sean O'Brien's *The Deregulated Muse: Essays on Contemporary British & Irish Poetry* (1998) is his account of poetry in the post-war period, from the generation of Larkin and Hughes to the new poets of the 80s and 90s.

The Bloodaxe bibliography (pages 263-72) shows how the balance of the list shifted in the course of the first ten years. The first American poets published by Bloodaxe were Hart Crane (1984), Denise Levertov (1986) and C.K. Williams (1988). The first translations from Bloodaxe included books by Marin Sorescu (1983), Leopold Staff (1983), Miroslav Holub (1984), Edith Södergran (1984), Irina Ratushinskaya (1986) and Tomas Tranströmer (1987), along with Fleur Adcock's translations of medieval Latin lyrics, *The Virgin & the Nightingale* (1983).

My Bookhouse knowledge helped here. I knew that Hart Crane's work was unavailable in Britain, and acquired the licence to publish a new edition of his *Complete Poems*, in 1984. However, this sold so

well that when the licence needed to be renewed seven years later, the American publisher decided to keep the rights and distribute its own edition, which is why Hart Crane's poetry is once again hard to find in UK bookshops. I was also aware from working in the shop that Denise Levertov had a sizeable following in Britain, but not many bookshops could be bothered to order import copies of her New Directions titles. In 1986 Bloodaxe published its own *Selected Poems* of Denise Levertov, together with her latest collection, *Oblique Prayers*; and thereafter Bloodaxe published every one of her US collections.

R.S. Thomas's *Selected Poems 1946-1968* was only available in an expensive hardback from Granada which few bookshops stocked; why no other publisher had thought to acquire the paperback rights, I couldn't understand, especially when Bloodaxe went on to sell over 20,000 copies of its paperback edition. We also made what appeared at first to be the mistake of sending copies of reviews of his book to RS, who sent a curt note in response saying he did not wish to know what the English critics thought of his work. Helped by Nansi, I wrote a polite letter of apology in Welsh, which his son later told me was the first time any publisher had written to RS in Welsh. This courtesy – along with Bloodaxe's devotion to poetry and royalty cheques bigger than any he'd received from Macmillan – persuaded RS to offer all his future poetry books to Bloodaxe.

In 1985 I made the first of many visits to Ireland, meeting writers and publishers in Dublin, Belfast and Galway, including Brendan Kennelly, Peter Fallon, Edna Longley, Julie O'Callaghan and Dennis O'Driscoll, who were to figure in Bloodaxe's publishing work in various ways. I'd wanted to publish Brendan Kennelly's *Cromwell* since reading extracts from the book in *The Rialto*. Brendan is Ireland's most popular poet, but until Bloodaxe took over his publishing he had seen little income from the sales of thousands of copies of books brought out by an assortment of Irish presses. After *Cromwell* in 1987, we published *A Time for Voices: Selected Poems 1960-1990*, and then in 1991, his 400-page epic poem *The Book of Judas*, which was even more controversial in Ireland than *Cromwell*. It topped the Irish bestsellers list that Christmas and sold nearly 10,000 copies. Dublin's *Sunday Press* picked up on Kennelly's influence on U2's lyrics (his Judas says 'If you want to serve the age, betray it'), publishing a special feature with Bono reviewing *The Book of Judas* and Kennelly response to U2's latest album, *Achtung Baby*.

As well as publishing 20 titles by Brendan Kennelly in Britain and Ireland, Bloodaxe took over the publication of Rita Ann Higgins and Julie O'Callaghan from Irish presses, and added several new Irish poets to its list. Irish publishers have always found it difficult to get their poetry titles distributed in Britain, and Bloodaxe was able to help them and their writers with co-publishing arrangements. Over a ten-year period from 1986, Bloodaxe published British co-editions of many leading poets from Peter Fallon's Gallery Press, including Ciaran

Carson, Harry Clifton, Medbh McGuckian, John Montague, Eiléan Ní Chuilleanáin and James Simmons. But while this helped give the individual poets more exposure in Britain, this "cherry-picking" made booksellers less inclined to order from the rest of Gallery's catalogue. There were also co-editions with New Island Books (Sara Berkeley) and Wolfhound Press (Richard Murphy's *The Mirror Wall*).

WORLD POETRY

My introduction to contemporary European poetry came both from working on *Stand* and from reading as many books as I could find from the Penguin Modern European Poets series. A good many were inexplicably out of print, and I had to be seek them out in second-hand bookshops. Even in translation, the East European poets I was reading the the 70s and 80s communicated far more than most of the English poets I'd come across. They seemed to achieve an eloquence, a purity of utterance, which I had not experienced in quite the same way in my reading of contemporary English poetry. They weren't concerned with how things looked, but how things *were*; like the English Metaphysicals, they were obsessed with ideas and human experience, not appearances. I couldn't reconcile a number of things. Firstly, that while many of these outstanding European poets were no longer available in Britain, most of the poets who were published here were producing work which was arid and inconsequential by comparison. And if poetry publishing had reached a dead end, where had all the readers gone? When I showed books by these European poets to friends, they found the writing very exciting, and wanted to get hold of copies for themselves. Why couldn't they? The publishers weren't interested. But readers were. And many of the younger British poets wanted to read the European poets also.

This was yet another realisation which was to nourish the Bloodaxe list. In its first two decades, Bloodaxe produced new editions of a number of poets from the old Penguin European series, including Anna Akhmatova, Hans Magnus Enzensberger, Odysseus Elytis, Guillevic, Josef Hanzlík, Miroslav Holub, Eugenio Montale, Marina Tsvetayeva and Tomas Tranströmer. To these were added newly commissioned editions of other major European poets, including Attilio Bertolucci, Jaan Kaplinski, Attila József, Federico García Lorca, Osip Mandelstam and Marin Sorescu. The Scandinavian strand in Bloodaxe's publishing has included three anthologies of poetry from Finland, books by two leading Danish poets, Inger Christensen and Pia Tafdrup, and editions of several major Swedish-language poets: Gösta Ågren, Karin Boye, Tua Forsström, Edith Södergran, Tomas Tranströmer and Mirjam Tuominen. The Bloodaxe Contemporary French Poets series ran from 1992 to 2003, with ten post-war French writers published in dual-language editions, in addition to other bilingual French editions published by Bloodaxe: *The New French Poetry* (1996) edited by David Kelley and Jean Khalfa, and titles by Jacques Dupin, Pierre Reverdy,

Jean Tardieu and Paul Valéry. Contemporary Russian poetry is not readily available in the original, and several of Bloodaxe's Russian titles have appeared in bilingual editions, including books by Tatiana Shcherbina, Evgeny Rein, Elena Shvarts and Tatiana Voltskaia.

Anthologies have made it possible to make an even greater range of modern and contemporary European poetry available to readers, including two seminal titles, Adam Czerniawski's translations of Polish poets in *The Burning Forest* (1988) and *The Colonnade of Teeth: Modern Hungarian Poetry* (1996), edited by George Szirtes and George Gömöri. Many books published by Bloodaxe have given a platform to poets responding to times of oppression, war, political unrest, social division and global change, including Geremie Barmé & John Minford's *Seeds of Fire: Chinese Voices of Conscience* (1989), Ken Smith & Judi Benson's *Klaonica: poems for Bosnia* (1993), John Fairleigh's *Where the Tunnels Meet: Contemporary Romanian Poetry* (1996), Chris Agee's *Scar on the Stone: contemporary poetry from Bosnia* (1998), J. Kates's *In the Grip of Strange Times: Russian poetry in a new era* (1999) and my own *Earth Shattering: ecopoems* (2007).

Irina Ratushinskaya's *No, I'm Not Afraid* was published in May 1986 when the young poet was imprisoned in a Soviet prison camp for the 'crime' of writing and distributing poems a judge had called 'a danger to the state'. At the age of 28, she had been sentenced to seven years' hard labour. Three years into her sentence, she was in desperate health, unaware that poems smuggled out of the camp had reached the West. As well as translations by David McDuff, *No, I'm Not Afraid* included documentary material on her imprisonment provided by Amnesty International, statements by her husband and friends, and extracts from a camp diary charting life in the 'Small Zone', the special unit for women prisoners of conscience in Mordovia where she was held. Many of her poems were first incised with burnt matchsticks onto bars of soap, and then memorised. An international campaign was mounted on her behalf, spearheaded by her own poetry, which led to her release in October 1986 on the eve of the Reykjavik summit after Mikhail Gorbachev and Ronald Reagan had been given copies of her Bloodaxe collection by David Owen. Allowed to come to Britain two months later for medical treatment, she settled in London for several years before moving back to Odessa. Her first reading in Britain was organised by Bloodaxe at Newcastle Playhouse in 1987, and followed a civic reception offered by Newcastle City Council and Newcastle University. *No, I'm Not Afraid* sold over 20,000 copies.

POETRY & THE ZEITGEIST

Many other writers and books published by Bloodaxe have hit the headlines, arousing controversy and debate outside the poetry world. Tom Paulin's essay collection *Ireland & the English Crisis* (1984) was savagely attacked by Enoch Powell for its political stance. Another *cause celebre* was provided by Tony Harrison's *v.* (1985), his book-length

poem set in a vandalised cemetery in Leeds during the Miners' Strike which captured the angry, desolate mood of Britain in the mid-1980s. Two years after its publication, Richard Eyre's film of the poem sparked a national furore not over Harrison's politics but over his skinhead protagonist's use of so-called 'bad language'. Attacked by Mary Whitehouse ('this work of singular nastiness') and by Tory MPs wanting Channel 4's broadcast to be stopped, the poem attracted lurid headlines in the tabloids. 'A torrent of four-letter filth' was the *Daily Mail*'s description: 'The most explicitly sexual language yet beamed into the nation's living rooms…the crudest, most offensive word is used 17 times.' When a reporter turned up on Harrison's doorstep in Newcastle to demand a comment, the poet used the same word to send him on his way: 'Mr Harrison was unavailable for comment' was the paper's prudish version of this (with a naked model on the next page). The second edition of *v.* (1989) documents the media reaction to the film.

Ken Smith received prominent national media coverage as the first writer-in-residence at London's Wormwood Scrubs prison (1985-87), even appearing on *Wogan*, but later received a taste of tabloid fury for his poem 'Lovesong to Kate Adie'. Benjamin Zephaniah has been called Britain's 'most filmed, photographed and identifiable poet' because of his stage and television appearances, bringing dub poetry straight into British living rooms. He is both a political activist and a much loved writer for children who has appeared on *Eastenders*. He was the first person to record with the Wailers after the death of Bob Marley, in a musical tribute to Nelson Mandela which Mandela heard on his prison radio on Robben Island.

Looking back now at the poetry books published by Bloodaxe over the past 30 years, I see numerous connections between what the British and Irish poets were writing and the *zeitgeist* of those times: Tony Harrison, Linton Kwesi Johnson, Sean O'Brien, Peter Reading and Ken Smith, powerful dissenting voices in Thatcherite Britain; Ken Smith roaming Eastern Europe after the break-up of the Soviet Union, writing from Berlin when the Wall came down; Benjamin Zephaniah, tireless fighter for racial tolerance, working with Michael Mansfield QC on the Stephen Lawrence case; Moniza Alvi, Imtiaz Dharker and Jackie Kay exploring urgent questions of cultural identity, race, gender and exile; books of essays by Edna Longley and Tom Paulin addressing the Irish question from diametrically opposed positions; Selina Guinness's *New Irish Poets* (2004) responding to a period of profound social, political and cultural change in the Republic and in Northern Ireland. Many of the books are marked by particular conflicts: Tony Harrison's *The Gaze of the Gorgon* (1992), an arc of poems connecting the cataclysmic end of the Second World War in 1945 with the first Gulf War in 1991; Choman Hardi's *Life for Us* (2004), charting lives marked by displacement, terror and flight from Kurdistan; Ciaran Carson's *The Irish for No* (1987/1988) and *Belfast Confetti* (1989/1990), an insider's view of Belfast before and during the Troubles.

The American poets too have been 'writing to the moment', to use Tom Paulin's phrase: Elizabeth Alexander and Naomi Shihab Nye on race, cultural identity and survival; Deborah Garrison and Galway Kinnell on 9/11; Brian Turner's harrowing, first-hand account of the Iraq War in *Here, Bullet* (2005/2007). In many ways their poetry has got much more under the skin of how it has felt to live through these changing times. Philip Levine, the authentic voice of America's urban poor in *Stranger to Nothing* (2006), chronicles the lives of the people he grew up with and worked with in Detroit, while Fred Voss is still living factory life as a machinist in *Carnegie Hall with Tin Walls* (1998).

C.K. Williams's *Collected Poems* (2006) takes us inside every decade from the 60s ('in those days there was still the race thing. / It was just at the time of civil rights: the neighborhood I was living in was mixed') right up to the present ('I was thinking, / as I often do these days of war'), but his focus is as much the self as the world. Many other American poets published by Bloodaxe are writing profound, essential poems, addressing the heart, spirit and mind to illuminate the human condition: Stephen Berg, Carolyn Forché, Tess Gallagher, Jack Gilbert, Ellen Hinsey, Jane Hirshfield, Galway Kinnell, Li-Young Lee, Denise Levertov, W.S. Merwin, Mary Oliver, Gjertrud Schnackenberg, Anne Stevenson and Chase Twichell (as well as the Canadian Alden Nowlan). And then there are other poets whose humanity is expressed through wit, linguistic verve and incisive social awareness: Dan Chiasson, Stephen Dobyns, Tony Hoagland, Julie O'Callaghan, Anne Rouse, Eva Salzman and the multi-faceted C.D. Wright.

In making the work of this particular range of poets available in Britain, Bloodaxe has helped correct the distorted and outdated picture readers would otherwise have had of contemporary American poetry. Anthologies don't help: the available selections of 'contemporary American poets' are far from contemporary, and the staggeringly high cost of permission fees charged for work by American poets has discouraged British publishers from commissioning new anthologies.

The major figures in the modernist canon are published by Faber and Carcanet. The New York "school" from Frank O'Hara to John Ashbery and his acolytes is well represented on the Carcanet list, as are a lively variety of American postmodernists, while Faber publish John Berryman, Robert Lowell and Sylvia Plath. However, apart from a few other poets published by Anvil (Donald Justice), Arc (David Baker, Thomas Lux, J.D. McClatchy), Cape (Mark Doty, Sharon Olds, with the Canadian Anne Carson), Carcanet (Louise Glück, Brigit Pegeen Kelly, Robert Pinsky, Mark Strand), Faber (August Kleinzahler, Charles Simic, Frederick Seidel) and Picador (Billy Collins, Yusef Komunyakaa), much of the most distinctive, powerful and innovative American poetry of the past 30 years would be unknown to readers here were it not for Bloodaxe's efforts. Frustratingly, very few books by these writers, either from Bloodaxe or from the other publishers,

has received much review coverage in Britain, and yet much of the most profound and original poetry written in English over the past 30 years has been by American poets.

CHANGING POETRY

In developing the Bloodaxe list over this period, I've tried to offer readers as wide a range as possible of contemporary poetry by all kinds of writers. One of Bloodaxe's most significant achievements has been to transform the publishing opportunities for women poets, not *because* they are women poets but because they are outstanding writers by any standard. For many years Bloodaxe has been unusual in having a poetry list which is 50:50 male: female. After starting from scratch, we've ended up with a list which reflects the population not the power of male patronage. The only positive discrimination I've exercised has been in commissioning anthologies including Carol Rumens's *New Women Poets* (1990), Linda France's *Sixty Women Poets* (1993), Maura Dooley's *Making for Planet Alice* (1997), and most recently, Deryn Rees-Jones's *Modern Women Poets* (2005), published as the companion anthology to her critical study *Consorting with Angels* (2005). While it is regrettable that such books are still necessary, they have been enormously valuable, and a number of poets have said that they only started taking their own writing seriously after reading one or other of these titles, especially Jeni Couzyn's *Bloodaxe Book of Contemporary Women Poets* (1985), published at a time when very little poetry by women was readily available to readers. It was adopted as a GCSE set text, and went on to sell over 40,000 copies.

As Bloodaxe has grown and expanded its publishing, it has been responsive to the changing literatures of Britain and of other countries. Talented writers have been emerging from all kinds of different backgrounds as Britain has become more culturally and ethnically diverse, and their poetry has evolved in ways which appeal to broader-based audiences. Enlightened government funding for the arts has enabled Bloodaxe to work for the benefit of writers and readers for 30 years, and we have seen it as our moral duty to respond to these changes in our literature and readership. But we have taken a pro-active stance in publishing and promoting the work of writers from diverse ethnic and cultural backgrounds not out of political correctness but because we have always had two primary concerns as poetry publishers: literary quality and broadening the readership of contemporary poetry. The diverse pool of writers Bloodaxe draws upon is the key to this. Bloodaxe has always been concerned to publish a range of writing which properly reflects the strengths of contemporary poetry from Britain and around the world, and which will appeal not just to the core poetry readership but to all kinds of readers from all kinds of backgrounds.

Bloodaxe has published some of the finest writers in the British-Caribbean diaspora – such as John Agard, James Berry, Kamau Brathwaite, Jean 'Binta' Breeze, Martin Carter, Fred d'Aguiar, Linton

Kwesi Johnson and Benjamin Zephaniah – as well as E.A. Markham's landmark Caribbean anthology *Hinterland* (1989). Our South Asian poets include Moniza Alvi, Imtiaz Dharker and Arundhathi Subramaniam, and Jeet Thayil's *Bloodaxe Book of Contemporary Indian Poets* (2008) looks set to be another seminal anthology. Other poets published by Bloodaxe include Bernardine Evaristo, Jackie Kay, Choman Hardi (from Kurdistan), Jack Mapanje (Malawi), Yang Lian and Yi Sha (China). Bloodaxe's international list includes not just numerous European poets but many poets from diverse ethnic backgrounds from other parts of the world, including Maram al-Massri (Syria), Aimé Césaire (Martinique), Mahmoud Darwish and Taha Muhammad Ali (Palestine), Salah Stétié (Lebanon) and the African American poet Elizabeth Alexander. The list also includes many writers who are Jewish or of Jewish extraction, such as Ruth Fainlight, Jenny Joseph, Denise Levertov, Philip Levine, Joanne Limburg, Evgeny Rein, Eva Salzman and George Szirtes.

CHANGING BLOODAXE

Nansi Thirsk came into her own when we were hit by the collapses of three distributors over a ten-year period. In 1985 Noonan Hurst went into liquidation, owing Bloodaxe over £9,000, a considerable sum at that time, amounting to three months' worth of sales income they had collected from bookshops but not passed on to us. This was our first experience of illegal trading by a company contracted to carry out our distribution. Bloodaxe had no working capital at that time, and was in immediate danger of going under because we couldn't pay the printer for large quantities of books just delivered. We had to stop publishing immediately and set about trying to raise funds with appeals to readers on the mailing list to buy books. One amazing woman sent a cheque for £1000 with a note on a postcard saying she 'hoped this would help'. Bloodaxe authors helped by buying up stocks of their own books.

Six months later, with some books supported by loans, we started up again, working with a new distributor, J.M. Dent Distribution in Letchworth. In 1986, Bloodaxe and Anvil approached the Arts Council for help in forming a new sales agency called Password (later re-named Signature), which took over the bookshop marketing work for a diverse group of small or independent poetry publishers. But as Bloodaxe's publishing grew, so did our marketing needs. Password was unable to give the larger imprints the nationwide coverage they needed without neglecting the individual requirements of the smaller presses.

We felt secure with Dent, but this was a distribution company created by a management buyout from the Dent publishing group. In 1988 Dent Distribution collapsed, owing Bloodaxe over £13,000. This time we were more successful in clawing back some of the debt. We took the opportunity to restructure our whole marketing operation, moving sales representation from Password to Drake Marketing

Services in Oxfordshire, and using Harper & Row in Plymouth for warehousing and distribution.

When Harper & Row became Plymbridge Distribution after another managemement buyout, Drake became nervous, and persuaded the publishers they represented to transfer their distribution to a new company they set up called Oxon Distribution. In the autumn of 1991, Oxon's service started to deteriorate, with late payments, complaints from bookshops and inefficient service. We knew the warning signs. After a series of heated publishers' meetings and belligerent correspondence and phone calls, we decided to act before it was too late. Nansi surprised their lawyers by obtaining an injunction against Oxon in the High Court, forcing them to pay half of the £54,000 they owed us into court while the dispute was resolved; when another publisher took legal action against them the following week, Oxon went into liquidation. We eventually recovered the money held by the court, and with Northern Arts guaranteeing the rest of the debt, Bloodaxe could carry on publishing. Plymbridge did not go bankrupt until 2003.

Each of these distributor collapses involved considerable disruption and extra costs on top of the bad debts tied up with the bankruptcies. Each time we had to rescue our stock from the warehouse. Container lorries and fork lift trucks had to be organised, and the administrator persuaded that the stock belonged to the publishers and should be released. After Oxon, we tried a new system, with books being warehoused with Clipper Distribution in Hampshire as well as in large storerooms attached to a new Bloodaxe office at Hawthorn House behind Newcastle Central Station. We established a sister company, Pandon Press, to take over the marketing work previously done by Umbrella, Password and Drake. Pandon managed a group of freelance sales reps visiting bookshops to solicit orders, and did the invoicing and credit control, with Clipper paid commission for warehousing, despatch and distribution software.

There was no longer any risk of losing our sales income to a distributor's bankruptcy, but the operation required more administrative staff. Then our landlord's business collapsed overnight, and we found ourselves occupying one end of an eerily empty office complex for several months. Our team in the Hawthorn House period included, at various times (as well as Karen Buchan), Andrew McAllister (assistant editor and publicist), Val Hannan and Salma Khan (production), Linda Healy (administration and rights), Margaret Akuamoah, Dennis Healy, Pat Manning and Stuart Turner (distribution), and Colin Ford, Mick Gill, Ryan Hewitt and Andrew Wildish (warehouse).

The main store-room was deluged twice, once from a burst watermain behind the station which cascaded down the car park and into our building, ruining all the lowest boxes of books in the stacks; and later from an overhead pipe which burst after a winter freeze-up, soaking all the top boxes in the stacks. It seemed we couldn't win either way, and when the new landlords quite properly decided that

the dilapidated premises needed upgrading, we were on the move again. The proposed new rent for the renovated offices set us thinking about other ways of housing and running the business.

Several things then came together to bring about the next big change in the Bloodaxe operation. Firstly, we realised that our turnover was now big enough for a large and financially secure distributor to be interested in taking over our warehousing and distribution; contracting all marketing and distribution via Pandon also offered financial protection to Bloodaxe. With distribution taken off our hands, we no longer needed our city centre premises (for which the rent was set to double), nor did we need as many staff to run everything. Next, Nansi had been offered her family law business in North Wales following the deaths of her father and uncle. By this time Simon had left the *Evening Chronicle* to work for a children's charity, and was working part-time for Bloodaxe as well as teaching marketing at a business college. I was finding it more and more difficult to do most of the editing and production work while also managing the day-to-day running of an increasingly complex business operation.

Our solution was to transfer the distribution to Littlehampton Book Services in Sussex, and split the publishing work between two offices, one in Northumberland and one in Wales. In 1995 Simon took over the business management and became full-time chairman managing the sales, marketing and finance side of the operation from Pandon's office in Bala; fortunately, our marketing manager Alison Davis was willing to move with the job, and Ruth Lewis joined as bookkeeper. At the same time I set up a new base for editorial, rights and publicity on a farm where I was living at Elrington in Hexhamshire. Peg Osterman joined as rights and publicity manager from Chicago Review Press, having just moved to Durham with her English husband.

The Bala office has since been the mainstay of the business part of the operation, with Simon at the helm, assisted by Alison and later Rita Black in sales and marketing, and by Ruth, Janice Dodd, Francis Mills and now Bethan Jones in finance. But the Northumberland office has been moved and expanded three times. The first of these moves was in 1997, to Otterburn, where Christine Macgregor took over publicity in 1998 and Peg Osterman stayed on to do rights work. Christine had moved back to Northumberland after working in London for art publisher Laurence King for some years. Also in 1998, the Forestry Commission offered us an office in a converted railway signal box attached to the old station at Falstone below Kielder Dam, where Liz Johnson and then Sally Best were publishing assistants. The other half of the building housed a cold store for deer, which the rangers brought down from the forest on Friday mornings, dumping rows of carcases along the old station platform. This was one of several deer stores, and when the culling arrangements changed and all the carcases were to be taken to one central store elsewhere, the Old Signal Box was put up for sale.

In 2000, we moved to our permanent office in the Tarset valley behind Highgreen Manor, to a building converted from a former granary and stable, where Suzanne Fairless-Aitken took over rights and permissions. The assistant's work was expanded first by Libby Marks and latterly by Rebecca Hodkinson, who works with Christine on publicity. We've also been well served during maternity periods by Kate Kirsopp-Reed in publicity and by Catherine Taylor in rights.

MUSICAL CHAIRS

Largely because of the difficulties with distributors and a consequent lack of working capital, the 1980s and 90s were a period of instability for Bloodaxe's publishing. When sales dipped, books due to be published a few months later had to be delayed. The publication schedule would go through wholesale changes in the course of a year. Some of the poets first published by Bloodaxe were wooed to join the supposedly more stable poetry lists of the larger trade publishers, including Simon Armitage (Faber), Glyn Maxwell (Faber), Sean O'Brien (OUP) and Jo Shapcott (OUP). While this always came as a blow, I could understand the writers' reasons for wanting to be with a more secure publisher: they made their living from work related to the books they published. As it turned out, some of these moves were less than secure: Glyn Maxwell was dropped by Faber after just one book (only to be picked up by Picador), and OUP made the extraordinary decision in 1999 to shut down its poetry list, not because it was making a loss but because it wasn't generating enough profit, and the reason for that was self-evident to the poets: their marketing was totally inadequate.

However, many more poets stayed with Bloodaxe, and their loyalty was a great encouragement as we tried to make Bloodaxe a much more effective poetry publishing house. Our marketing is tailored to the needs of a specialist poetry imprint, and integral to this has been a strategy of designing, devising, commissioning and accepting books which appeal not just to existing poetry readers but to people who might read more poetry with the right kind of encouragement. Most of the poets have felt that this helps their own work as well as addressing the need to broaden the readership of contemporary poetry at a critical time. Following the abolition of the Net Book Agreement in 1995, bookshops now have to compete with the supermarkets for the sales of the bestsellers from which they derive most of their income, with the result that their stock range of poetry and many other kinds of books has been decimated. Despite this, Bloodaxe has persevered and has become highly effective in all areas of marketing, especially press and radio publicity, rights and readings, as well as maintaining high production standards and operating a pricing policy which has meant the books have remained affordable.

As a result of this strengthening of the operation, Bloodaxe was soon the winner in poetry publishing's game of musical chairs. In this, the music stops whenever a publisher goes under or axes its poetry

list. Then all the poets run about frantically looking for a new home for their work. The music starts up again but comes to another sudden halt when a poetry editor leaves and is replaced by a new broom with different tastes or with friends to be published. Or sometimes a poetry editor leaves and isn't replaced for a year or more, which sends all the poets into a mad panic. More rarely, a large publishing house has a new director who decides he wants a prestigious poetry list, and appoints a well-known poet as his poetry editor, giving him a budget like a football manager to buy in the players he wants, which means luring them from other teams as well as nurturing new talent. Not all the poets playing for the different teams remain in the game: some don't stay match fit, or they fall out with the manager, and at the end of the season their contracts aren't renewed, or they storm off. (Or more tragically, they are so disheartened that they stop writing, or give up on publishing their work, which is what happened to Freda Downie after the closure of the Secker poetry list and her subsequent rejection by OUP.)

Thus Bloodaxe lost Ian Duhig and Kathleen Jamie to the new Picador list, Linton Kwesi Johnson to Penguin and John Hartley Williams to Cape, but gained one poet from Allison & Busby, one from Canongate, one from Cape, three from Chatto, two from Dent, three from Faber, two from Heinemann, four from Hutchinson, one from Macmillan, ten from Oxford University Press, two from Paladin, two from Peterloo, three from Secker, one from Serpent's Tail and two from Virago. In the early years most of the poets published by Bloodaxe in book form were either new writers or American and European poets. Then, during the last 15 years of the 20th century, over 30 of Britain's leading poets decided to bring their work to Bloodaxe, including Fleur Adcock, John Agard, Gillian Allnutt, Moniza Alvi, Elizabeth Bartlett, Connie Bensley, James Berry, Jean 'Binta' Breeze, Stewart Conn, Ruth Fainlight, Roy Fisher, Andrew Greig, Philip Gross, Selima Hill, Jenny Joseph, Barry MacSweeney, Jack Mapanje, Adrian Mitchell, Peter Reading, Carol Rumens, Lawrence Sail, Carole Satyamurti, Penelope Shuttle, Anne Stevenson, George Szirtes, R.S. Thomas, Susan Wicks and Benjamin Zephaniah. Bloodaxe also took over the publication of Basil Bunting's work in 2000, following the OUP debacle, and published two collected editions of J.H. Prynne's poetry in 1999 and 2005 after he had decided that work only previously available in limited editions from small presses should be made available to a wider readership.

Bringing together the work of these poets with books by writers published from the beginning has greatly strengthened Bloodaxe's effectiveness as a poetry publishing house. Anthologies serving both broad and specialist readerships have provided further stability. When Bloodaxe was having to cope with distributor collapses and unreliable income from sales or rights, it was difficult to plan more than six months ahead, and books were frequently delayed, often more than

once. But now Bloodaxe has become a much more stable publishing operation – steadied by Simon working full-time as head of the business – a publication schedule is set well in advance and followed.

REACHING MORE READERS

Over the years Simon has developed our thinking about widening the audience for poetry, and I have responded with ideas for anthologies or groups of books to take this forward. For some time he tried to involve other poetry publishers in these initiatives, believing that the more of this kind of work we did jointly, the more we could achieve collectively in broadening the readership of poetry in Britain, which would help all the poets and publishers as well as the readers. But everyone else seemed to want to just carry on doing what they had always done. So we went it alone, and I came up with *Staying Alive: real poems for unreal times* (2002), which became Britain's bestselling poetry book within a fortnight of publication.

When I first had the idea for *Staying Alive*, it was for a diverse and lively book to introduce new readers to contemporary poetry as well as to show existing poetry readers a wider range of poems from around the world than is generally available from British poetry publishers. I had no idea then that the book would be championed so enthusiastically by readers, or savaged in furious, apparently co-ordinated attacks by snooty academics who were angered especially by endorsements on the cover by 'a mindboggling selection of famous people' (Mark Ford, *Guardian*). 'There are readerships and there are markets,' declared Michael Schmidt in *PN Review*. 'There is selling poetry and selling poetry out.' Writing in *Poetry Review*, Robert Potts and David Herd howled from the same songsheet: 'There is a difference between selling poetry and selling it out.' Six years later, elitist critics are still berating me for *Staying Alive* in lectures printed in *PN Review*.

There's a big a difference between dumbing down and reaching out to new readers, which is what Bloodaxe did in its publication and promotion of *Staying Alive*. Those "celebrity endorsements" scorned by Mark Ford and his chums were vital to the book's success. John Berger, Jane Campion, Mia Farrow, Anne Michaels, Philip Pullman and others who wanted to help Bloodaxe with *Staying Alive* are not just famous people, they are avid readers and passionate advocates of poetry. Their comments helped us reach thousands of people interested in fiction, film, theatre and other arts who until then hadn't been sufficiently engaged by contemporary poetry. We included their quotes with sample poems from the anthology in a brochure sent out to a quarter of a million people, using a variety of mailing lists, from *Granta* to Tate Modern. And because we had those endorsements, the bookshops were willing to put in big orders, and to stack up copies on the display tables with the latest paperback novels.

Staying Alive reached a broad popular readership, and was Britain's no.1 poetry title for five consecutive months, displacing the perennial

bestseller *The Nation's Favourite Poems*. It has sold over 100,000 copies in Britain and over 30,000 in America, where it was launched in New York in a reading by Meryl Streep and Claire Danes with Paul Muldoon and other poets to a packed house in the Cooper Union's 700-seater auditorium (where Whitman listened to Abraham Lincoln's speeches). It was followed in 2004 by a sequel anthology, *Being Alive* (with endorsements by Van Morrison, Kamila Shamsie and Meryl Streep); a third volume in the "trilogy", *Being Human*, is planned for 2009.

Staying Alive was Bloodaxe's response to the findings of a readership survey commissioned by the Arts Council, *Rhyme and Reason: developing contemporary poetry* (2000), a thoroughly researched and alarming survey which others seemed more inclined to disbelieve, dispute or disregard. This presented a damning picture of how poetry was viewed by the general public: how people whose knowledge of modern poetry was limited would dismiss it as obscure, difficult, dull, boring or pretentious. Modern poetry, according to their comments, was irrelevant and incomprehensible, so they didn't bother with it, not even readers of literary fiction and people interested in other arts which use language, such as theatre and film; and not even people who read Shakespeare and the classics: one of the most surprising findings of that research was that only 5% of the poetry books sold in British bookshops were by living poets.

The anthology was my attempt to show all those people who love literature and language and traditional poetry that contemporary poetry *is* relevant to their own lives; and that much of it is lively, imaginative and accessible to intelligent readers who might not have given it much of a chance before. And that didn't involve "dumbing down", but choosing lucid poems to entice new readers. There's no conflict here between "access" and excellence.

And *Staying Alive* won thousands of new readers for poetry largely because of word of mouth: reader power. Those readers didn't just buy one copy for themselves, they bought more and more to give to friends and family as presents. *Staying Alive* is still being discovered by new readers. Six years after the book appeared, I'm still receiving letters, postcards and e-mails expressing people's appreciation, messages of support and thanks, all saying how much *Staying Alive* had helped or stimulated them and fired up their interest in poetry.

Staying Alive was not a one-off phenomenon for Bloodaxe. In any year we will not just be working on the latest collections by our poets, but researching and trying out new ways to take contemporary poetry to a broader audience. In 1995 Bloodaxe began a project with the British Council to originate audio recordings for the *Poetry Quartets* series of cassettes which eventually covered 36 poets on nine double-cassettes; however, by the time the last of these appeared in 2004, CDs had taken over.

Two of Bloodaxe's initiatives were inspired in part by Penguin Modern Poets. The Bloodaxe World Poets series features selections

of work by major modern writers whose work appeared in *Staying Alive* and its companion anthologies, and has so far included titles by Mary Oliver, Alden Nowlan, Jane Kenyon, Li-Young Lee and Naomi Shihab Nye. This was followed by the Bloodaxe Poetry Introductions series, in which each book covers four poets in depth, with substantial selections of each writer's poetry introduced by background material, including profiles, interviews, essays and commentary by the poets.

In 2000 Bloodaxe received funding from the Millennium Festival and the National Lottery through the Arts Council for an educational initiative to build a stronger awareness of 20th century poetry. This involved the publication of two books, Edna Longley's *Bloodaxe Book of 20th Century Poetry from Britain and Ireland*, an anthology of 60 poets presented with informative introductions, and *Strong Words: modern poets on modern poetry*, a book of key essays on poetry by poets (half of these specially commissioned), edited by W.N. Herbert and Matthew Hollis. The books were presented at schools conferences and university seminars, and both have quickly become set texts.

In 2001 Jo Shapcott gave the first of the Newcastle/Bloodaxe poetry lectures at Newcastle University. Several other poets have since spoken about the craft and practice of poetry to audiences drawn from both the city and the university. These public lectures are later published in book form by Bloodaxe, giving readers everywhere the opportunity to discover what leading poets have to say about their own subject.

Other initiatives to introduce contemporary poetry to new readers have included working with reading groups in Nottingham and in libraries across the West Midlands. And in Birmingham, Jonathan Davidson's team at Book Communications have produced three touring theatre shows which have taken live poetry performances to venues across Britain: the first drew on *Staying Alive*, the second on *Being Alive*, and the most recent, *Changing Lives*, was a theatre piece using poems from books published by Bloodaxe over the past 30 years.

In Person is the latest and most innovative of Bloodaxe's poetry initiatives. Because we've done all the film and DVD work ourselves, the project is affordable for a small publishing house (with some help from Arts Council England). We have also posted sample videos from *In Person* on YouTube, linked to the Bloodaxe website, and this will continue with subsequent recordings, enabling Bloodaxe to promote contemporary poetry to a new online generation.

For 30 years Bloodaxe has been fostering a poetry revolution in Britain which has helped to reconnect poets with their grassroots readership. This revolution would not have succeeded had it not been for the support of both the readers and the writers. Poetry readings have helped feed the growth of Bloodaxe's publishing over three decades. *In Person* has symbolic resonance with this: the poets have been speaking to readers through their writing, but now new technology makes it possible for them to be seen and heard reading their work all over the world.

BLOODAXE BOOKS BIBLIOGRAPHY: 1978-2008

All titles published were poetry, except where shown otherwise:
F FICTION   LC LITERARY CRITICISM   P PROSE   V VERSE DRAMA
All titles were published in paperback only, except where shown otherwise:
† HARDBACK   ‡ HARDBACK & PAPERBACK   § PAMPHLET   ☆ OTHER MEDIA
* Asterisked titles were first collections (book or pamphlet)

1978
Ken Smith *Tristan Crazy* §

1979
Fleur Adcock *Below Loughrigg* §
John Cassidy *Changes of Light* §
John Cassidy *The Fountain* §
* Vincent Morrison *The Season of Comfort* §

1980
Neil Astley (ed.) *Ten North-East Poets*
Basil Bunting: *Basil Bunting reads 'Briggflatts'*
☆ LP RECORD
* David Constantine *A Brightness to Cast Shadows*
* Stephen Dunstan *Tarot Poems*
* Tony Flynn *A Strange Routine*
John Oldham *Selected Poems*
* Nigel Wells *The Winter Festivals*

1981
Tony Harrison *A Kumquat for John Keats* §
Tony Harrison *U.S. Martial* §
Tom Paulin & Noel Connor *The Book of Juniper* POETRY & ART §
Ken Smith *Burned Books*
Ken Smith *Fox Running* §

1982
John Cassidy *Night Cries*
* Peter Didsbury *The Butchers of Hull*
Douglas Dunn *Europa's Lover* §
Douglas Dunn (ed.) *A Rumoured City: new poets from Hull*
* Paul Hyland *Poems of Z*
Carol Rumens *Scenes from the Gingerbread House* §
* Matt Simpson *Making Arrangements*
Ken Smith *Abel Baker Charlie Delta Epic Sonnets* §
Ken Smith *The Poet Reclining: Selected Poems 1962-1980* ‡

1983
Fleur Adcock *The Virgin & the Nightingale: Medieval Latin Poems* ‡
Martin Booth *Looking for the Rainbow Sign* §
Noel Connor (ed.) *Talitha Cumi* POETRY/ART
David Constantine *Watching for Dolphins*

* Helen Dunmore *The Apple Fall*
Ruth Fainlight *Climates* §
Eva Figes *Days* F
Frances Horovitz *Snow Light, Water Light* §
Shena Mackay *An Advent Calendar* F
* Sean O'Brien *The Indoor Park*
Marin Sorescu *Selected Poems*
Leopold Staff *An Empty Room*

1984
Hart Crane *Complete Poems*
Miroslav Holub *On the Contrary* ‡
Paul Hyland *The Stubborn Forest*
B.S. Johnson *House Mother Normal* F
Tom Paulin *Ireland & the English Crisis* LC‡
* David Scott *A Quiet Gathering*
Edith Södergran *Complete Poems* ‡

1985
David Constantine *Davies* F†
Angela Carter *Come unto these Yellow Sands: Four Radio Plays* RADIO DRAMA‡
Jeni Couzyn *Life by Drowning: Selected Poems*
Jeni Couzyn (ed.) *The Bloodaxe Book of Contemporary Women Poets* ‡
Tony Harrison *Dramatic Verse 1973-1985* V†
Tony Harrison *The Fire-Gap* §
Tony Harrison *v.* POETRY & PHOTOGRAPHY‡
Frances Horovitz *Collected Poems* ‡
Sirkka-Liisa Konttinen *Byker* PHOTOGRAPHY

1986
* Fleur Adcock *Hotspur* POETRY/ART §
Fleur Adcock, Maura Dooley, S.J. Litherland, Jill Maughan *Fourpack #1*
* Maura Dooley *Ivy Leaves & Arrows* §
* John Drew *The Lesser Vehicle*
Helen Dunmore *The Sea Skater*
G.F. Dutton *Squaring the Waves*
Lauris Edmond *Seasons and Creatures*
Jimmy Forsyth *Scotswood Road* PHOTOGRAPHY
* Pamela Gillilan *That Winter*
* Douglas Houston *With the Offal Eaters*
Andrew Greig & Kathleen Jamie *A Flame in Your Heart*
Jenny Joseph *Persephone* F‡
Denise Levertov *Oblique Prayers*
Denise Levertov *Selected Poems*
* S.J. Litherland *The Long Interval* §

263

Edna Longley *Poetry in the Wars* LC‡
* Jill Maughan *Ghosts at four o'clock* §
Eiléan Ní Chuilleanáin *The Second Voyage:*
  Selected Poems ‡
Irina Ratushinskaya *No, I'm Not Afraid* ‡
James Simmons *Poems 1956-1986* ‡
Ken Smith *Terra*
R.S. Thomas *Selected Poems 1946-1968*

1987

Neil Astley (ed.) *Bossy Parrot: Newcastle*
  Evening Chronicle children's poetry
  competition anthology
Sid Chaplin *In Blackberry Time* F‡
David Constantine *Madder*
Stewart Conn *In the Kibble Palace:*
  New & Selected Poems
Peter Didsbury *The Classical Farm*
* Steve Ellis *Home and Away*
* Arthur Gibson *Boundless Function*
Miroslav Holub: *The Fly*
Brendan Kennelly *Cromwell*
* Kathleen Jamie *The Way We Live*
Sean O'Brien *The Frighteners*
Ken Smith *A Book of Chinese Whispers* P
Ken Smith *Wormwood*
Marin Sorescu *The Biggest Egg in the World*
* Martin Stokes *The First Death of Venice*
Tomas Tranströmer *Collected Poems*
Marina Tsvetayeva *Selected Poems*
Alan Wearne *Out Here*
John Hartley Williams *Bright River Yonder*

1988

Fleur Adcock *Meeting the Comet* §†
Neil Astley (ed.) *Poetry with an Edge*
Martin Bell *Complete Poems* ‡
Ciaran Carson *The Irish for No*
Jaroslav Cejka, Michal Cernik & Karel Sys
  The New Czech Poetry
Jack Clemo *Selected Poems*
Adam Czerniawski (ed.) *The Burning Forest:*
  Modern Polish Poetry
Helen Dunmore *The Raw Garden*
Philip Gross & Sylvia Kantaris *The Air*
  Mines of Mistila
Vladimír Janovic *The House of the Tragic Poet*
* Jean Hanff Korelitz *The Properties of Breath*
Denise Levertov *Breathing the Water*
Irina Ratushinskaya *Pencil Letter* ‡
Carol Rumens *The Greening of the Snow Beach*
* Jo Shapcott *Electroplating the Baby*
Nigel Wells *Wilderness / Just Bounce*
C.K. Williams *Flesh and Blood*
C.K. Williams *Poems 1963-1983*

1989

Anna Akhmatova *Selected Poems*
* Simon Armitage *Zoom!*
Shirley Baker *Street Photographs: Manchester*
  & Salford PHOTOGRAPHY
Geremie Barmé & John Minford (eds.) *Seeds*
  of Fire: Chinese Voices of Conscience
John Cassidy *Walking on Frogs*
* George Charlton *Nightshift Workers*
Richard Falkner (ed.) *Tyneside: where's*
  the buzz P
Tony Harrison *v.* SECOND EDITION
Friedrich Hölderlin *Selected Poems*
Sylvia Kantaris *Dirty Washing: New &*
  Selected Poems ‡
Sirkka-Liisa Konttinen *Step by Step*
  PHOTOGRAPHY
* Marion Lomax [Robyn Bolam]
  The Peepshow Girl
* Peter McDonald *Biting the Wax*
E.A. Markham (ed.) *Hinterland: Caribbean*
  Poetry from the West Indies & Britain ‡
John Montague *Mount Eagle* ‡
Richard Murphy *The Mirror Wall* ‡
David McDuff (ed.) *Ice Around Our Lips:*
  Finland Swedish Poetry
* Deborah Randall *The Sin Eater*
David Scott *Playing for England*
* Pauline Stainer *The Honeycomb*

1990

Neil Astley (ed.) *Dear Next Prime Minister* P
Connie Bensley *Central Reservations:*
  New & Selected Poems
Gordon Brown (ed.) *High on the Walls:*
  A Morden Tower Anthology
Ciaran Carson *Belfast Confetti*
Jack Common *Kiddar's Luck* F
Odysseus Elytis *The Sovereign Sun:*
  Selected Poems
Sylva Fischerová *The Tremor of Racehorses:*
  Selected Poems
Tua Forsström *Snow Leopard*
Andrew Greig *The Order of the Day*
Dorothy Hewett *Alice in Wormland:*
  Selected Poems
Miroslav Holub *Poems Before & After:*
  Collected English Translations ‡
Brendan Kennelly *A Time for Voices:*
  Selected Poems 1960-1990 ‡
Joolz *Emotional Terrorism*
* Gerald Mangan *Waiting for the Storm*
* Glyn Maxwell *Tale of the Mayor's Son*
John Montague *New Selected Poems* ‡
John Montague *The Rough Field*

Eugenio Montale & Jeremy Reed
The Coastguard's House
Carol Rumens (ed.) *New Women Poets*
Matt Simpson *An Elegy for the Galosherman:
New & Selected Poems*
Ken Smith *The heart, the border*
R.S. Thomas *Counterpoint* ‡
John Hartley Williams *Cornerless People*

1991
Neil Astley (ed.) *Tony Harrison* LC‡
Noel Connor (ed.) *Confounded Language*
David Constantine *Selected Poems*
Stephen Dobyns *Cemetery Nights*
Maura Dooley *Explaining Magnetism*
* Ian Duhig *The Bradford Count*
Helen Dunmore *Short Days, Long Nights:
New & Selected Poems*
G.F. Dutton *The Concrete Garden*
Alistair Elliot (tr.) *French Love Poems*
Victoria Forde *The Poetry of Basil Bunting* LC‡
* Elizabeth Garrett *The Rule of Three*
John Greening *The Tutankhamun Variations*
Tony Harrison *A Cold Coming* §†
John Hughes *Negotiations with the Chill Wind*
Linton Kwesi Johnson *Tings an Times:
Selected Poems*
* Jackie Kay *The Adoption Papers*
Brendan Kennelly *The Book of Judas* ‡
Brendan Kennelly/Euripides *Medea* V ‡
Herbert Lomas (ed.) *Contemporary Finnish
Poetry*
Osip Mandelstam *The Moscow Notebooks*
Adrian Mitchell *Greatest Hits*
David Morley *Under the Rainbow: Writers
& Artists in Schools* P
Julie O'Callaghan *What's What*
György Petri *Night Song of the Personal
Shadow: Selected Poems*
Simon Rae & Willie Rushton *Soft Targets*
Pierre Reverdy *Selected Poems*
William Scammell (ed.) *The New Lake Poets*
Piotr Sommer *Things to Translate*
Rabindranath Tagore *I Won't Let You Go:
Selected Poems*
Jean Tardieu *The River Underground:
Selected Poems & Prose*
* Fred Voss *Goodstone*

1992
Gösta Ågren *A Valley in the Midst of Violence:
Selected Poems*
Simon Armitage *Xanadu*
Neil Astley & Mark Lavender (eds.) *Wordworks*
Stephen Berg *New & Selected Poems*

Yves Bonnefoy *On the Motion and Immobility
of Douve*
Kamau Brathwaite *Middle Passages*
René Char *The Dawn Breakers*
Harry Clifton *The Desert Route: Selected Poems*
Stewart Conn *The Luncheon of the Boating
Party*
Jacques Dupin *Selected Poems*
Lauris Edmond *New and Selected Poems*
Tony Flynn *Body Politic*
* Linda France *Red*
Tony Harrison *The Gaze of the Gorgon* ‡
Miroslav Holub *The Jingle Bell Principle* P
Paul Hyland *Getting into Poetry* P
Jenny Joseph *Selected Poems*
Brendan Kennelly *Breathing Spaces:
Early Poems* ‡
Federico García Lorca *Selected Poems*
George MacBeth & Martin Booth (eds.)
The Book of Cats
Medbh McGuckian *Marconi's Cottage*
Glyn Maxwell *Out of the Rain*
Henri Michaux *Spaced, Displaced*
Micheal O'Siadhail *Hail! Madam Jazz:
New & Selected Poems* ‡
Irina Ratushinskaya *Dance with a Shadow* ‡
Lawrence Sail *Out of Land: New & Selected
Poems*
* Eva Salzman *The English Earthquake*
Sappho *Poems & Fragments*
Lemn Sissay *Rebel Without Applause*
Dave Smith *Night Pleasures: New & Selected
Poems*
Pauline Stainer *Sighting the Slave Ship*
Eira Stenberg *Wings of Hope and Daring:
Selected Poems*
Attila the Stockbroker *Scornflakes*
D.M. Thomas *Puberty Tree: New &
Selected Poems*
R.S. Thomas *Mass for Hard Times* ‡
C.K. Williams *A Dream of Mind*
James Wright *Above the River:
The Complete Poems*
Benjamin Zephaniah *City Psalms*

1993
Annemarie Austin *On the Border*
Attilio Bertolucci *Selected Poems*
* Killarney Clary *Who Whispered Near Me*
Brendan Cleary *The Irish Card*
Jack Clemo *Approach to Murano*
Jeni Couzyn *In the Skin House*
Fred D'Aguiar *British Subjects*
* Katie Donovan *Watermelon Man*
Alistair Elliot (tr.) *Italian Landscape Poems*

265

Steve Ellis *West Pathway*
David Ferry (tr.) *Gilgamesh*
Linda France (ed.) *Sixty Women Poets*
Pamela Gillilan & Charlotte Cory
  The Turnspit Dog: poems & woodcuts
Josef Hanzlík *Selected Poems*
Selima Hill *A Little Book of Meat*
Michael Hulse, David Kennedy & David
  Morley (eds.) *The New Poetry*
Kathleen Jamie & Sean Mayne Smith
  *The Autonomous Region: poems &
  photographs from Tibet*
Sylvia Kantaris *Lad's Love*
Jackie Kay *Other Lovers*
* Stephen Knight *Flowering Limbs*
Brendan Kennelly/Euripides *The Trojan
  Women* V ‡
Denise Levertov *A Door in the Hive /
  Evening Train*
Mairi MacInnes *Elsewhere & Back: New &
  Selected Poems*
* Christine McNeill *Kissing the Night*
William Martin *Marra Familia*
Henry Normal *Nude Modelling for the
  Afterlife*
Ottó Orbán *The Blood of the Walsungs:
  Selected Poems*
Ruth Padel *Angel*
Jill Pirrie (ed.) *Apple Fire: The Halesworth
  Middle School Anthology*
Deborah Randall *White Eyes, Dark Ages*
Peter Redgrove *The Cyclopean Mistress:
  Selected Short Fiction* F
* Anne Rouse *Sunset Grill*
Carol Rumens *Thinking of Skins: New &
  Selected Poems*
Roy Shaw (ed.) *The Spread of Sponsorship* P
Elena Shvarts: *'Paradise': Selected Poems*
Ken Smith *Tender to the Queen of Spain*
Ken Smith & Judi Benson (eds.) *Klaonica:
  Poems for Bosnia*
* Stephen Smith *The Fabulous Relatives*

1994
Gillian Allnutt *Blackthorn*
Connie Bensley *Choosing To Be a Swan*
Sara Berkeley *Facts About Water*
Karin Boye *Complete Poems*
George Charlton *City of Dog*
David Constantine *Caspar Hauser*
Peter Didsbury *That Old-Time Religion*
Helen Dunmore *Recovering a Body*
Hans Magnus Enzensberger *Selected Poems* ‡
Carolyn Forché *The Angel of History*
Linda France *The Gentleness of the Very Tall*

Pamela Gillilan *All-Steel Traveller: New
  & Selected Poems*
* Chris Greenhalgh *Stealing the Mona Lisa*
Andrew Greig *Western Swing*
Geoff Hattersley: *Don't Worry*
Adrian Henri *Not Fade Away*
W.N. Herbert *Forked Tongue*
Harold Heslop *Out of the Old Earth* P‡
Selima Hill *Trembling Hearts in the Bodies
  of Dogs: New & Selected Poems*
Douglas Houston *The Hunters in the Snow*
Philippe Jaccottet *Under Clouded Skies &
  Beauregard*
Kathleen Jamie *The Queen of Sheba*
Joolz *The Pride of Lions*
Brendan Kennelly *Journey into Joy: Selected
  Prose* LC ‡
Edna Longley *The Living Stream: Literature
  & Revisionism in Ireland* LC‡
Douglas Oliver *Penniless Politics*
Tom Pickard *Tiepin Eros: New & Selected
  Poems*
Richard Pine (ed.) *Dark Fathers into Light:
  Brendan Kennelly* LC ‡
Maria Razumovsky *Marina Tsvetayeva:
  A Critical Biography* LC†
* Ann Sansom *Romance*
Peter Sansom *Writing Poems* P
Pauline Stainer *The Ice-Pilot Speaks*
John Tranter & Philip Meads (eds.) *The
  Bloodaxe Book of Modern Australian Poetry*
Mirjam Tuominen *Selected Writings*
Poetry Virgins: *Sauce*
John Hartley Williams *Double*

1995
Neil Astley *Biting My Tongue*
Annemarie Austin *The Flaying of Marsyas*
Elizabeth Bartlett *Two Women Dancing:
  New & Selected Poems*
James Berry *Hot Earth Cold Earth*
Ron Butlin *Histories of Desire*
Aimé Césaire *Notebook of a Return to My
  Native Land*
Jack Clemo *Approach to Murano*
Stewart Conn *In the Blood*
Jane Cooper *Green Notebook, Winter Road*
* Julia Copus *The Shuttered Eye*
Freda Downie *Collected Poems*
Ian Duhig *The Mersey Goldfish*
Tess Gallagher *My Black Horse: New &
  Selected Poems*
* Maggie Hannan *Liar, Jones*
Tony Harrison *Permanently Bard: Selected
  Poetry*

Paul Hyland *Kicking Sawdust*
Jenny Joseph *Ghosts and other company*
Brendan Kennelly *Poetry My Arse* ‡
* Helen Kitson *Love Among the Guilty*
* Gwyneth Lewis *Parables & Faxes*
Glyn Maxwell *Rest for the Wicked*
Bill Naughton *Neither Use Nor Ornament* P‡
Micheal O'Siadhail *A Fragile City*
Peter Reading *Collected Poems 1: Poems 1970-1984* ‡
Carol Rumens *Best China Sky*
Lawrence Sail *Building into Air*
Olive Senior *Gardening in the Tropics*
Matt Simpson *Catching up with History*
R.S. Thomas *No Truce with the Furies* ‡
C.K. Williams *New & Selected Poems*

1996

Josephine Balmer (tr.) *Classical Women Poets*
* Eleanor Brown *Maiden Speech*
Judi Benson & Agneta Falk (eds.)
    The Long Pale Corridor: contemporary poems of bereavement
Ciaran Carson *Opera Et Cetera*
Stephen Dobyns *Velocities: New & Selected Poems*
Maura Dooley *Kissing a Bone*
Menna Elfyn *Cell Angel*
Paul Éluard *Unbroken Poetry II*
John Fairleigh (ed.) *When the Tunnels Meet: Contemporary Romanian Poetry*
Roy Fisher *The Dow Low Drop: New & Selected Poems*
André Frénaud *Rome the Sorceress*
Tess Gallagher *Portable Kisses*
George Gömöri & George Szirtes (eds)
    The Colonnade of Teeth: Modern Hungarian Poetry
W.N. Herbert *Cabaret McGonagall*
* Tracey Herd *No Hiding Place*
Rita Ann Higgins *Sunny Side Plucked: New & Selected Poems*
Friedrich Hölderlin *Selected Poems*
    SECOND EDITION
Miroslav Holub *Supposed to Fly*
Paul Hyland *Getting into Poetry* P
    SECOND EDITION
David Kelley & Jean Khalfa (eds.) *The New French Poetry*
Brendan Kennelly & Katie Donovan (eds.)
    Dublines ‡
Brendan Kennelly/Federico García Lorca
    Blood Wedding V ‡
Brendan Kennelly/Sophocles *Antigone* V ‡
Stephen Knight *Dream City Cinema*

Marion Lomax [Robyn Bolam] *Raiding the Borders*
Andrew McAllister (ed.) *The Objectivists*
Peter McDonald *Adam's Dream*
Osip Mandelstam *The Voronezh Notebooks*
Don Marquis *Archyology*
Paula Meehan *Mysteries of the Home*
Adrian Mitchell *Blue Coffee: Poems 1985-1996*
Åke Persson (ed.) *The Fellow with the Fabulous Smile: A Tribute to Brendan Kennelly*
* Katrina Porteous *The Lost Music*
Tom Pow *Red Letter Day*
Peter Reading *Collected Poems 2: Poems 1985-1996* ‡
Pauline Stainer *The Wound-dresser's Dream*
Miroslav Válek *The Ground Beneath Our Feet: Selected Poems*
Benjamin Zephaniah *Propa Propaganda*

1997

John Agard *From the Devil's Pulpit*
Gillian Allnutt *Nantucket and the Angel*
Keith Bosley (tr.) *Skating on the Sea: Poetry from Finland*
Jean 'Binta' Breeze *On the Edge of an Island*
David Constantine *The Pelt of Wasps*
Lauris Edmond *In Position*
Imtiaz Dharker *Postcards from god*
Stephen Dobyns *Common Carnage*
Katie Donovan *Entering the Mare*
Maura Dooley (ed.) *Making for Planet Alice: Women Poets*
Helen Dunmore *Bestiary*
Hans Magnus Enzensberger *Kiosk*
Ruth Fainlight *Sugar-Paper Blue*
* Gillian Ferguson *Air for Sleeping Fish*
Linda France *Storyville*
Miguel Hernández *I Have Lots of Heart: Selected Poems*
Selima Hill *Violet*
* Jane Holland *Brief History of a Disreputable Woman*
Jenny Joseph *Extended Similes* P
Denise Levertov *Tesserae* P
* Roddy Lumsden *Yeah Yeah Yeah*
Barry MacSweeney *The Book of Demons*
Adrian Mitchell *Heart on the Left: Poems 1953-1984*
Peter Reading *Work in Regress*
Anne Rouse *Timing*
Carol Rumens & Viv Quillin *The Miracle Diet*
Tomas Tranströmer *New Collected Poems*
Liliana Ursu *The Sky Behind the Forest: Selected Poems*

Paul Valéry *La Jeune Parque*
C.K. Williams *The Vigil*
John Hartley Williams *Canada*
Glyn Wright *Shindig*

1998
Chris Agee (ed.) *Scar on the Stone:
    contemporary poetry from Bosnia*
Beverliey Braune *Camouflage*
Brendan Cleary *Sacrilege*
Ian Duhig *Nominies*
Elizabeth Garrett *A Two-Part Invention*
Pamela Gillilan *The Rashomon Syndrome*
Philip Gross *The Wasting Game*
* Jackie Hardy *Canuting the Waves*
Geoff Hattersley *'On the Buses' with
    Dostoyevsky*
W.N. Herbert *The Laurelude*
Jackie Kay *Off Colour*
Brendan Kennelly *The Man Made of Rain* ‡
Brendan Kennelly *The Man Made of Rain*
    ☆ CASSETTE
John Kinsella *The Hunt*
John Kinsella *Poems 1980-1994*
Denise Levertov *Sands of the Well*
Gwyneth Lewis *Zero Gravity*
Jack Mapanje *Skipping Without Ropes*
Sean O'Brien *The Deregulated Muse: Essays on
    Contemporary British & Irish Poetry* LC‡
Julie O'Callaghan *Two Barks*
Micheal O'Siadhail *Our Double Time*
The Poetry Quartets 1: Armitage, Jamie,
    Kay, Maxwell ☆ CASSETTE
The Poetry Quartets 2: Adcock, Duffy, Hill,
    Rumens ☆ CASSETTE
The Poetry Quartets 3: Fenton, Harrison,
    Reading, Smith ☆ CASSETTE
* Clare Pollard *The Heavy-Petting Zoo*
David Scott *Selected Poems*
Ken Smith *Wild Root*
Fred Voss *Carnegie Hall with Tin Walls*
Clair Wills *Reading Paul Muldoon* LC‡

1999
Neil Astley (ed.) *New Blood*
Annemarie Austin *Door Upon Door*
Stewart Conn *Stolen Light: Selected Poems*
* Amanda Dalton *How to Disappear*
* Nick Drake *The Man in the White Suit*
Guillevic *Carnac*
* Frieda Hughes *Wooroloo*
Attila József *The Iron-Blue Vault: Selected
    Poems*
J. Kates (ed.) *In the Grip of Strange Thoughts:
    Russian Poetry in a New Era*

Brendan Kennelly *Begin*
John Kinsella *Visitants*
Mairi MacInnes *The Ghostwriter*
Micheal O'Siadhail *Poems 1975-1995*
Andrew Fusek Peters (ed.) *Sheep Don't Go
    to School: mad & magical children's poetry
    from Eastern Europe*
György Petri *Eternal Monday: New &
    Selected Poems*
The Poetry Quartets 4: Durcan, Kennelly,
    Longley, McGuckian ☆ CASSETTE
The Poetry Quartets 5: Dunmore, Fanthorpe,
    Jennings, Shapcott ☆ CASSETTE
J.H. Prynne *Poems* ‡
Peter Reading *Ob.*
Tracy Ryan *The Willing Eye*
Pauline Stainer *Parable Island*
E.P. Thompson *Collected Poems*
Chase Twichell *The Snow Watcher*
* Christiana Whitehead *The Garden of Slender
    Trust*
C.K. Williams *Repair*
Yang Lian *Where the Sea Stands Still*

2000
Fleur Adcock *Poems 1960-2000* ‡
John Agard *Weblines*
Moniza Alvi *Carrying My Wife*
Connie Bensley *The Back and the Front of It*
Jean 'Binta' Breeze *The Arrival of Brighteye*
Basil Bunting *Complete Poems*
Basil Bunting *Basil Bunting reads 'Briggflatts'*
    ☆ CASSETTE
Inger Christensen *alphabet*
* Polly Clark *Kiss*
Stephen Dobyns *Pallbearers Envying the One
    Who Rides*
Chris Greenhalgh *Of Love, Death and the
    Sea-squirt*
* Jane Griffiths *A Grip on Thin Air*
W.N. Herbert & Matthew Hollis (eds)
    *Strong Words: modern poets on modern
    poetry*
Ioana Ieronim *The Triumph of the Water Witch*
John Kinsella *The Hierarchy of Sheep*
* Joanne Limburg *Femenismo*
Edna Longley (ed.) *The Bloodaxe Book of
    20th Century Poetry from Britain & Ireland*
Edna Longley: *Poetry & Posterity*
Roddy Lumsden *The Book of Love*
Don Marquis *Archyology II (The Final Dig)*
Isabel Martin *Reading Peter Reading* LC‡
William Martin *Lammas Alanna*
Glyn Maxwell *The Boys at Twilight: Poems
    1990-1995*

Adrian Mitchell *All Shook Up: Poems 1997–2000*
Julie O'Callaghan *No Can Do*
Douglas Oliver *A Salvo for Africa*
Alan Plater *Close the Coalhouse Door: from stories by Sid Chaplin, a stage play in three acts with songs by Alex Glasgow*
The Poetry Quartets 6: Alvi, Donaghy, Stevenson, Szirtes ☆ CASSETTE
The Poetry Quartets 7: Burnside, Herbert, Lochhead, Paterson ☆ CASSETTE
Peter Reading *Marfan*
Carole Satyamurti *Love and Variations*
Carole Satyamurti *Selected Poems*
Salah Stétié *Cold Water Shielded: Selected Poems*
Anne Stevenson *The Collected Poems 1955–1995*
Anne Stevenson *Granny Scarecrow*
George Szirtes *The Budapest File*

2001
Gillian Allnutt *Lintel*
Elizabeth Bartlett *Appetites of Love*
David Constantine (tr.) *Hölderlin's Sophocles: Oedipus* AND *Antigone* V
Imtiaz Dharker *I Speak for the Devil*
Helen Dunmore *Out of the Blue: Poems 1975–2001*
Menna Elfyn *Cusan Dyn Dall / Blind Man's Kiss*
John Fairleigh (ed.) *Sorescu's Choice: Young Romanian Poets*
Andrew Greig *Into You*
Philip Gross *Changes of Light: Poems 1980–1988*
Tracey Herd *Dead Redhead*
Rita Ann Higgins *An Awful Racket*
Selima Hill *Bunny*
Frieda Hughes *Stonepicker*
Brendan Kennelly *Glimpses* ‡
Galway Kinnell *Selected Poems*
Denise Levertov *This Great Unknowing: Last Poems*
* Esther Morgan *Beyond Calling Distance*
* Caitríona O'Reilly *The Nowhere Birds*
* Jem Poster *Brought to Light*
Peter Reading *[untitled]*
Evgeny Rein *Selected Poems*
Gjertrud Schnackenberg *Supernatural Love: Poems 1976–2000*
Marin Sorescu *Censored Poems*
George Szirtes *An English Apocalypse*
Pia Tafdrup *Queen's Gate*
Benjamin Zephaniah *Too Black Too Strong*

2002
Moniza Alvi *Souls*
Linda Anderson & Jo Shapcott (eds.) *Elizabeth Bishop: Poet of the Periphery* LC
Neil Astley (ed.) *Pleased to See Me: 69 very sexy poems*
Neil Astley (ed.) *Staying Alive: real poems for unreal times*
David Constantine *Something for the Ghosts*
Katie Donovan *Day of the Dead*
Maura Dooley *Sound Barrier: Poems 1982–2002*
G.F. Dutton *The Bare Abundance: Selected Poems 1975–2001*
Hans Magnus Enzensberger *Lighter than Air*
Ruth Fainlight *Burning Wire*
Linda France *The Simultaneous Dress*
Kevin Hart *Flame Tree: Selected Poems*
Selima Hill *Portrait of My Lover as a Horse*
Frieda Hughes *Waxworks*
* Helen Ivory *The Double Life of Clocks*
Kathleen Jamie *Mr and Mrs Scotland Are Dead: Poems 1980–1994*
Brendan Kennelly *The Little Book of Judas*
Micheal O'Siadhail *The Gossamer Wall: poems in witness to the Holocaust*
Clare Pollard *Bedtime*
Peter Reading *Faunal*
Carol Rumens *Hex*
Lawrence Sail *The World Returning*
Ken Smith *Shed: Poems 1980–2001*
R.S. Thomas *Residues* ‡

2003
Nin Andrews *The Book of Orgasms* F
Neil Astley (ed.) *Do Not Go Gentle: poems for funerals*
Neil Astley (ed.) *Bloodaxe Poems of the Year: 2003*
Annemarie Austin *Back from the Moon*
Julia Copus *In Defence of Adultery*
Peter Didsbury *Scenes from a Long Sleep: New & Collected Poems*
Stephen Dobyns *The Porcupine's Kisses*
Maura Dooley (ed.) *The Honey Gatherers: a book of love poems*
Freda Downie *There'll Always Be an England: a poet's childhood, 1929–1945* P
Menna Elfyn & John Rowlands (eds.) *The Bloodaxe Book of Modern Welsh Poetry: 20th-Century Welsh Language Poetry in Translation*
Peter Forbes (ed.) *We Have Come Through: 100 poems celebrating courage in overcoming depression and trauma*

Carolyn Forché *Blue Hour*
Philip Gross *Mappa Mundi*
Ellen Hinsey *The White Fire of Time*
Kapka Kassabova *Someone else's life*
Brendan Kennelly *Martial Art* ‡
Denise Levertov *New Selected Poems*
Gwyneth Lewis *Keeping Mum*
Barry MacSweeney *Wolf Tongue:*
Selected Poems 1965-2000
Gérard Macé *Wood Asleep*
Osip Mandelstam *The Moscow & Voronezh*
Notebooks
W.S. Merwin (tr.) *Sir Gawain and the Green*
Knight
Peter Reading *Collected Poems 3: Poems*
1997-2003 ‡
Ann Sansom *In Praise of Men and Other*
People
Esta Spalding *Anchoress*
Pauline Stainer *The Lady & the Hare:*
New & Selected Poems
Anne Stevenson *A Report from the Border*
* Sarah Wardle *Fields Away*
Susan Wicks *Night Toad:*
New & Selected Poems
C.K. Williams *The Singing*

2004

Robert Adamson *Reading the River:*
Selected Poems
Gillian Allnutt *Sojourner*
Maram al-Massri *A Red Cherry on a White-*
tiled Floor: Selected Poems
Neil Astley (ed.) *Being Alive: the sequel to*
'Staying Alive'
Josephine Balmer *Chasing Catullus*
Elizabeth Bartlett *Mrs Perkins and Oedipus*
David Constantine *Collected Poems*
David Constantine *A Living Language*
(Newcastle/Bloodaxe Poetry Lectures) LC
* Matthew Hollis *Ground Water*
Catullus *Poems of Love and Hate*
* Cheryl Follon *All Your Talk*
Selina Guinness (ed.) *The New Irish Poets*
* Choman Hardi *Life for Us*
Selima Hill *Lou-Lou*
Paul Hyland *Art of the Impossible:*
New & Selected Poems 1974-2004
Jaan Kaplinski *Evening Brings Everything Back*
Brendan Kennelly *Familiar Strangers:*
New & Selected Poems 1960-2004
Radmila Lazic *A Wake for the Living*
Roddy Lumsden *Mischief Night:*
New & Selected Poems
* Kona Macphee *Tails*

Jack Mapanje *The Last of the Sweet Bananas:*
Selected Poems
Adrian Mitchell *The Shadow Knows:*
Poems 2000-2004
Ágnes Nemes Nagy *The Night of Akhenaton:*
Selected Poems
Alden Nowlan *Between Tears and Laughter:*
Selected Poems
Mary Oliver *Wild Geese: Selected Poems*
* Leanne O'Sullivan *Waiting for My Clothes*
The Poetry Quartets 8: Causley, Greenlaw,
Constantine, Motion ☆ CASSETTE
The Poetry Quartets 9: Duhig, Rouse,
Sweeney, Zephaniah ☆ CASSETTE
Anne Rouse *The School of Night*
Carol Rumens *Poems 1968-2004*
Eva Salzman *Double Crossing:*
New & Selected Poems
Tatiana Shcherbina: *Life Without:*
Selected Poetry & Prose 1992-2003
Ken Smith *You Again: last poems &*
other words
Marin Sorescu *The Bridge*
George Szirtes *Reel*
R.S. Thomas *Collected Later Poems* ‡

2005

Moniza Alvi *How the Stone Found Its Voice*
Neil Astley (ed.) *Passionfood: 100 Love Poems*
Robyn Bolam (ed.) *Eliza's Babes: four centuries*
of women's poetry in English, c.1500-1900
Polly Clark *Take Me with You*
Stewart Conn *Ghosts at Cockcrow*
Julia Darling & Cynthia Fuller (ed.)
The Poetry Cure
Roy Fisher *The Long and the Short of It:*
Poems 1955-2005
Linda France *The Toast of the Kit-Cat Club:*
A Life of Mary Wortley Montagu
Jane Griffiths *Icarus on Earth*
Jen Hadfield *Almanacs*
Rita Ann Higgins *Throw in the Vowels:*
New & Selected Poems
Jane Hirshfield *Each Happiness Ringed by*
Lions: Selected Poems
Tony Hoagland *What Narcissism Means*
to Me: Selected Poems
Jackie Kay *Life Mask*
Jane Kenyon *Let Evening Come:*
Selected Poems
Gwyneth Lewis *Chaotic Angels:*
poems in English
Esther Morgan *The Silence Living in Houses*
Micheal O'Siadhail *Love Life*
Clare Pollard *Look, Clare! Look!*

J.H. Prynne *Poems* SECOND EDITION
* Sally Read *The Point of Splitting*
Peter Reading *-273.15*
Deryn Rees-Jones *Consorting with Angels:*
Essays on Modern Women Poets LC
Deryn Rees-Jones (ed.) *Modern Women Poets*
Carole Satyamurti *Stitching the Dark:*
New & Selected Poems
David Scott *Piecing Together*
Piotr Sommer *Continued*
Anne Stevenson *Poems 1955-2005* ‡
Sarah Wardle *Score!*
Yang Lian *Concentric Circles*

2006

John Agard *We Brits*
Elizabeth Alexander *American Blue:*
Selected Poems
Neil Astley (ed.) *Poetry Introductions 1:*
Alexander, Alvi, Dharker, Kay
Neil Astley (ed.) *Poetry Introductions 2:*
Enzensberger, Holub, Sorescu, Tranströmer
Fran Brearton *Reading Michael Longley* ‡
Jean 'Binta' Breeze *The Fifth Figure*
Martin Carter *University of Hunger:*
Collected Poems & Selected Prose
Dan Chiasson *Natural History*
& other poems
Imtiaz Dharker *The terrorist at my table*
Ruth Fainlight *Moon Wheels*
Tua Forsström *I studied once at a wonderful*
faculty
Jack Gilbert *Transgressions: Selected Poems*
Andrew Greig *This Life, This Life:*
New & Selected Poems 1970-2006
Philip Gross *The Egg of Zero*
W.N. Herbert *Bad Shaman Blues*
Selima Hill *Red Roses*
Jane Hirshfield *After*
Miroslav Holub *Poems Before & After:*
Collected English Translations
SECOND EDITION
Helen Ivory *The Dog in the Sky*
Brendan Kennelly *Now* ‡
Brendan Kennelly (tr.) *When Then Is Now:*
Three Greek Tragedies
Jenny Joseph *Extreme of things*
Philip Levine *Stranger to Nothing:*
Selected Poems
Joan Margarit *Tugs in the Fog: Selected Poems*
Dennis O'Driscoll *The Bloodaxe Book of*
Poetry Quotations
Caitríona O'Reilly *The Sea Cabinet*
Lawrence Sail *Eye-Baby*
* Clare Shaw *Straight Ahead*

Penelope Shuttle *Redgrove's Wife*
Anne Stevenson *Five Looks at Elizabeth*
Bishop LC
Chase Twichell *Dog Language*
Tatiana Voltskaia *Cicada: Selected Poetry*
& Prose
C.K. Williams *Collected Poems*

2007

Gillian Allnutt *How the Bicycle Shone:*
New & Selected Poems
Neil Astley (ed.) *Earth Shattering: ecopoems*
Neil Astley (ed.) *Poetry Introductions 3:*
Gilbert, Hirshfield, Kinnell, Merwin
Neil Astley & Pamela Robertson-Pearce (eds)
Soul Food: nourishing poems for starved
minds
* Suzanne Batty *The Barking Thing*
Connie Bensley *Private Pleasures*
James Berry *Windrush Songs*
Robyn Bolam *New Wings: Poems 1977-2007*
* Zoë Brigley *The Secret*
Jackie Kay *Darling: New & Selected Poems*
Mahmoud Darwish *The Butterfly's Burden*
Nick Drake *From the Word Go*
Helen Dunmore *Glad of These Times*
Menna Elfyn *Perfect Blemish: New & Selected*
Poems 1995-2007 / Perffaith Nam: Dau
ddetholiad & Cherddi Newydd 1995-2007
Tess Gallagher *Dear Ghosts,*
Desmond Graham *Making Poems and their*
Meanings (Newcastle/ Bloodaxe Poetry
Lectures) LC
Chris Greenhalgh *The Invention of Zero*
Kapka Kassabova *Geography for the Lost*
Galway Kinnell *Strong Is Your Hold*
☆ PAPERBACK WITH AUDIO CD
Li-Young Lee *From Blossoms:*
Selected Poems
Joanne Limburg *Paraphernalia*
Jack Mapanje *Beasts of Nalunga*
W.S. Merwin *Selected Poems*
Kenji Miyazawa *Strong in the Rain:*
Selected Poems
Taha Muhammad Ali *So What: New &*
Selected Poems 1971-2005
Mary Oliver *Thirst*
Micheal O'Siadhail *Globe*
Carol Rumens *Self into Song (Newcastle/*
Bloodaxe Poetry Lectures) LC
Anne Stevenson *Stone Milk*
Brian Turner *Here, Bullet*
Susan Wicks *De-iced*
C.D. Wright *Like Something Flying*
Backwards: New & Selected Poems

2008

Moniza Alvi *Europa*
Moniza Alvi *Split World: Poems 1990-2005*
In Person: 30 Poets filmed by Pamela
   Robertson-Pearce, (ed.) Neil Astley
   ☆ DVD-BOOK
Annemarie Austin *Very: New & Selected*
   Poems
* Paul Batchelor *The Sinking Road*
Maura Dooley *Life Under Water*
Deborah Garrison *The Second Child*
Janet Frame *Storms Will Tell: Selected Poems*
Jane Griffiths *Another Country:*
   New & Selected Poems
Jen Hadfield *Nigh-No-Place*
Selima Hill *Gloria: Selected Poems*
Selima Hill *The Hat*
Jane Hirshfield *Hiddenness, Uncertainty,*
   Surprise: Three Generative Energies of
   Poetry (Newcastle/ Bloodaxe Poetry
   Lectures) LC
Esther Jansma *What It Is: Selected Poems*

Jackie Kay *The Lamplighter* RADIO PLAY
   ☆ PAPERBACK WITH AUDIO CD
* Stephanie Norgate *Hidden River*
Naomi Shihab Nye *Tender Spot:*
   Selected Poems
Julie O'Callaghan *Tell Me This Is Normal:*
   New & Selected Poems
Mary Oliver *Red Bird*
Anne Rouse *The Upshot: New & Selected*
   Poems
Elena Shvarts *Birdsong on the Seabed*
John Sears *Reading George Szirtes*
Pauline Stainer *Crossing the Snowline*
George Szirtes *New & Collected Poems*
Jeet Thayil (ed.) *The Bloodaxe Book of*
   Contemporary Indian Poets
Edward Thomas *The Annotated Collected*
   Poems
Tomas Venclova *The Junction:*
   Selected Poems
Yi Sha *Starve the Poets! Selected Poems*

DVD FORMAT

Since our primary readership is the UK, our films have been converted to PAL format. Whether you can play our DVDs will depend upon what kind of DVD player you have, or whether you watch DVDs on a PC. If you live in Britain, you should have no problem.

PAL/SECAM is the TV format used in Britain and most of Europe, most of Africa, China, India, Australia, New Zealand, Israel, North Korea, and other countries. NTSC is the TV format used in Canada, Japan, Mexico, Philippines, Taiwan, the United States, and other countries.

DVD players sold in Britain and Europe will play PAL DVDs (and most will play NTSC DVDs also).

However, most players sold in the US only play NTSC DVDs (but some recent models will play both PAL and NTSC DVDs). A very small number of NTSC players sold in the US (such as Apex and SMC) can convert PAL to NTSC. But most NTSC TVs don't work with PAL video.

If you live in the US, it is unlikely that you will be able to play our DVDs using a DVD player. However, if you can play DVDs on your computer, you should have no problems.

Most DVD PC software and hardware can play both NTSC and PAL video. Some PCs can only display the converted video on the computer monitor, but others can output it as a video signal for a TV.

In an ideal world we'd produce our DVD-book with DVDs in either format and give overseas readers the choice, but unfortunately that would be much too costly. If the manufacturers had agreed upon a standard worldwide format ten years ago, no one would have this problem now.

Making Poetry

THE FICTION-MAKERS 1985

'You have to inhabit poetry
if you want to make it.'

And what's 'to inhabit'?

To be in the habit of, to wear
words, sitting in the plainest light,
in the silk of morning, in the shoe of night;
a feeling bare and frondish in surprising air;
familiar...rare.

And what's 'to make'?

To be and to become words' passing
weather; to serve a girl on terrible
terms, embark on voyages over voices,
evade the ego-hill, the misery-well,
the siren hiss of *publish, success, publish,*
success, success, success.

And why inhabit, make, inherit poetry?

Oh, it's the shared comedy of the worst
blessed; the sound leading the hand;
a wordlife running from mind to mind
through the washed rooms of the simple senses;
one of those haunted, undefendable, unpoetic
crosses we have to find.

Poem for a Daughter

MINUTE BY GLASS MINUTE 1982

'I think I'm going to have it,'
I said, joking between pains.
The midwife rolled competent
sleeves over corpulent milky arms.
'Dear, you never have it,
we deliver it.'
A judgement years proved true.
Certainly I've never had you

192